Angels Among Us

Living Dream Series

ERWIN LAZARO

LLD
BOOKS

authorHOUSE®

AuthorHouse™
1663 Liberty Drive
Bloomington, IN 47403
www.authorhouse.com
Phone: 1 (800) 839-8640

Editing by: Katy Rubinkowski

Published by AuthorHouse 09/22/2017

ISBN: 978-1-5462-0405-3 (sc)
ISBN: 978-1-5462-0404-6 (hc)
ISBN: 978-1-5462-0403-9 (e)

Library of Congress Control Number: 2017912514

Printed in the USA.

The following memoirs are the expression of my passion. These are my truths revealed. Nobody can dictate otherwise. I do not offer any professional advice or service. I am laying my life out as an open book, an offering for any who empathize, sympathize, or are interested. My intention is to accurately convey my experiences with sincerity. I acknowledge all who shaped the soul I am. My living dream is my lifelong prayer, full of hope, pleas, and thanksgiving. Finally, I am not expressing or implying any of my actions or accounts as guarantees, viable solutions, or warranties. Each person is without equal, living special circumstances, and responsible for their own choices, actions, and results. Please use wisdom as a guide in understanding and acting upon personal truths.

Please feel welcome to visit the author, Erwin Lazaro, at www.lazarolivingdream.com or contact by email at erwin@lazarolivingdream.com or lldbooks2017@gmail.com for an open dialogue inspired by the expressions within these pages. Erwin will sincerely respond in a considerate manner.

To my heart …
no longer tied to the rhythm of this world …
set free to guide, only if you are willing and if God will allow …
You are an angel for all, though you dedicated all to me and
family. If my selfishness continues to bind you, I proclaim and
release you, my heart, so you can do as you please …
or disperse entirely to share all that you are with as many as possible,
born into the rhythm of this world, who innately know what you offer.
Mom, I never deserved you and thank you …

Prologue

Living Dream

AMBER WAVES OF SPLENDOR FLOWING. Teeming with life, its brilliance stretched to and fro, here and there, rhythmic by nature. This dynamic ipseity whispered a golden calling. An ethereal trail cascaded from its motion, allowing a lasting impression to temporarily play, thousands of sparkling elements fluttering outward before rejoining its massive core. Movement without pattern, alive and vibrant, this presence thrived within a space otherwise devoid, discernible splendor indeed.

The presence appeared two dimensional, limited to one plane, distant and separate from my being. I quietly observed. Yet, playfully, its brilliance beckoned. It was an invitation akin to a ceremony of sorts. It took a formal approach and then launched into a mirthful gait. Radiant and projecting, directing its energy towards me, its presence grew. Or rather, I was getting closer. It drew me in. My surroundings bore no reference. I could not tell. I felt its gentle embrace pulling me closer. I could sense the ripples of movement back and forth, swaying easily and constantly, following the rhythm of a tune that was not heard. The melodic waves ebbed and flowed. That rhythm charmed me, leading me by a meandering path. In a sense, its motion mimicked living, slow, purposeful breaths; visible as my own on a cold, brisk morn. A bit amused, I looked for a giant that could possibly be the source.

I felt its presence more boldly, surrounded by a warm embrace. Protective arms cradled me. It permeated my entirety, making me comfortable. I could get used to this feeling. Closing my eyes, I enjoyed the serenity. I sighed and soaked it all in just as I would the warm rays of the sun. The presence projected golden tendrils and when we touched, the exhilaration charged me with waves of harmony, in the sense that we were becoming one or I was becoming a part of this presence. With a warm smile and peace within, I drifted. This was marvelous.

But, as quickly as calm soothed me it was taken away. Tranquility was repelled. I was in motion again, no longer supported; drifting away from the auric brilliance. My mind began playing tricks with me. I was a little dazed and my thoughts began sliding in and out of awareness. My mind was not clear nor was my vision. I seemed to be blinking, but I was not sure.

That beautiful radiance invited me to focus and pay attention, but my senses continued being distorted. Another was interfering. I could feel it. I did not recognize what I saw nor could I determine if I was seeing at all. Suddenly, I was injected with a nagging feeling. I was supposed to seek a special place, a hallowed place that I may never find again.

I sensed the golden tendrils retracting. The warmth was being driven away. Urgency took the place of comfort as my attention further waned and I drifted farther and farther. No longer within the ethereal embrace, I felt a great distance from the pleasure that had invited me. At least, radiating warmth kept me facing in the general direction I wanted to move. I relied on this feeling for guidance. My eyes betrayed me and focusing bred frustration beneath the veil obscuring my vision. I kept trying to identify what I was experiencing before it was lost. I certainly felt treasure yearning to be found.

An abrupt separation is already heartrending, but the presence imparted more. It's nurturing embrace was tainted with a perception of loss. Not prevalent, but hints of sorrow drifted within the movement that had impassioned me. I did not sense regret. The encounter left the impression of a bittersweet sensation from something palatable that was cherished for its time and the inevitability of moving onward. In other words, it was a reaction in the way a memory cannot be relived, recollection that provides small comfort, and the touch of loss in tow.

My desperation grew, battling against the compulsion to succumb. I tried shaking it off, but the more I tried to focus, the less aware I became. The warmth was all but gone now. I continued struggling but I was slipping away, anesthetized under a growing shroud of darkness. The tender caress that cradled me earlier was replaced by oppressive claws closing in. Vaporous, clawed wires slithered straight towards me, distinctly visible through a hazy vision. I had earlier considered the void in which I drifted as darkness, but that was a mistake. The void was more an absence of light compared to this opaque shadow confronting me now, an existence that suppressed my senses. These converging coiled claws wanted me to fully realize my pending capture. They were not touching me yet, but I felt their gloom closing in. I continued wrestling that which threatened my potential discovery, but I was caught and restrained. Cold and uninviting, the shadows slowly twisted around my body. It wound around my hands and feet, darting in and out of me as stitches for a seam, binding me in place. My limbs were frozen, my chest was heavy, but I fought. I thrashed my head left and right as if I could still escape. I refused to relinquish. Worming, wriggling, and writhing; I swore to break free. My mouth was wide open, emitting a voiceless scream. I yelled, but I could not hear a sound or I was screaming so loud it was deafening. I screamed at the top of my lungs. I kept screaming without taking any breaths. I felt tears, but I was not scared. I was angry. I was losing. I was losing this precious chance.

I started feeling lightheaded. I was near the edge of hope, during the last moment of a last breath. I could no longer function, drifting even farther from the allure that had appeared. It had teased me with hopeful yearning in the beginning. My senses dulled to the point of the urgency vanishing. I was almost unaware of what I sought ... almost unaware.

An impression of hands grabbed and pulled me ... somewhere.

In my weakness, in those final moments of complete loss, I no longer felt any kind of sensation, except for endless drifting towards obscurity; neither suppressed nor free. The shadows almost enveloped everything. Yet, a hint of the presence persisted to shine, though so distant now. Even the warmth was gone.

But then ... I felt it.

A familiar approached me. A gentle presence moved around me and then, through me. I reacted. It urged me to calm myself. It teased my curiosity. It lured me back, drawing me back, leading me back. The warmth returned. The comfort returned. This aid restored my sensibilities. The exhilaration led me back to self-awareness. Washing aside the troublesome insecurities that plagued my manifestation here, an overwhelming sense of peace swept over me and with peace, I let go. My mind, my body, my soul … I let go and found what I sought. It was in this moment, when I let go, that everything in front of me started to make sense. I did not lose hope.

This was the cue for me to revive. My sight was returning and I could feel once again. In regaining my senses, I quickly realized that I had never lost them to begin with. The shadows had manipulated me and as the shadows receded, the absence of light started filtering into place. The further the shadows, the clearer my senses became. The veil that had clouded my vision and suppressed my senses lifted away with what felt like a calm breeze. It was this breeze that brought my senses under control and calmed my frantic reflex in order to understand I was about to lose a precious connection. And, as the soothing breeze continued to lure me back into a state of awareness, the calm strengthened my resolve. I was supposed to be here. I was getting help. This wonderful breeze set me free and gently guided me in the direction I was supposed to go when I was about to be consumed by oblivion.

Thankfully, that was behind me now. Before me, a portal took shape. I started feeling anticipation. I felt the grogginess from a long, deep slumber burning away, even though I was certain that only a few moments had passed. My sense of time was skewed, but I did not care. I wanted what lay ahead. I let go. I let it take me and finally …

Golden light adorned the rustling leaves of the trees, shimmering as the wind danced. Back and forth, I could almost see its form as it traveled in a random path. My eyes followed the wind that looked like the coat tails of a child whisking playfully through the air. The path of the wind was clearly marked by gleeful leaves reacting to the frolicsome force of nature. The air was light and a sense of tranquility permeated everything. It was breathtaking to be in this place. My smile could not be any greater as my eyes were drawn towards the blinding azure of the summer sky. The sky was so bright. No clouds, not even a wisp. This scene was perfect. The sun's golden light was everywhere and yet I was not aware of the sun. As bright as it was, I was not squinting. I was not sweating from any overbearing heat.

Whatever tried to pull me away was completely gone now. I became fully aware of this place. My eyes came back to the flying leaves. The playful breeze continued darting about, but I could no longer feel nor hear it. I was not being physically affected in any way, but I could see its effect on other objects. I should have considered all that to be peculiar, but I did not.

I did not realize I was moving until I noticed the environment changing. That is also when I became aware that I was not moving by my own power. For the span of an eager breath, it felt odd to be sitting. I was sitting in an open vehicle that had seats. It appeared to be a small, open boxcar travelling by rail. I could see one set of tracks laid before the car's path as I glanced ahead. I touched the car, once for security, and twice to make sure I was really in this car. It had a rustic feel to it, made from wood; aged and worn. It was warm to the touch from soaking in the sun's rays that I could not feel nor see for myself. Again, this sensation should have been out of place, but I accepted it for what it was. I defined the warmth for myself, maybe so I would not be afraid. The warmth felt as that of the touch of a person's living skin.

I sat quietly, using only sight to guide my thoughts. I had this feeling that I was present and that I was also not present. I could observe myself as a spectator. I could also look at my own hands and confirm I was witnessing this from my own perspective. I thought this felt like a movie and the cut scenes between cameras. Instead of dwelling on these matters, I smiled and noticed a situation which had escaped me.

I was not alone. How did I not realize that my sister was sitting by my side? I did not notice my sister until I turned my head and looked at eye level. I was looking up. I was looking down. I was looking ahead, but not to my side. I guess that made sense. We were sitting in this open car together. I was glad my sister was with me. Her presence was comforting.

We moved in the direction of a familiar area. No words were exchanged between us, but we communicated our awe of this experience as our eyes met. Attracted to the evolving scenery, we basked in the visual story unfolding. My gaze turned to the path ahead.

My sister and I found ourselves moving amongst mundane items. Without transition, we were inside a place that evoked a reassuring intimacy. We still traveled by open car as observers not allowed to touch the objects appearing around us. Everything here was covered by a golden hue. I could not tell if it was light playing with my perception or the objects themselves that were golden. Everything sparkled with a nostalgic sense of being. A natural affinity emanated from this place. Together, we advanced amid clothing, furniture, toys, and tables loaded with books and delicate items such as dishes, glasses, photo frames, and vases. These items were memories from our home. Identifying items that belonged to my family, the mundane had transformed into personal effects, but the more I focused on each piece, the nostalgic glow further transformed into a preservative golden coating that blended everything together into a single mass.

It did not matter though. I did not care to identify anymore because my heart started racing. A feeling of anticipation welled within me. My eyes darted everywhere. I turned to my side to confirm this anticipation with my sister but, I could not identify her any longer. My sister became part of the environment and blended with the golden hue of everything too.

I was shocked and reached for the area where my sister sat, but it was indeed empty. My shock turned into concern and I became worried by her disappearance, or maybe it was better to describe a transformation of my sister related to the objects within this place. Her presence next to me was comforting and now she was gone. My eyes darted faster and my heart raced faster. I did not care earlier about things, but my sister leaving my side disturbed me. She was my security in this familiar yet foreign place. Now she was gone.

I gripped the warm car and it slowed by my pressure, reacting to my fear. I braced myself as if preparing for an impact, but the car gently came to a halt. I kept a firm grip because I was clearly uncomfortable and holding fast for what might happen next. Trying to calm myself, I wondered why I became so scared without my sister by my side. I am her older brother, after all. Why am I scared? Or, was it my concern for her wellbeing? Or, was it because I shared this experience with her and her displacement was unnatural?

Sitting in a stationary position, I was lost in thought, distracted by my own questions. Then I turned to my side and my sister was looking at me with concern. I should have thought her re-emergence to be out of place and yet again, I did not. This little hiccup was a strange ripple because the car was moving as if it had never stopped. What just happened anyway? What was wrong in the first place? I could not remember, but I was excited by what lay ahead.

Sluggish action almost compelled me to jump out. I hardly contained myself, but I was convinced of fulfillment once we reached our destination, whenever and wherever that might be. A child waiting in anticipation, I was wide-eyed. My instincts warned that if I acted poorly, the opportunity to find out what lay at the end of these tracks might disappear, so I patiently anticipated and imagined the expression on my face. My smile must be as wide as a platter. I could hardly stand this confinement. I wanted to run ahead.

I noticed the sky outside through golden window panes and shimmering glass. The view was almost blinding and I was forced to focus on everything that lay within this nostalgic scene. Apparently, I was being encouraged to engage the activity here and not have my attention wander any further than this space we were moving through. I was not sure if my sister felt the same way. We could not speak to one another or we simply did not speak to one another. I could not determine exactly which situation was the truth. It might have been because we were both in shock for being here and sharing this experience together. But, how could this be? Was any of this real? It felt real.

My thoughts kept straying. I was regressing. This distraction of pondering my situation was enough to change my perspective. I witnessed the two of us riding in the open boxcar, moving along the singular set of tracks from a point of view that would seem to place me above and outside of this enclosure. I watched the two of us glance at everything with wonder. I noticed that my sister and I in the car were the only entities in focus from this position. The sum of the objects that were once familiar to us merged into one another, slowly at first, and then accelerating into a massive blur ... *amber waves of splendor flowing.*

It made sense now. We were inside the presence that had beckoned me. It was irresistible. I was enjoying this. I saw that mirthful gait and that rhythmic flowing. The brilliance charmed me. The radiance soothed me. I was so happy. The movement was so playful.

But then, I sensed a change about to take place. I could see an opening ahead of the tracks. We continued moving at the same meager velocity as I looked ahead from our approach within the open boxcar. My heart raced. My pulse became more prominent. I tried to ignore the throbbing in my head. My heart was pumping hard and the strain forcibly created the sensation of sound within my ears. My pulse became audible. I was going to burst from the building pressure, but I refused to let up. I also strained to keep my eyes fixed ahead of the car. I did not want to blink. I did not want to miss what lay ahead. I centered myself in breathing. I fixated on breathing steadily and calmly. The last thing I wanted was to lose control.

As much as I tried to contain the tension, I became more and more excited. Despite my best efforts, my breathing hastened, fixated with hope. All this provocation ignited an epiphany come to light. I had an idea of what lay ahead being led to believe a miracle was about to come true. This had to be the answer to deeply rooted prayers I had protected and held so dear. The time had finally come. The realization propelled me further into a frenzy of emotions. My mind, heart, and soul charged forward. I moved forward.

Is this really it? Is this the time I had planned for over the years, not rushing for it to come to pass, but knowing that the opportunity may arrive and I must be prepared at any time? But, it still seems too soon. Is this really the right time? My wife ... My children ... Regardless of what lay ahead, I cannot look back. There is no backwards. Time knows no mercy. Time moves onward regardless of circumstances, regardless of anything, though it is not really time.

The opening was clear now. It was strange to become aware of the size and shape of it. What appeared to be so far away and seemingly large was merely the size and shape of a normal doorway. The scale of the opening seemed unnatural over the distance we had just travelled. It was not ominous or overbearing. It was a simple doorway just large enough for our open boxcar to pass through. And, to make the anticipation grow further, we slowed down as we drew near. This waiting was excruciating and worse, I could not see anything beyond. Whatever lay ahead was guarded by a pale illumination on the other side.

I wanted to scream, and do anything but sit in place, to set this pent-up energy free. I was about to burst into tears, scarcely containing myself. We were so close and the boxcar slowing down made me quiver. I grasped the car even tighter, but this time, not out of fear. Again, the car reacted to my tightening grip and slowed even more. I could not remember anything more consuming. As our movement slowed, my impression of time slowed down with it. This agonizing transition heightened my anticipation beyond anything I could normally tolerate. Barely breathing, I was frozen in place. My unblinking gaze was fixated on the doorway. I was about to crush the car with my hand. Every muscle in my body was taut, not sure if I was breathing any longer. I could not sense anything beyond the pounding of my own heartbeat, praying that my heart would endure this immense pressure.

Nearly at the opening, I could finally see the tracks extending beyond the doorway. I automatically thought about how much further we would have to travel before finally arriving at our coveted destination. The doorway was so close now. I could almost step through on my own. This was so cruel and comprehending the purpose for this journey was beyond me. This entire odyssey was forever etched into my psyche. As strong as my grip was on this car, I burned every image into my mind's eye so that I would not forget any detail. Almost from the beginning I knew this was a hallowed place that I may never find again. I continued to believe that this was my one and only occasion to be here. I reaffirmed my resolve.

In that singular recollection, by reclaiming the allure which brought me here in the first place, my anxious yearning evolved into a calming prescience. I finally knew WHY we were here. I was not breathing and by releasing the tension, I inhaled everything, drawing in the environment surrounding me. And, as I drew in life itself with that great breath, time sped up and flowed freely once again. The momentum of our vehicle traversed the threshold of that doorway and we were on the other side.

I was in awe. Only the single set of tracks extended beyond. Nothing else existed. It was natural to fixate on those tracks and for the first time, a bend in the path appeared. It was a ninety-degree turn. I could not take my gaze away from the path. The car accelerated and then the car turned.

My chest was still. I kept my mouth shut, desperately trying not to move a muscle. I threw all the determination I could muster into holding everything inside. I willed myself not to let go. I clawed at myself to keep everything together. I am so close. Please, no. I am so very close. I just need a little more time, just a little longer. But, I could no longer hold everything in. I was suffocating. I choked. It was gone. Everything was gone. Desperate to live, I exhaled everything. My body reacted instinctively. A short breath and I jolted in place. Convulsive and violent, my entire body shook. I opened my eyes.

A series of abrupt inhales marked my return. One long, stuttering exhale confirmed my reality. Gasping for air turned into sobbing. That was all I could do for the moment. My eyes welled with tears as streams of mucus, water, and oil flowed freely down my cheeks, passing across my lips, making me taste the full magnitude of loss washing over me. Short, abbreviated, abrupt breaths were all I could manage from weeping out loud. The noise in my mind was an unbearable wailing, but as far as my home was concerned, I laid virtually motionless, the silence broken only by my halted breathing, the soft breaths of my wife beside me, and our children sleeping well beneath their protective comforters within their respective rooms.

I rallied my thoughts and steadied my breathing. I settled myself so I could return as quickly as possible. It was my only chance to return, if there was any chance at all. I concentrated on every detail of my experience so that I could be projected back to that sacred place. Closing my eyes, I relaxed, submitting.

Sometimes an observer, sometimes an active participant, always human, and always myself, I never choose where I am or what I am. I remember fragments of what I had just done and thankfully, tragedy rarely opens its door for me. But, when tragedy appears to strike, at the nth moment before a point of no return, I am whisked back to my familiar place and time. One moment of self-awareness serves as the gateway. One swiftly drawn breath brings me back to this reality. My eyes open to greet the morning light, as faint or as bright as it may be. I immediately know this is the place where I belong because I am fully aware of what will happen next. I do not need to focus or gain my bearings. I just know. It is possible that I could be passing through, but my love here is great and serves as a beacon for my return. This is where I am rooted. This is the place and time I call home. Documenting this also serves to anchor me in this reality. I cannot believe any other way.

Within my dreams I am not aware of any other existence as is the case for this reality. I openly remark, "My life is a dream." I am doing what I am supposed to be doing, without question, but it is more like I am observing myself or others in a different time and place. The ability to differentiate between reality and dreams seems to lie in the when and where I wake. It is the sensation I immediately recall of feelings that linger and images of places I had just been. Waking with my heart pounding or waking with tears flowing, these are signs that I had just returned from conditions I could no longer bear. I assume I am hastened back to my point of origin.

I

The Second And The First

I LURCHED AND squinted at the glaring red digits of my bedside
clock. My face was soaked with tears. My pillow was soaked too.
It's too early to get out of bed and too early to begin the day. I woke
up before the alarm sounded … again. My forehead was drenched in
sweat. I ran my fingers over my face and wiped the sweat and tears
through my hair. It's so cold. This is happening a lot lately. I breathed
deeply, propped on one arm, fixed in place. Confirming the time on
the clock again, "I really need the sleep …" or else I'm going to be in a
world of hurt. "What a waste," I sighed aloud. I'm normally up and out
of bed as the alarm sounds. One sweeping motion and I'm on my feet.
I had never lingered in bed, but waking up before the alarm doing its
thing is really getting on my nerves. I can't go back to sleep either. I'd
fall asleep and then the alarm would sound. So, I've been taking this
unwanted waking time to dwell more than I normally would, recalling
memories of places I had just visited, places as clear as my view now,
casually looking around my room in the dull light of this new day.
Consequently, as days and nights have passed in this manner, the haze
in my mind has grown thick. I am physically affected as well. My mind
and my body are growing numb. It's getting more and more difficult
to focus.

My arm started to fall asleep. Go figure. I wish I could make the rest
of my body do that as easily, just go numb and live without sensation,
turning it off when I want. I guess I'm already on my way, but that's
probably a bad thing. Who am I kidding? I'm describing what's inside
that's numb and that's not so good either. I've been desensitized for

1

a while now, so this numbness in my arm is kind of refreshing. It's electrifying in a way. The nerves are screaming at me to move my sorry ass. The tingling grew stronger, but I challenged the reaction. The discomfort is stimulating. I held out for as long as I could. "Ouch," I whispered to myself, laying back, trying to feel my limp arm. It's always weird trying to move my fingers when my arm is asleep. I stared at my spiritless limb, massaging it until sensation returned. I always get a rush feeling that burn. The blood flowed back to where it had been denied. It's a good feeling.

The burn reached my hand and I slowly began to move each finger. Twitching turned into opening and closing my fist. The motion helped the blood flow while I stared at the ceiling. My waking eyes adjusted, but I turned to my mind's eye and converged on once clear scenes becoming fading memories. I tried to recall details of experiences elsewhere from the dreams I just had, but the images of people and places swirled into a blanketing fog that would no longer focus. "What a waste," I sighed again. I'd get frustrated if I had experienced this sensation randomly, but this is how it has been every single morning. It's kind of expected now.

I dream many dreams. I know they're not just dreams. They're experiences and have their own place, their own special identity within my life. Honing my ability to recall, I hope to learn a little more about the places I'd just been. I don't want to forget the people involved. I don't want to leave the experiences behind. I know I'm capable. I just haven't figured out how to manage this ability yet. Maybe that's why I'm waking before my prescheduled time. I'm practicing. I exhaled for what seemed a minute or two ...

I pondered some more, giving importance to this time before its time to begin my day. Everything serves a purpose, after all. That's probably why I'm uneasy. I'm trying to learn from these experiences in hopes to apply the wisdom I might gain. These are opportunities I can't ignore. I've much to accomplish if I can only harness the potential within reach ... yet so far away. "This is some deep shit," I muttered to myself.

Unfortunately, I'm no longer relaxed. This is a horrible way to

Erwin Lazaro

start my day. It's frustrating when I can't reclaim my dreams. Oddly enough, I'm also energized. It's inspiring to know I'm on the verge of something great. I can feel it. I think I'm going crazy, but I can feel it. This is how every day is beginning for me lately. It's a bit conflicting. It sounds taxing too, but it's not. Somehow, I'm encouraged to keep seeking considering how I'm feeling. It's expected now.

Now it's time to get back to this life. I don't know which direction this life is heading. More unsettling feelings rise with each morning. I don't have much to look forward on this day or any other day for that matter. It's just another ordinary work day, nothing to look forward to after work, but go home and repeat the same dull routine the following day. I just can't get over this nagging feeling that I'm supposed to do something magnificent, dare I describe it that way, but I cannot, for the life of me, figure out exactly what it is I am supposed to do. Every day is an exercise in futility. It really is. I'm so pathetic. This is a horrible way to start my day.

I clasped my hands together, placed them under my head and kept speculating. I'm healthy. Dad always says, "If you don't have your health, you've got nothin'." Can't argue with that, so okay, I've got more than nothing. I'm doing alright, I guess. I'm living comfortably. I have the greatest family and the greatest friends. Mom, Dad, and my sister will always be there for me. I know my friends will help me if I ever ask for help. I have a great job with the best boss. I think a lot of people would love to have what I have. In fact, I know so. Is it fair for me to ask for more?

Millions of people suffer without water, food, and/or shelter. Millions of people suffer from disabilities, disease, and disorders. Crimes beyond my imagination are taking place. I've tried to consider a fraction of the unfortunate circumstances that plague people, but a few minutes of dwelling upon those adverse conditions and my mind is on the verge of exploding. Sometimes, I can't help but feel guilty when these selfish thoughts cross my mind. What's worse is that I can't easily let them go. Contemplating on the direction of this life seems so insignificant as compared to the tragic situations that so many others face day in and day out. What right do I have to complain? I should feel guilty and I do. Maybe, guilt is freezing me in place. I want more, but I don't deserve it.

If I'm being honest with myself, I am having this silent conversation in my brain, so I can't lie. Well … I could, but I'm not. I laughed quietly. I know … I'm living someone else's life. I'm not myself. Something's off, but I just can't figure it out. I'm hovering over this body trying to knock sense into this husk of a man that's supposed to be somewhat intelligent. Well, maybe the problem is that I believe I'm intelligent. "Crap …" scoffing at the notion. How do I manage to do this every morning? I'm a broken record. Something is broken. What's wrong with me?

I continued dwelling and followed my seemingly not-so-random thoughts … Sure, as a kid, I did what I was told. I was kind of a slow starter in elementary school, but that's kind of an oxymoron … As an eight-year-old, I was forced to grow up through the mental and physical abuse from my second-grade teacher. I'm not the only student from that class that suffered either. I think because of that ordeal, I refused to let go of other things I probably should have outgrown. My spirit was and is unrelenting. I cried a lot. I'm still crying … but I also learned how to handle adversity by smiling and laughing too. The smiles and laughter are real, great medicine really. It's amazing what people do to protect themselves, especially when forced by traumatic situations. I did eventually get it together. I'm not ashamed to cry. I never was. Crying is cleansing, so is laughter. As an eight-year-old, it took a while for me to figure out I was growing up, but I did. That should count for something. No, I know it was important. Plus, Mom and Dad would never let me go so wrong. Their love made all the difference. I am so blessed by my family.

Outside of that second-grade classroom, I didn't get into too much trouble. I mean, what boy hasn't stumbled upon a stash of dirty magazines hidden in a plastic bag under a bush in a parking lot? Right? I was too embarrassed to ask, but I was certain all my guy friends had their own private stashes. That's what I told myself. It was natural. Some guy wanted a boy like me to carry on and learn about manhood. How else are tween boys supposed to learn how to manage their stuff without dirty magazines? Use our imaginations? Come on. I was so embarrassed

Erwin Lazaro

when Mom found them in the rec room closet. But, Mom, the angel that she is, didn't get mad. She just told me to throw them away. So, I threw them into another hiding spot. It worked as far as I know because she didn't find them again or, more likely, she never told me she found them again. Chuckling to myself, "Yeah, that last bit's probably more like Mom."

"My poor mom" I sighed deeply. I don't know how she's done it for all these years. Well heck, even now. I'm sure I'm worrying her with my moping about. It doesn't matter what I do. Mom never raises her voice, let alone a single finger at me regardless of how bad I am. I was the most spoiled and ungrateful brat growing up. Numerous times I ran from her in public places and the times I made her cry when I purposefully hid from her in the stores. And my relatives … out of respect for my parents, I'm glad I wasn't walloped for my mindless selfishness. I certainly don't think my uncle appreciated me stabbing him in the ear with a pencil while he was sleeping. And my grandpa, who was also sleeping, got a rolled-up newspaper square on his face as I used his peaceful demeanor for target practice. I don't know what it was about targeting helpless relatives in their sleep. I was a mean and mischievous child and yet I had a smile of an angel. "I hope God doesn't make me pay when I become a dad." I shook my head at myself. At least, those were a few occasions and not a daily activity for me. And, it wasn't for lack of trying on my mom's part. Mom's loving efforts are boundless. Thankfully, her gentle smile and gentle ways eventually won. Her efforts in combination with the birth of my sister, I believe.

By the time my sister was born, I started practicing good manners and making better choices. Mom's pregnancy and Kristine's birth changed my behavior. I instinctively reacted to being a big brother. But, for nine years, not only my mom, but my relatives had to endure my ridiculous antics. Thank goodness, my sister was born. Otherwise, I don't know how much worse I would have turned out to be. It's no wonder that Mom and Dad waited so long before having another child. They were probably afraid of another me. I'm sure they were happy when they received an angel for their daughter. The two of us could not have been more opposite as children. Again, thank goodness for my sister. Even being nine years apart, birth order traits still held true. Kristine is the angel and I'm not. Whatever the case, I'm just glad that Mom and Dad didn't have to brave another me.

I reflected on the thought of another me and shuddered. Then I noticed the morning light spreading around the drapes of my bedroom window. That's it. Every day is a new beginning. Get inspired about something. Something, but what exactly should I get inspired about? That's been the question lately at roughly the same time during this recent morning routine. I see the light and my hopes rise. It makes me think of glory days when life was grand and I was genuinely happy. I fondly recall high school memories. Those were incredible times. High school was a blast for so many reasons, but I can't go backwards, nor do I want to live in the past. The past has its place … but I can't get beyond this rut.

And so, what do I do? I must be real with myself. When my dreams fade to the point that I can't remember any further, I go back through my own life. I go back as far as I can recall, almost as an exercise so I don't forget. It makes me feel real. I know I just patted myself on the back for not living in the past, but that was a quick, pathetic turnaround. I just can't help it. Apparently, I don't know any better nor do I want to try to know any better. Mornings have been this way lately. I guess this is the way it is for the time being. With these feelings, I'm not surprised at how easily I stray from my own determination and contradict myself so readily. I can't believe I've sunk so low. I'm having my own pity party. It really is pathetic. I looked at the morning light spreading even further and shook my head. Nope. I'm going to figure this out and search for whatever it is I lost so I can move forward again. Or, maybe it's more accurate to think that I'm stuck and I feel like I'm wasting my life. Whatever the case, the sooner I figure this out the faster I can get out of this horrible groove. If only I could make my conviction last. It probably isn't conviction to begin with if I let it go so easily. I've been dedicating myself every morning, but my determination vanishes by the time I return home. It's a cruel cycle.

I inhaled deeply and sighed. No, it was more of a cleansing breath. It's not so bad dwelling in the past, especially when I've learned so much from experiences I'll never forget. In fact, I've worked very hard at honoring the memories that have shaped my life. At the same time, I also can't help but feel guilty too. I've had many close friends come and go, but I especially think of two of my closest friends whose lives were cut short, one best friend's accidental death, and another best friend taking his own life. My gut tightened and I took in another deep breath. Contemplating death is scary enough, but then I think about one best friend's desperation to live in his final moments and my other best friend's will to follow through and take his own life. I think about the three of us being so close, playing hours upon hours of ping pong together having fun growing up. At least, I thought so, but I found that their reality was different than the innocent one I enjoyed when we were together. I shouldn't feel guilty, but I think about my own role … maybe I was a poor friend for not doing something more to somehow prevent those tragedies from taking place. I am alive while two of my best friends are dead. I think of their families who were also my friends. But, I also think of both best friends and the promise I later made for living life to the fullest. I want to think I promised for the three of us, but the reality is that I was selfish. I was scared and I didn't want my life cut short. That was it. I want to believe that it was not selfish, but I learned from their short lives. I knew them well and we were best friends, but I also know that we were no longer the best of friends by the time their lives passed from this earth.

My sixth and seventh grade years were our best times together. But, I didn't realize until later that one of my best friends had already been mending from a broken family. That's why Randy came to live in my neighborhood in the first place. He was entirely new to the Pacific Northwest. In fact, I'll never forget the way we met. I quietly snicker while recalling. Randy's situation was no laughing matter, but mine was. Mine was a scenario like someone had scripted for a movie. It's a perfect backstory for a character in a comedy.

During the summer before my sixth grade, my mom was convinced that I needed to perm my hair. I was adamant in my opinion for not getting a permanent and I remained obstinate throughout the entire ordeal, but I lost in the end. I can still recall my ungrateful disposition with my arms tightly crossed on the way to the salon when my hair was straight, and on the way home when the big curls flowed all over my head. It was not as bad as a Medusa-look-alike, but it sure was a nightmare-come-to-life for an upcoming sixth grade boy. I don't think my expression changed for several weeks and my mom had warned me, in her gentle way, that if I didn't change that look on my face, my face would stay that way for the rest of my life. I think that's when I began to question my resolve and relaxed a bit.

Unfortunately, the new school year was about to start. I didn't know what I was going to do about this, what I felt to be, an unacceptably embarrassing situation. I ended up brainstorming what I thought to be a very clever remedy to hopefully last until the perm straightened out on its own. I decided to wear my winter parka to school with the hood on and keep my perm hidden until I made it back home after each school day. The perm was my awkward secret to keep. I did exactly that and roasted in the summer weather while everyone else enjoyed it. I thought that I would simply endure the unbearable heat gain in the classroom, outdoors at recess time, and especially during P.E. class. I doubt that anyone appreciated the sweat I was dripping everywhere, not to mention the odor I regrettably gifted as the resident pigpen. I was a wide, pudgy kid at the beginning of the school year and easily lost pounds in the double digits by the time I conceded. The last straw was when I was sitting in music class and the teacher demanded that I take off my hood as well as my coat. I was unyielding and that determination landed me in the principal's office. That was the one and only time I was ordered to visit the principal and entirely because of my vanity. To the very end, I stood tall in my hooded parka. I remember being alone in a room next to the principal's office. I waited for a long while because when the door finally opened, the principal was accompanied by my mom. The conversation was peaceful, reassuring, and brief overall. The two of them made me believe that my friends and teachers would accept me no matter what I looked like. "It's the person that I am that makes friendships." Those words of encouragement softened me and I conceded my clever ploy to my mom and the principal. Reluctantly, I peeled off my hood, took off my parka altogether, and gave it to my mom to take home. That was probably so I wouldn't scurry to put it on again, just in case I was greeted with rousing laughter by the other students upon my return. My mom also probably wanted to give my sweaty parka a good wash, too.

Music class had already ended by the time I finished with the principal and when I walked back into to my classroom, it was as if nothing out of the ordinary had happened. No one stared at me or gave me any extra attention because of my abrupt and ordered departure. I was worried and a little stunned, but being a boy helped a lot, because as soon as the next fun activity started, all was forgotten as if I had never created a spectacle of myself in the first place. Boys seem to move on easily, but I might have only been thinking about myself.

Years later, I wasn't surprised to find out from my mom, that while I was waiting in the room, the principal had made an official school-wide announcement. I don't know what the exact words were, but the statement was effective. My fear of being teased or ridiculed never came to pass and I will always be grateful to every person there who honored that direct order from the principal. Because I wasn't made into a laughing stock, that first perm grew on me in more ways than one. I continued to visit the salon and happily endured the three-hour process for every perm over the next few years. Karen, the stylist became my friend for life. I did eventually grow out of that perming stage. For ten years Karen permed and cut my hair until it was too difficult for me to visit her. My endless nights at the university for the school of architecture took me away from my childhood friend. We stayed in touch by phone, but life has its way of evolving. "I hope you're doing well, Karen." I whispered.

My comedy didn't conclude with my visit to the principal's office. I was so focused on myself at the beginning of sixth grade, when I had put myself and everyone around me through that absurd fiasco, I had not noticed that our classroom had welcomed a new student. My jumbled curly locks and I finally met the new boy from Florida. Randy was so cool because he had the Floridian accent and I could understand almost everything he said too. Before we knew it, we had become best of friends. That's when he finally told me that, for the first few days of class, he thought I was girl. Nothing but curls spilling from my hood and he thought it was odd that anyone would be wearing a heavy coat like that in the summertime. He was also perplexed and thought I was a bit large for a girl. I would have liked to say I laughed at his first impressions of me, but it was more like I muttered, "Uh, what do you wanna do now?" to break the awkward silence during that admission. The good thing was that, once that came to light, the niceties disappeared and nothing was left to hide, except when Randy wanted to share the story of how we met. I shrunk every time it was brought up and then I would try to hide. Randy meant no harm in his telling. It is a hilarious story.

We were best buds and during our sixth-grade school year, Randy met another boy while roaming around our neighborhood. They had soon become best of friends too. I finally met the other boy during a weekend when I could play with my friends. He was a bit loud and had a crazy, distinct, high-pitched laugh. When he laughed, he laughed for a really, really, long time and he turned bright red. He'd turn so red that I could no longer distinguish his freckles from the rest of his face. He was also a bit obnoxious, but I got used to him. He probably had an opinion about me too, but it didn't matter. His name was Patrick.

The three of us got along well together. I was surprised to learn that Patrick was a year older than Randy and me, but that didn't matter either. For only a little while, I thought it was odd that a middle school guy was hanging out with us sixth graders. But once they both learned I had a ping pong table at home, we spent the next two years in my rec room, slamming ping pong balls at each other every chance we got.

None of us were very good at ping pong when we first started playing, but our addiction to the game quickly made us champions in our own minds. The rec room in my home was not very spacious. We had about three feet around three sides of the table. The remaining side had just enough room for a walking path and the washer and dryer. The room had one small window and a door to the backyard. The previous homeowner had converted the existing garage to a rec room before my parents bought the house in 1977. The remodel lent itself well to our great passion while my mom and dad carried on with their tasks; moving between the kitchen and our raucous gameplay to take care of laundry and work in the yard when it was nice outside. We opened the tiny window and the back door as much as possible while the three of us projected all our energy into the game. We worked up quite the appetites and my mom always had food ready for us when we took breaks. Guys don't talk a lot, so we argued about the scores, who was better, laughed at the number of times we got slammed in the face with the ping pong ball, and thanked my mom for the delicious food. Grinning from ear-to-ear, I thought it was a miracle that we didn't break anything like the walls, for example. We'd lunge for the ball countless times, refusing to lose. Then again, we didn't have much room to lunge so when we lurched towards the ball, we simply braced ourselves against those walls and used the method to our advantage as we propelled in the opposite direction to get back into position. We were competitive. We were ping pong champions.

Sadly, the unpredictability of life fell upon our friendships during the summer after my seventh grade. Patrick, Randy, and I grew apart. Our primary interests swiftly changed. Ping pong became less important and the ping pong table became silent.

During the summer before I entered the eighth grade, I experienced tragedy for the first time in my life. It was a horrible and numbing feeling. Other things lured my two best friends away. One was death, a crude way of putting it. The other learned more about grownup stuff, things that never attracted me. The rules were strict in my home. I was never allowed to go out during school days, but I didn't mind. It might have even saved my life. I spent my days and nights learning how to draw, learning how to compose stories, and learning how to sing with pop music from the radio. Plus, having an angel as my mom was more than enough for me to enjoy being home. Dad worked a lot, but Mom always had dinner ready on the table when Dad came home. We ate home-cooked meals together every evening. I always expected it. At that time, my home was my world and I didn't need any more. I didn't know any more nor did I seek any more. It was so simple. I miss those times. But, for my friends, it was different. During the summer of my thirteenth year, Patrick died.

Numbness came after the jolting shock dealt by the death of one of my best friends. At least, I had still considered Patrick to be one of my best friends. His younger sister, Theresa, had relayed the grim news to those who had been close to him. Under the darkness of night, while inebriated, Patrick and one of his friends, that I didn't know, had jumped into a neighborhood manmade lake. Both being impaired, the friend climbed onto Patrick's shoulders while they were in the water. It was said that Patrick had been entangled by the growth below the surface of the lake and his friend didn't understand that Patrick was in trouble. My friend drowned. I was shocked and dumbfounded. It didn't make any sense to my thirteen-year-old mind. I know he didn't want to die. Even now, it's still so hard to believe. Since that awful time, Patrick has been in my prayers before I sleep every night. "I continue to pray that you are resting in peace, Patrick."

After Patrick's death, the growing pains started bearing more heavily on my shoulders and on Randy's shoulders too. I didn't realize how severe life's adversities had affected my remaining best friend though. When the two of us were together, as limited as those times became, we still played ping pong, but just the two of us. It wasn't the same. Randy and I knew it. That end of summer marked the closing of ping pong in the rec room and the beginning of the two of us growing apart.

Patrick's death was actually the second time in my young, sheltered life that I realized the world was crueler than I could have imagined. The first time still makes me quiver recalling my emotional scars. Only after the undesirable effort to remember my second-grade school year do bits and pieces resurface, under the guise of the lights turned off, and an entire classroom of students with our heads down on desks. I don't want to imagine the horrors other children have faced within a school, but our suffering was public. We suffered together. I cried a lot in that classroom. I was labeled a "crybaby." No one told me I wasn't supposed to cry after being beaten and humiliated. Yes, I sobbed openly. I wasn't ashamed to cry. I survived, I overcame, and I eventually became stronger. Was that the teacher's purpose? I'll never know.

I'm a little scatterbrained, but the trauma I suffered by the hand of my second-grade teacher hasn't faded. The details may be fuzzy in order to protect myself from horrible memories in her classroom, but the fear in my heart is still present. Sometimes, I try to believe those things never really happened. The whole idea is so foreign to my world, but unfortunately, I was a victim of emotional and physical abuse at my elementary school. I was once told that teachers in the olden days used to beat their students with objects, but for someone like me who grew up in a loving home with an angel, violence of any kind was completely barbaric. I was eight years old. This was 1976, a few months before my sister was born.

Oh my … my thoughts strayed even further. I smirked and felt proud recalling the day I punched a bigger, older kid. Some punk wouldn't stop making fun of my mom when she was pregnant. Because my mom continually walked back and forth to school in her condition, lots of students and teachers saw her on school grounds. During one recess, a stupid kid came up to me and started calling my mom fat. I told him to knock it off, but he wouldn't stop, so I decked him. One punch, square on the nose and that wimp was down on the grass field. I don't remember getting in trouble for that, but I was proud of what I did. I told my dad and he was proud of me, too. I was never harassed again. That was the only time I was compelled to punch anybody. No one makes fun of my mom.

My poor mom, the final trimester of her pregnancy started when I returned to school in September. She did a lot of walking for me. She was not very mobile and she didn't know how to drive at that time. Thankfully, we lived within a few blocks from my elementary school, but any extended length of walking under the heat of the summer sun while pregnant is asking too much. Almost every week, my mom would show up after school and find me crying. It burns me up thinking about my kind mom arguing with that HORRIBLE teacher about the HORRIBLE things that were happening in that HORRIBLE classroom. My mom walked back and forth to school every weekday because she was afraid of what might happen to me. I don't know what was worse, my mom walking back and forth and the ensuing stress that grew or the fact that, no matter how many times my mom complained to the principal, nothing changed. All of it was bad. Without question, it was a big mess.

Tears started welling in my eyes. I sniffled a few times as images rushed back to me about some of the abuse taken from that teacher. The entire class was being disciplined and we were required to place our heads down on our desks between our arms. We had to do this often and it always felt like a long time passing whenever we were in this position. I was always scared. Unfortunately, on one occasion, I needed to go to the bathroom and I had pleaded that I couldn't hold it in, but that teacher refused to let me go relieve myself. I held out for as long as I could. Even now, I still feel that once I had told her of my need to go pee, she had purposefully waited until I couldn't hold out any longer. She didn't give me any other choice, but to pee in my chair. That's how mean she was. And, that's exactly what happened. I peed in my chair with my head down on the table between my arms. I started crying. I reeked of urine. The rest of that disgusting memory is mostly a blur. Of course, I remember that teacher's disgust towards me. Of course, I remember my shame. The only consolation I remember from that situation was a few of my friends offering me paper towels so that I could clean up my area.

I bit my lip, but I continued down this awful trail in my life. I consoled myself by thinking this is nothing compared to other children being abused somewhere else in the world. Those children need help. So much worse is happening around the world, I shouldn't even emotionally react to what happened to me. That was a small event. It's in the past. The worst part of that experience was the horrified reaction of my mom when she came to pick me up after school. My mom had so many heated discussions with that teacher. I didn't realize how significant it was at the time, but now, I realize the true strength of my mom's nature. During those heated confrontations with the employees of that elementary, my mom never raised her voice. She never lost her temper. She never violated any social etiquette. In the end, her gentle ways might have been the very reasons why no actions were taken to rectify the debilitating conditions in that second-grade classroom. What those people didn't realize was that my mom protected them from my dad. If my dad had become involved, things might have gotten out of hand. That's why my poor mom shouldered all the pain, hers and mine. My dad didn't find out for a very long time. It wasn't until after that elementary school was shut down that these awful memories were revealed to my dad when there was no longer reason for him to be filled with rage on my behalf.

I breathed slowly as I recalled a recent chat with an old friend who happened to be part of that second-grade nightmare. She had been looking at old yearbooks and came across our second-grade class photo. That's when she revealed her own torment in that classroom. She asked me if I remembered "that" dreadful situation. I really didn't know which dreadful situation she was referring to, since there were many, so I asked her to relay her memories to me.

Soon after she started speaking, I could barely breathe. I listened in anguish as the images came pouring into my head. She started with, "That second-grade teacher was mad about something and made everyone put their heads down on their desks. Then, she turned out the lights, and I could hear her angrily rummaging through her drawers for T H E P A D D L E. No one knew WHO was going to get it... terrifying. Then, I heard you bawling your eyes out while she paddled the crap out of you. I totally remember that you threw up and she made you just suffer through it. The lights turned back on and I saw you crying, but your head was still down on the desk. I'll never forget what I saw next. That second-grade teacher wouldn't let you lift your head from your vomit. You had to stay that way until you stopped crying. I felt so bad for you. I had no idea why she was so mad. I just knew it was unfair and scary. What a horrible woman. She would never get away with that nowadays, thankfully. At least your mom was sticking up for you behind the scenes!"

As she relayed details, I'm not sure if I was breathing, but tears were running down my face. I was listening in complete horror as the memories came flooding back. I had not remembered that incident with clarity. I had buried those appalling circumstances to protect myself. I had only recalled the crying and vomiting, but as soon as she started evoking those flashbacks something unlocked within me. I automatically relived the terror and the tears of my eight-year-old self. I quietly laughed as I wiped them away.

My friend proceeded to tell me one of her own incidents. "One time, that second-grade teacher RIPPED me out of line because I was talking too much (I still do) and made me lie on the floor in the front of the classroom, face down, while everyone filed in and did their lesson. It lasted forever and I wanted to die. It was total and complete public humiliation. She broke me, temporarily. My mom was always in the principal's office complaining about her. Our family called her "The Drill Sergeant" ... Remember those multiplication drills? BANG! BANG! BANG! BANG! Scary ... but I will say that her fear-and-loathing technique permanently jammed those equations in my head. So, at least I got something out of it!"

I replied with, "I'm sorry that you have your own traumatic memories from that second-grade teacher. I'm sorry that I can't personally recall what had happened to you or any of our other classmates during that time. When you relayed the details of that incident with me and the vomit, I started bawling my eyes out like I was in second-grade again. And then, I started laughing because I was crying. Apparently, I'm repressing memories from that time. I've always let people know that I don't remember many details about my childhood. I get flashbacks of imagery and specific instances, but I cannot recall memories like you were able to relay with detail. I do want to add that I wasn't crying because of the incident itself. I started crying, thinking of my mom living with great personal adversities and I certainly made life more difficult for her. Even now, I pause in awe because my mom is the only person I know who never raises her voice or shows any signs of anger. Even when she tries to get angry, she bows her head and starts smiling. I'm very happy that I have a part of that within me, but I'm not as strong as she is. I let anger get the best of me while my mom lets the anger roll off her."

After our exchange of awful memories, it became clear to me that I was not the only victim of that second-grade teacher. I was too fixated on my own misery and I have zero memories of other students being mistreated. It makes me wonder how many victims she terrorized over her tenure as an elementary school teacher. As far as I know, that second-grade teacher retired without incident.

It wasn't until much later that I learned it was common for teachers to carry paddles and threaten students. Those paddles are used for disciplinary actions against students who break school rules. I also learned that most states banned corporal punishment, as it was called, but several states still allow it. Even after learning that, I think of the eight-year-old child I was, never abused outside of that second-grade classroom. I think of the eight-year-old child I was that didn't know that violence was acceptable in school. It didn't feel like it should've been accepted especially when it was discretionary. I only remember my tears. I can't remember what I had done wrong. I probably did misbehave to some degree, but enough to get physically disciplined and publicly humiliated? I just don't know if any measure is justifiable. At the end of each of those nightmarish second-grade days, I knew my mom would save me. That's what pulled me through.

The strange thing is that, fifteen years later when I was a university student, as my mom and I were exiting a neighborhood grocery store, we crossed paths with that second-grade teacher. I even smiled and greeted her. My mom did not. My mom smiled downward and quietly walked by. Then, she slapped my arm. My mom was visibly agitated as we passed her. I clearly saw my second-grade teacher's genuine smile for that instant. I don't know what possessed me to greet her. I credit my reaction to my strong upbringing of good and proper manners. I was happy that I didn't harbor any ill will towards my second-grade teacher. I really don't.

When we arrived at my mom's '69 Chevy Nova, I opened the passenger door for her, placed the groceries in the back seat, and faced my mom. Mom then said with furrowed brows and repressed smile, "That teacher still makes me mad for what she did to you." My mom's sweet expression was the visible extent of her anger. I smiled for my mom, hugged my mom, and assured her, "Mom, don't be angry. Let it go. It's not our place to judge. Sure, those things that happened were wrong and I do react when I think about it, but I can honestly tell you that I have no feelings for her or those times. I simply don't want to waste any more time on her. You and I are happy. God knows the truth. God takes care of everything. Consider how we are so Blessed. We are Blessed because we live the best we can. That's what matters." I smiled even wider, "Plus, I have great memories of wonderful teachers. Giving praise to them is important. One horrible teacher is easily forgotten. I think of the wonderful teachers throughout my life."

"You're right, son." Mom softly placed her hand on my cheek and gave me that knowing, comforting smile. The furrowed brows and repressed smile were gone. She sat down into the front passenger seat and I closed the car door.

I got in and turned to my mom, "… and Mom, you're the greatest teacher of all." We moved on with life. We never crossed paths with that second-grade teacher again. We never spoke of her again either.

The next thing I knew, "Time of Your Life" was playing on the radio. In one instance, I was driving my mom home and then I blinked and stared at the ceiling of my bedroom. This is Green Day. Disoriented and confused, I looked around and realized I had drifted off to sleep. The radio playing meant it's time for my work day to begin. That day with my mom at the grocery store was about seven years ago and hearing "Time of Your Life" was appropriate, but it should have been the Paul Anka song playing in 1991. Green Day's song with the same title is from the *Nimrod* album released in 1997. I get the chills when something doesn't make sense. Staring at my bedroom ceiling when I thought I was driving and hearing a song that doesn't fit the scene. That's plain freaky. At least I'm feeling something. That's more than I've been feeling for a while now.

Erwin Lazaro

II

The Third

NOW THAT IT really is time to get out of bed and get ready for work, I am exhausted ... I should call in sick ... The guys wouldn't mind ... Yawn ... I have deadlines, though ... It'd be pretty lame if I didn't go to work ... Yawn ... What would I do if I stayed home anyway? I don't have anything else to do ... I guess that pretty much seals the deal ... What a drag ... Yawn ... It's so pathetic.

I exhaled deeply with the lethargic weight of the world upon my shoulders. I rolled out of bed, bumped into everything possible getting ready, and managed to get out the door without breaking anything. I couldn't stop yawning as I started up my baby. "You know, I love you." I affectionately greeted my '95 Jeep Grand Cherokee Limited on this sunny, lackadaisical Friday morning. Looking forward to the weekend would be great if I had something to look forward to. I chuckled to myself and yawned again. I slowly stroked the driver's wheel, made the sign of the cross, and quietly began saying my morning prayers.

I sighed and promptly yawned again, an appropriate tandem for this kind of day.

I started my normal prayers and paused. Because I pray during the morning commute, the radio is always off. I could change my routine today ... but, I always use this time to gather myself for the day ahead. Meditation is vital for my sanity. With a fifty-mile commute to work and lots of thinking to do, I'm too distracted to focus on my daily routine. Instead of repeating prayers today, I'll pray for help. Now where did I leave off, before I fell back asleep and was rudely awakened by this new day of doldrums? These kinds of days are more suited for my selfish conversations with God. It's happening a lot and I'm getting terribly annoyed by this status quo. "Sorry, Lord God in Heaven, I'm not annoyed by having conversations with you. I'm annoyed by my situation. I need your help, as always." I'm so pathetic. I can't do anything on my own.

The gears immediately churned in my brain while I drove. Within my limited context, I've gained reliable insight from observing people, especially when those being observed think no one is paying attention. That's when I learn the most about the people around me. Awareness has helped me accurately gauge behavior and that insight has protected me well. I've purposefully honed my perception of my environment. Being abused made me think this way. I steer clear of trouble when my "spidey senses" kick in and I actively seek positive influences. When a person is lost in thought or engaged within a special moment or caught by surprise; those are instances when a person is most genuine. Maybe I'm the fool who paints everything in a positive light, but that's the light I want to see. The brighter side of life helps me navigate through my own darkness. Smiles especially, I enjoy smiles. Genuine smiles are to be admired. I enjoy people smiling so much that I can't help but smile too. It's such a simple way to warm my heart. No intentions involved, just good-natured behavior. Of course, if I was in shady part of town and witnessed people smiling, I wouldn't react the same way. In fact, I'd be much more guarded. But, for the random stroll among people within a festive setting or during the hustle and bustle of everyday living, when people are smiling, I smile too. Rarely do I smile back at a stranger, usually diverting my attention. Even I'd think that a stranger smiling back at me is a bit creepy. I chuckled to myself and then sighed.

I have worked hard at not judging people, regardless of the wrongs done to me. My second-grade teacher was a grand test for the eight-year-old I was. Second-grade was a defining time for my young life because in addition to my abusive teacher, people made fun of my weight. I was quite the round boy. I was often called "earwig" because my name sounded so much like the insect. I cried a lot during class so I was also called a cry baby, not much empathy from some kids around me. I couldn't blame them, but because of these experiences, I was forced to mature. I learned how to protect my spirit.

I learned to laugh when people made fun of me. I learned to smile after wiping away the tears. I paid attention and found that when I was carefree about the name calling, people simply stopped harassing me. I wasn't much fun to tease when I was happy. People moved on, except for my second-grade teacher, of course. Now that I think about it, I'm not sure if she considered her students as people in the first place. I think we were more like cattle that she was training. It seemed that way.

It's strange thinking about this stuff now. Back then, I kept the pain and humiliation to myself and found wisdom. Only my mom knew. I took what I learned from home and naturally applied that love to my growing pains in school. Children are naturally resilient, but I also protected my heart at that young age, although it's probably more accurate to give credit to my mom for protecting my heart for me. Her love healed my wounds.

I also inherited the innate sense of peace that my mom possesses. My mom is a living angel. I remember smiling at my mom after we passed my second-grade teacher at the grocery store. I knew she was upset, but her "upset" consists of looking down and smiling at the floor or ground or whatever is below the other person's eye level, if they are the object of her anger. On top of that, if I'm next to her, my mom's reaction usually includes a gentle slap on my arm. I wouldn't even call it a slap. It's more like bracing herself for support. If I had to explain what I thought my mom was feeling, I'd say my mom was being coy because she was embarrassed for feeling angry in the first place. And then, she'd laugh about being angry. That's how my mom is. It makes me smile when she's angry, but making light of my mom's reaction is not appropriate. I know she really gets upset, but her nature is so calming. My mom seems to immediately let go of any anger she feels. I think it's a gift, though it's more likely she's learned how to cope in this manner. "Nope, I'll go with her nature on this one. That's what I believe …"

"… and I'm sorry, Mom." As a young child, I didn't know any better. Mom had so much patience for the spoiled brat I was. Who am I kidding? I'm still a spoiled brat, but along the way I learned to take notice and appreciate my mom. Her benevolence is incomparable. Mom's kindness inspires me to give back so I've shared what I've learned with everyone I meet, especially to those who appreciate my offering. Being around my mom is the closest to my ideal of a heavenly experience on earth. I can't imagine anything or anyone being as wonderful as my mom.

Now that I think about my childhood overall, if I remember correctly, I don't think anyone ever witnessed me being angry or sad after second-grade. Forget the witnessing. I was never angry or sad, period. It could be that I'm choosing selective memories, but regardless, the feelings were real. That bubble was wonderful. I did yell once in high school. I still feel deep guilt about that incident. I have no excuse. A girl crushing on me never deserves that kind of treatment. That was an immature reaction that I can never take back and will always regret. I have yet to apologize for that stupidity. "Dee Dee, wherever you are, I'm sorry." I hope I'll choose wisely if our paths cross again. I don't have much confidence in what I'll do. I hope I do the right thing.

Where was I? Oh yes, I was always genuinely happy, otherwise. I can't remember everything, of course, but happiness permeated my life. It wasn't that I was hiding my emotions either. That is what is so incredible about how I grew up. If anything was troubling me, I knew that once I got home everything would be perfect again. Being home healed me in every way. Being home washed away my troubles. So, it didn't matter what happened outside. I always had my home.

Facing great adversity at a young age can ruin or bolster growth. Thankfully, I have the advantage of being born from a compassionate mom and a powerhouse of a dad. The reinforcement I receive from my family is the core of my strength. I recognized that source of strength as a young child and I continue building upon that strength every day. My dad was super strict and I didn't completely appreciate his rules at that time, but now I understand the wisdom of his ways. Even so, I'll try to find a balance between my parents when I become a parent myself. I will be a dad and I'll work to become the best dad I'm capable of being by nurturing my future family with unconditional love. And, when my children become parents, I'll expect them to outshine me. That's my goal as a parent. I will raise my children to become better than their old man in every possible way. I can help teach them to reach the level of their grandma Josie ... "Well, *you'd* have to teach them to potentially reach your level, Mom ..."

There I go again. It's so easy to wander and so difficult to get back on my train of thought. Though, reinforcing my dreams is always a good thing. Okay. Okay. Right ... I shared my loving ways from home with everyone I met and invested in friendships, making lasting connections. My amiable personality and my mom's cooking that won over the bellies of my peers were more than enough to create strong bonds. It wasn't until my senior year in high school when my swelling bubble burst, destroying the cushion I developed to protect myself; the cushion carefully sewn with love, humility, and appreciation from my home. I forgot the person I worked hard at being and the invaluable lessons that guided me. My ego outgrew my wisdom and I ruined the altruistic sense I cherished, including the ability to potentially help others when they might have needed my help the most, especially the best friend I failed, my best friend who lost hope. "Randy. I'm so sorry."

I grasped the crystal hanging from my rearview mirror, a precious gift from Randy. "I really let you down." I thought we felt the same way after Patrick drowned, but I was wrong. I knew shit. I knew we were both changing, but I didn't do anything when we outgrew the best friends we were. I was too busy becoming full of myself, especially during our senior year in high school. I didn't realize my efforts beginning as a thirteen-year-old would lead me to become a self-absorbed eighteen-year-old.

Patrick's passing from this world made Randy and I take more notice of our own lives, making us think about what we were actually doing. I became inspired to make more effort and do better with my own life. On top of Randy's broken past, something else went through Randy's mind as he withdrew from the normalcy of life around him. I didn't notice and because I didn't notice, I didn't recognize his declining situation.

Since the day we met, I knew Randy was brilliant. That was and that wasn't the problem. His brilliance naturally shined. It was the thoughts that he kept to himself that turned him into someone else. This was our transition into high school.

After the accidental drowning of our mutual best friend, Randy dove into music. Randy was another tragedy in the making, but I didn't recognize the signs. I'll confirm the fact again, the fact that I was too consumed by my own ego, especially during my senior year in high school. I know I failed you, Randy. I hope you will forgive me or must I forgive myself first?

I know what people will tell me. It's not my fault because I wasn't anywhere near you when you committed suicide. I don't believe anyone was aware of your intention to take your own life. Only those who were near you at that time might have had a clue, but even they could not stop you. It sounds like common sense to me, but this reasoning doesn't account for the times you and I did communicate and I failed to perceive the value of your expressions to me. I'm the egotistical idiot who missed the signs.

I have so much to thank you for and I never thanked you in person. You're always within my heart and you know the deepest truth of everything, but I can't rewind and do it again. That's my fault. What kind of best friend did I turn out to be for you? I'll never forget what you did for me.

You opened doors to music for me that I never knew existed, Randy. I already had a nostalgic impression about music with my dad's love for anything Elvis Presley. Because of my dad, I also enjoyed the music of Chuck Berry, Johnny Cash, Jerry Lee Lewis, Barbara Mandrell, The Righteous Brothers, Conway Twitty, Matt Monro, and many more. My mom always had music playing in our home and I quickly fell in love with the music of Barry Manilow, Dionne Warwick, Bee Gees, Crystal Gayle, Linda Ronstadt, John Denver, Billy Joel, and many more. And then I had my own preferences for Earth, Wind & Fire, Stevie Wonder, Queen, Kool & the Gang, America, Commodores, Heatwave, and many more. And because of you, Randy, I was entranced by Black Sabbath, Blue Öyster Cult, Sammy Hagar, Cheap Trick, Led Zepplin, Pink Floyd, Donald Fagen, and many more too. I'll never forget when you asked me if I knew about the animated film *Heavy Metal*. I can't remember exactly how I watched it for the first time because I was shocked by what I was experiencing. I had never seen anything like that and it was animated. It is an adult-themed animation. That really piqued my interest, especially as an adolescent boy. *Heavy Metal* really changed my perspective about animation because of those adult themes. I chuckled. *Star Blazers* was always my thing, but *Heavy Metal* easily became my favorite movie for many years. Beyond the imaginative perversity, the music from *Heavy Metal* is still my favorite sound-track of all-time. I had never listened to music like that before and I was hooked. Thus, was my introduction to heavy metal and its variations as a genre of music. Heavy metal music automatically clicked with me and a large part of that, I'm certain, is because of you, Randy.

You dove into music and so did I. Music became your true refuge and music became my refuge, too. You picked up a guitar and you rarely put it down while I developed my singing voice. Our mutual discovery and love for music marked the outset of our bond loosening. We both found something no one else could touch. You bound yourself to music and the culture that came along with the music you loved. I added music to the love I already nurtured for life. Your clothes transformed to black and you grew long, unkempt hair. You started smoking and experimented with other things. You made new friends. You got into trouble. You became the lead vocalist and lead guitarist of a band you put together. Your world completely transformed into something so foreign to me, but I don't ever recall saying anything about those transformations. "I was an idiot, wasn't I, Randy? Did you want me to say something? Were you waiting for me to step in and tell you how I felt?"

I was too dense to understand. You didn't hesitate to tell me how you felt through your actions. You were always upfront and true to your feelings. You did what you needed to do and faced the consequences. I didn't realize that you were yelling out loud for someone to intervene. You just didn't use words. "Was that it, Randy?"

Tears began to well. They began from my heart and emerged from my eyes. With those tears, angst filled my heart. My chest started aching and I clutched at my chest. I was trying to stop those tears from flowing, but they flowed freely, unwanted.

I'm not saying your new friends or the culture you dove into was bad. You made choices that I couldn't appreciate. I absorbed the parts of what I learned from you and incorporated them into my lifestyle, but it didn't transform me. From my perspective, you appeared to walk a dangerous path, but I never said anything. I'm not sure if I ever told you how I felt and if I'm unsure, it's most likely I never really did. My silence was unacceptable.

On the surface, everything you did was cool. You were the blue-eyed, blond kid from Florida with the cool accent. You had it all. You had genius-level intelligence. You spoke well. You had a great singing voice. You were a leader. You were a good-looking guy. I knew the girls thought you were so good looking, but you weren't very approachable. Heck, you were my eternal rival in competitive ping pong from our pepperoni stick betting days in junior high. You and your Lego ping pong paddle. Your secret weapon was the super random deflection that negated every spin that came your way. I was pissed and threatened by your superior paddle technology. On the surface, you seemed to have so many good things going for you.

Those were the days, Randy. I witnessed each of the changes you projected and wanted people to see, but I rarely made comment or acknowledged those changes. I'd come over from time to time and enjoyed your jam sessions on your guitar. It was your escape from the things that were slowly eating you from the inside out. I was too stupid to say anything even when you got into trouble. You might have gotten mad at me and told me I wasn't your father, but at least, I would have let you know how I felt. You could have gotten angry with me, cussed me out, and lashed out at me. It would have been better for you to know that I cared instead of appearing indifferent. That's probably how you thought I felt. We're guys. That's how guys are, right? We don't have long conversations and hug each other to make each other feel better. Maybe that was wrong. Maybe I should have said more to you. You had Jon. You had other friends. I figured you didn't need me to tell you how I felt. I figured you didn't need me. "Is that an excuse for my indifference?" The tears continued.

We even performed on the same stage during the high school variety show. I wore a carnation pink-colored, puffy, long-sleeve shirt with leopard print suspenders and serenaded our classmates with "Tender Love" by Force MDs. You and your band rocked out to some heavy metal jam. I remember you sounded awesome and you looked so confident on stage. I remember the lighters going up. It was awesome. You were awesome. I genuinely felt those things and I genuinely thought those things. I was proud of you, but I don't remember congratulating you after your performance. I was too caught up in myself. I didn't take the time to greet you. Maybe, I felt you were going to come up to me and then we'd exchange compliments. But time passed quickly and before I knew it, the show was over. Everyone left and I went on my merry way, forgetting to compliment you. I really wanted to take the time, but I just plain forgot and moved on. I did care, but I didn't make the effort to let you know, Randy. Maybe, I figured that you already knew I was happy for you. It was a guy thing. By that time in high school, we weren't really speaking to each other, anyway. We had our own lives and we were happy for each other. Right, Randy?

"RIGHT?!" I screamed out loud. I couldn't help sobbing.

Tears were flowing and I desperately gripped the steering wheel, trying to control my emotions, focusing my feelings into my clenched fists. Clenching the wheel, I rubbed my hands back and forth across my grip. "Right, Randy?" I sobbed. "Right?" You didn't need me to tell you how awesome you were. You didn't need your former best friend to tell you that I admired you for all that you were. You didn't need me to tell you that you mattered to me, right? You didn't need me, right? You got that from other people, didn't you? "Didn't you?" I whispered under my breath as I could barely see through my tears. This torrent of regret obscured my vision through the grueling morning commute.

As the last days of high school began winding down, Randy and I were almost strangers, but we held onto an unspoken bond not even time could take away from us. I remember our senior trip to the ranch. Our senior class hopped on a charter bus rented by our school and we were all whisked off to an undisclosed destination. This was our senior spree. Many of us danced and we partied all night long at that ranch. I brought a camera and so did a lot of our classmates. Lots of pictures were taken. I took a picture of you sleeping on the way home when the sun had already risen for the new day. We didn't sit together on the bus. We didn't spend any time together at the ranch and hang out. We didn't reminisce about old times. In addition to celebrating a last hurrah as a senior class, our union on this trip also encouraged me to reminisce about my memories with my classmates as we were about to embark on a new phase of our lives away from the comfort of our high school. That's how I remember feeling. For those few hours, together, we could have had similar feelings. That's what I wanted to believe.

A few weeks later we graduated from high school. The summer after our graduation passed quickly. Some of us found jobs or started working full-time. Some went to local community colleges. Some left the state to pursue a higher education. I accompanied a few friends and attended the University of Washington. You moved back to your hometown in Florida. It all seemed rather mundane.

I struggled through the university. I fooled myself into believing I could pursue something I didn't have any interest in. My dad had his dream for me, but it wasn't my own. I did eventually figure out that architecture was the path I should pursue and I found something important to claim for myself. I had a real goal and I believed in it. In the meantime, I lost all contact with you, Randy. Out of sight, out of mind; disturbingly lame of me.

I can't remember how much time passed, but you called me out of the blue. I was really surprised. I was really happy to speak with you. You let me know you were coming to visit. I was happy thinking about seeing you. I paused to focus on my driving as I switched lanes. My thoughts drifted and I turned my attention to the beautiful crystal hanging from my rearview mirror. I gently cupped it with my right hand, closed my eyes, and exhaled. With my breath, I let go. I refocused on the road and recalled more memories of Randy.

You did visit and during your time with me, I tried to convince you to move back to Washington. You refused, but while you were with me, you gave me a beautiful hanging crystal ball. You told me it had power and it would protect me. I was grateful for your gift, but I didn't place that much value in it at that time. I guess that might have represented my feelings about our distant friendship after the years that had passed after high school. We had grown farther and farther apart.

As preadolescents, we exchanged the customary birthday gifts, but other than that, I don't recall giving one another gifts, maybe a Christmas gift? I can't recall. I was such an idiot, not realizing the significance of the crystal at the time you gave it to me, that self-absorbed me with the density of a rock. If I was aware, if I was only given a sign that knocked me in the head, if I could have sensed your pain, if I was a better friend ... Would you be alive now?

I swiped across my face with the back of my hand. What really sucks is that I don't recall any part of our conversations while you were visiting. I can't remember what we did or where we went when you visited. I don't remember what time of year you visited. I can't remember the season. I don't remember if you were telling me something important that was supposed to make me react. I can't even remember the day when your sister called me and gave me the awful news about your suicide.

I had stopped crying and I had stopped breathing. I was fixed in that moment. Maybe, the shock of your death made me forget everything important about the last moments I spent with you. I didn't have a clue that your visit was going to be the last chance I'd have to tell you how important you have been in my life. I should have understood the signs. I should have realized when you made that trip from Florida to see your family and friends in Washington, and especially after giving me a precious gift, I should have realized that act was also your goodbye.

I had learned a little about suicide. I know that a person suddenly giving an important personal item is a telltale sign for a tragedy potentially going to happen. When the situation is neatly defined by someone else, it's easy to see the whole picture. I was given warning. Randy travelled thousands of miles and gave me a purposeful gift. He did that for me and I wasn't smart enough to put the pieces together. "I didn't understand. I should have at least considered your phone call and your visit and your gift … I should have. That was all sudden. I didn't figure it out." I sank in my seat. My heart ached tremendously.

My attention returned to the beautiful crystal hanging from my rearview mirror. I gently cupped it with my right hand again. I kept my hand in place and spoke to it as if Randy's spirit was contained within. "This crystal has become my most precious memento, Randy. You will always be with me." With my words, I let go. I pray for Randy. I pray for Patrick. I closed my eyes and prayed for the souls of both of my friends. I would never have imagined that two lives that were both my best of friends would both end in tragedy. I keep them both in my daily prayers and this day I feel like I'm going mad as my ravings are clawing at me from within. This uncertainty is eating me from the inside out. I just can't get a handle on it, but it feels like I'm near the end of something. I just don't know what it is and it's driving me crazy.

III

Frozen

MY PREOCCUPATION WITH this deep-seated guilt about Randy brought me to work in a daze. I drove, but I don't remember any of my commute. I was on autopilot. Thank God, I made it to work in one piece. That's crazy scary because I could have done something stupid. Maybe, Randy was looking out for me. Patrick is probably laughing at me. "Both of you guys …" I pulled into my regular parking spot, facing away from the two-story commercial building where I work, and stared at the Wendy's fast food sign across the parking lot.

I turned the engine off and sat frozen in place, still staring at the sign, trying to settle myself. I don't feel like moving, but the work day is starting. I don't want to work, but I'm already at the office. I made the effort to get here and now I'm just sitting in the parking lot. Ross is probably wondering why I'm not moving from my vehicle. He's the boss and I know he's up there looking out of his second-floor window. "Come, come on, move. Move, move already," I stammered out loud. I don't understand what's happening to me. Getting out of my baby is tormenting. I'm supposed to start working as I would any other work day, otherwise the guys are going to ask me if I'm doing okay and then I'll have to say something when I clearly don't want to say anything at all. It hasn't been this bad before. I hope it doesn't get any worse. I should have stayed home if I can't even face the guys. I gripped my steering wheel, "Come on, man."

I made an unspoken promise to Patrick and then to Randy that I would live my life as if there is no tomorrow. I promised to live for the three of us, but here I am wasting time wallowing in self-pity. I'm a detailed-oriented person, meticulous to a fault, but I've slowly decomposed over the last two years. Even knowing this, I still can't believe I've sunk so low. I artlessly ignored the warnings being too desensitized to notice. I've hit rock bottom and I'm wound up, slowly and methodically twisting myself with my own thoughts. I'm a selfish fool for being self-destructive.

My glass was always half full and then I threw it as far as I could. It shattered somewhere. I don't even have a glass to fill anymore. I can't decide anything for myself and maybe that's why it's so bad this morning. My mind is being flooded with regret, with pain, with confusion, with toxic feelings that are ruining my life. I have only myself to blame. It really does sound pathetic and it is.

This morning is different in an unbearable way. My feelings are concentrated. I'm conscious, but I feel an undeniable sensation that I'm waking up in some strange manner. I can't remember how long it's been since I've experienced such intense emotions. These ordeals are horrendous and exhilarating at the same time. I'm being injected with feelings I can't control. I already lost track of the last fifty miles and the last sixty minutes. Is this why I'm frozen? Are my senses telling me that I'm about to do something I'm going to regret? Or, am I afraid of the future that's about to unfold from which I'm no longer going to be able to hide? Let me think about this before I move. Calmly, I must breathe calmly. Clearly, I must think clearly.

Since waking this morning, I've focused on some rough patches in my life that's left me feeling helpless. I could care less about my second-grade teacher, but Patrick and Randy are in my daily thoughts and prayers. "It's been roughly eighteen years, Patrick. It's been four years, Randy. Time has moved quickly, but I will never forget." Or, from the time I promised each of you, has my commitment diminished and sifted through my fingers? Did I get lazy and drift too far? Did I drift to the point where the two of you couldn't stand it any longer? It seems neither of you can rest until something is done. "I'm quite lame for the two of you to be stirring in the afterlife for me." My world is being shaken by feelings I can't ignore, fed up with the person I've become. My two friends are kicking my ass from wherever they are because I'm failing my promise to them. I apparently can't do this on my own and I can't keep living like this either. I'm nearly at my breaking point.

"I'm sorry guys," I looked towards the sky. I somehow lost my place. Everyone and everything is passing me by. I'm moving around, but I'm going nowhere. It's so true about the adage, "Idle hands are the devil's workshop." Some people make ridiculously stupid choices with idle hands. Me, apparently, I've come to the point where I can't do anything at all. I think I have enough sense not to do anything too rash, but I don't know how long that will last. I'm pissing my life away. I also think I know what my problem is but I don't know how to kick-start myself. It was so much easier when I had clear goals. I could focus and act with purpose.

My mind found stillness and I blinked at the sky a few times. Turning my head, my gaze settled upon my boss' window before I looked down upon my steering wheel, trying to change my perspective and delve deeper.

My professional status is a blessing. I know my design work is meaningful and people are depending on me. I always have simultaneous deadlines and I aim for top results every time. Architectural design is not my vocation, though. If it were then I'd feel differently. Designing is a secure part of my life if I produce positive results, but my work alone is not enough. It's only a small part of the equation that contributes towards fulfilling the life I'm aspiring to build. Working for Ross is a blessed stepping stone to making my dreams come true, dreams that feel so distant at this point in my life.

Every person faces their own battles. No one goes through life without facing adversity; which can be overwhelming, at times. I am mindful of that for every person I meet. I do my best to express the kindness that an open mind offers especially to those who are not friendly in the first place. A smile and an energetic tone of voice can often work wonders. I work hard to be nonjudgmental, but even through my focused efforts I discriminate instinctively. I always criticize myself without mercy and I try to moderate my social reactions. But sometimes, my actions betray my intentions and I become emotionally charged.

I think about my first two years at the University of Washington and I become irate with myself. I have certainly faced unmotivated, self-destructive challenges since graduating from high school, floundering at the university, wasting time and money while trying to figure out exactly what I was going to do with my life. The most significant situation for me to challenge was my dad's dream for me. Inherently, there is nothing wrong with a parent's dream for or with their child. The challenge arose from my inability to walk on the same path with my dad and truly share the same dream he wanted for us. My dad always had the dream that the two of us would develop a partnership once I secured my degree in electrical engineering. Following his dream was the least I could do to show my gratitude. My dad's a genius and after all that he has done for me I thought I could muscle my way to the goal he had set for me. He paid for my education.

As it turned out, muscling through hurdles didn't work out in any way, shape, or form. I frequently found my face in the dirt. I found it more and more difficult to stand up after each hurdle I failed to overcome. My mind wanted to win this race for my dad while my heart screamed to be heard, telling me that living for my dad's dream was not acceptable.

It wasn't until the approaching deadline for submitting applications to the electrical engineering department at the University of Washington that forced me to choose. I chose a path for myself, remembering my promise to my two best friends. The time came when I was required to fully commit towards my dad's dream. My heart finally hurt so badly that I could not willingly give up my future, even if it was for the sake of my dad. I was too selfish to sacrifice myself for my dad's dream. That's how I felt. I've always had a strong sense of duty and making a choice against my dad made me feel as if I was ripping apart the ties that bind. I felt I was betraying and disappointing my dad, but these feelings did not outweigh the strong sense of responsibility that I had for my own future.

I lived with my family while I attended the university, but forced myself to leave for a few days to gather my thoughts. I stayed at a vacant rental property owned by a close friend's family. Clearing my mind and gathering courage, I finally addressed my dilemma with my dad. I confronted him. I had no desire to become an electrical engineer. The conversation with my dad started calmly, but it escalated into a shouting match. My mom tried to keep the peace. My sister sought refuge in her bedroom. Though I was relentless, I felt my willpower losing to my sense of duty as we went back and forth with our arguments. The conclusion of the verbal bout was determined by my answer to the questions my dad yelled at me, "What are you going to do with your life?! If you're not going to be an electrical engineer what are you going to be?! HUH!?!"

The truth is that I had not thought that far ahead. I had mustered the courage to reveal my anguish, but I could not think beyond that effort. We were in the living room and I had instinctively backed myself towards the door as our voices grew louder and louder. I stopped when I had nowhere else to go. My back was against the wall. I remember my exact position. I was adjacent to the front door, a wall mirror behind me, I had made my way there as a means of escape if cowardice took over. When I had no further to go, when I had nothing left to say, instead of fleeing, I looked my dad straight in the eyes and I screamed with my loudest roar, "ARCHITECTURE!!!" Silence took over. That was the end of that drama. I opened that front door, walked out, and began the next phase of my life. No further comments. No further questions.

After completing a few prerequisites, I designed my portfolio and applied to the School of Architecture at the University of Washington. I received the good news for being accepted into the department and took my first step towards my own goal. That was the spring of 1990. It was the first time I did something for my future that I could call my own. I felt proud.

My journey within the architectural program was an incredible experience. I worked tirelessly to overcome the demanding pace of the curriculum. My personal record was seventy-two hours without rest or sleep to meet a project deadline. I believe some of my peers were even crazier, going without sleep for an even longer stretch. I chuckled.

Architectural design is not easy and it's subjective, to boot. Professionally, I do all-nighters, from time to time. I've gone two days without sleep as my max, thus far. But, seventy-two hours for a graded school project without pay? I was motivated. That was certain. That was crazy. Three days. At that time, I was carpooling with my ex-girlfriend's little sister, Marv. It was my responsibility to get her to school. I remember, by the third morning, Marv was really worried about me and said I didn't have to get her, but I insisted. I picked her up as usual, driving from the university, to her home in Shoreline, and back to the university. I distinctly remember falling asleep at the wheel and she was so nice about it. I was too stubborn to let fatigue defeat me and I endangered both of our lives. Somehow, we made it to school in one piece. I made it through the rest of that day, completed my deadline, and managed to drive home before collapsing in bed. I don't think I moved for at least twelve hours after I did a face plant. The college of architecture taught me how to persevere under stressful conditions, face responsibilities head on without hesitation, meet deadlines like nobody's business, and stay awake without rest for extended intervals; all definitely not the best actions for my physical health and overall well-being, but absolutely essential for appreciating the demands of becoming successful. That is to say, hard work pays off, though no guarantees exist. Thankfully, hard work has continually paid off for me, thus far.

With regards to my school of architecture days I also have a significant, personal feat I am proud to acknowledge. I grew balls: "big cohones". Design presentations for peers and professors taught me how to objectively handle criticism on campus. Motivated higher learning paid off in spades. But, even more significantly, off campus, I didn't anticipate that as I developed a relationship with only the second girlfriend in my life, I'd undergo serious humiliation training exercises as a countermeasure to our relationship? Yes, my relationship was not approved by my girlfriend's mother and tears flowed over our growing bond. I'm not certain about tears from her mother, but rivers flowed from the conviction of my girlfriend. My girlfriend, who later became my fiancée, endured most of the direct fire. She protected our relationship and we both endured the agony that came with disrespectful and belittling behavior towards our bond. I learned how to fight for my own causes during that period, but not in an aggressive or even vocal manner. It was the exact opposite. I utilized the loving ways my family taught me to combat the indirect, malicious nature towards me. I should make clear that as a human being, no issues existed, but because of the relationship, I was invisible. I was barely and rarely acknowledged. I was often referred to in third person even though I was present. Again, coming from a loving home gave me the strength to withstand the emotional animosity towards me. I had to maintain a peaceful demeanor on behalf of our relationship, while my girlfriend was the opposite. She was continually engaged in vocal violence. In addition to her mother, her younger sister fed from the malice and continually threw salt deep within every wound.

Imagine three grown women consumed in rage. I am within the same space, but invisible, silent. Out of respect for the wishes of my girlfriend, I had no ability to protect my position or our relationship against her mother. My girlfriend took everything upon her shoulders to speak for the both of us. She protected her mother out of respect for their relationship. She also would not accept criticism from me or allow me to openly criticize her mother. I understood and honored her stance. In return, my girlfriend protected me in honor of our relationship. So many times, my girlfriend insisted we should go our separate ways so I would not be treated so poorly and we could both have peace. I continually disapproved and reminded her we made a commitment to one another. Other people were not going to be the reason we abandon our relationship.

I planned on proposing to my girlfriend and I conferred with my parents about my intentions. Their blessings are significant to me. After hearing me out, they expressed their reservations about our future entirely because of our difference in faith. She is Hindu. I am Catholic. Though conflicting with their personal opinions, they respected my choice and gave me their blessings, willing to accept our union. I know that was not easy for them, but their love for me and their trust in my ability to make wise choices outweighed their concerns. "You know what you're doing, son." my mom said as she gave me her comforting smile.

My girlfriend's mother, on the other hand, refused any consideration beyond her predetermined opinion and her actions spoke loud and clear. I sighed. My heart softens though, when I think of her relatives in British Columbia. The warmth they exude is much like my own family and I will always remember their kind spirit and support. They simply wished the best for us and showed us great hospitality. Their kindness is the model I perceive of the Indian culture, gracious and inviting. They will always remain fondly within my heart.

I had always dreamed of a fairytale wedding proposal and this situation was far from ideal, but I continued forward with my plans. My parent's blessings plus the blessings of her B.C. relatives was enough for me to believe I had gained ample support for a marriage proposal. I planned through the strife. A great opportunity soon served as the venue for my desire. I proposed to my girlfriend during a flight to California. We were accompanied by close friends for this momentous occasion. The flight attendants helped me by placing the engagement ring within a glass of champagne being served to my girlfriend. She graciously accepted, disregarding our pending struggles with her mother, and together we accepted a roar of congratulations from the other passengers and flight staff. For the time being, we enjoyed the excitement of the occasion.

For six years my fiancée and I endured emotional anguish in the presence of her mother and/or sister. My fiancée lived with her sister and that was a daily challenge. Unless her mother was visiting, I basically lived with the two sisters. Though turbulence erupted into chaos from time to time, the living conditions were tolerable. The two of us cherished our time together when outside forces weren't prying at us. The rest of the time we managed the circumstances, less than ideal for two people considering a lifetime together. Nonetheless, our relationship worked well because we sought something incredibly vital from one another. I provided her comfort, peace, and stability; a refuge from her continual struggles. She taught me how to live passionately, made my cohones bigger, and invigorated my already optimistic outlook for the potential of each new day. That's how we balanced our lives together.

For six years I geared myself for emotional combat, the pending turmoil with embattled veterans of psychological warfare. I tried to look forward to a life beyond this reality and then, one day, I woke up and considered my reality in a different light. That day, my fiancée asked me again about separating, abandoning our future together. Basically, she said this wasn't going to work. We weren't going to gain peace. No guarantees existed that would allow us to live without the constant pressures when the four of us were together. The tears may never stop.

That time, that one and only time, I agreed with her. I never looked backwards. Our relationship concluded amicably. We remained close for a while and eventually drifted apart. We still spend time together within our group of close friends, but I never entertain thoughts of a future reunion, only friends. I had no regrets and my heart was at peace, finally.

But, before concluding that phase of my painful reminiscing, in addition to the mom and sister of my ex-fiancée, she also had a "best friend" who completely despised me. And, I can't help but think how strange people can be. It's oddly humorous in a way because it's so ridiculous.

I can't even say that my ex-fiancée's mom and sister despised me. Her mom simply didn't approve of me for her daughter. Her sister is simply immature. I promised my ex-fiancée that I would never confront them, but I also can't lie to myself and be at peace without acknowledging the truth of my experience.

Now, back to the "best friend" … it's best to forget about her. She's only worth a little more time than I've already given. And, I gave solely for the sake of a woman I once loved. The "best friend" with the white windbreaker and casual manner, both incessantly disguising her wicked nature. Though, she never actually hid her wickedness because the vicious lashings emanated from her forked tongue and not from her demeanor. She was a "best friend" because of her efforts to be as sweet as sugar to my ex-fiancée. She was proud of her twisted existence to mock me and butter my ex.

I understood her position as a jealous friend. I personally believe that jealousy is an emotion to suppress at all costs, completely destructive, with no redeeming value. I also believe that jealousy is the demon on my shoulder telling me what to do and I must always fight it because it's always wrong. This woman accepted jealousy with open arms and continually asked her demon for as many ideas as possible. I had no choice but to endure this passive-aggressive assault in addition to the other two, a constant three-pronged attack from a sharpened pitch fork.

I'm certain that this "best friend" considered me to be weak and never understood how much resolve was required for me not to react to the constant humiliation she inflicted. I had prior training from second grade that adequately prepared me for people like her, but I still had to endure the stings regardless of how thick my skin became. That's enough about her.

Gratefully, to help alleviate those unpleasant memories, my ex-fiancée had a true best friend who was like a little sister to me. Thank goodness for her. She is the kind of person that I exchanged feelings with through simple gestures. She is Filipino and because of our shared culture, I am her kuya and she respected that tradition. Even so, I don't believe she would have acted differently because of her inherently kind nature. She teased me as a younger sibling would, but she never exuded any malicious intent. I am grateful to still call her my friend. My ex and my honorary baby sis were roommates at the university dorms and I'm certain they will remain lifelong friends. It's good to know they have those strong bonds. I took comfort in her friendship. She helped me tolerate those conditions. I'd like to think that she understood my position, as well, doing my best to maintain peace. Her quiet manner and quick laughter were comforting for me. I hope she knew that.

In hindsight, I find it fascinating that between the four UW students, with my ex and I being in the middle, we had an angel on one side and a demon on the other. One man constantly with three UW women and each of us were playing a distinct role for one another within the UW culture. The only way I can spin the entire picture into a positive light is that everything I learned from that time with them added to the knowledge I hope will become wisdom when I finally do meet the woman of my dreams. The lessons I've learnt are invaluable for my future.

Being engaged to be married reminded me to look beyond myself.

Erwin Lazaro

My mom and dad have been married for over thirty-one years, from May 20, 1967 to this present day. Wow. That is what I want. I have no doubt that my parents will be married until death do they part. I pray. I pray my parent's union will be for many, many, many more years to come. I cherish my mom and dad. My only dream since childhood is to find the "woman of my dreams," dedicate our lives to one another, and help bring new lives into this world so we can develop and nurture a wonderful family for the rest of our lives, together, in holy matrimony. My family reminded me of the future I seek for myself. I revisited my lifelong dream. I remembered my dad's advice that when I find the "woman of my dreams," that woman includes her family. I wouldn't just be marrying her. I'd also be marrying her family. That belief is essential to my well-being and to the well-being of our lifelong commitment to one another. I want to be married to one woman for the rest of my life and life is a journey with a learning curve. Achieving maximum competence for any given skill is always a challenge and life, in general, will offer a growing number of challenges with every experience. And, because I know and accept that to be the case, I need a strong foundation. I don't want to build a family upon a fragile condition, knowing that two important people in the lives of my ex-fiancée have no respect for our relationship. The bottom line is that I thought of our future family and considered my children more than likely witnessing that hell. When that revelation became clear to me, my decision was final. I was not going to subject the dream of my future children to that horrific environment. I did us a favor by finally agreeing upon our separation. We didn't abandon our future together. We improved the potential of our future apart and I certainly learned much about what I didn't want in my life, in my potential life with a growing family. This was the common sense I did not anticipate while dating. I'm grateful. I eventually came to my senses and we both moved forward.

I focused on the fast food sign again before continuing. Two years have passed since my ex-fiancée and I parted ways. I had to learn how to be single again. At that time, winter was transitioning into spring. I had gained an extraordinary amount of weight and my ten-year high school reunion was fast approaching. At first, my newfound freedom was refreshing, but I didn't want to see my glory day friends with my poor health. For the second time in my life, I had to pound the pavements to regain good heart health. I wanted to walk through my alma mater with pride. Three years earlier, I had ruptured my Achilles tendon while playing basketball during the summer of 1993. I gained forty pounds after being bed-ridden for four months. Once my physician gave me the green light, I ran the weight off, and recaptured a healthy lifestyle. It took me one year to lose that weight. Unfortunately, by the time I became single three years later, my complacent behavior gained me another forty pounds. That was entirely my fault. Second time around, I had four months to lose forty pounds, and reach my target weight before my ten-year reunion.

Goal in mind, I awoke each weekday morning at 5 a.m., ran roughly four miles around my neighborhood, left home by 7 a.m. for a fifty-mile commute, worked my typical eight-hour day, drove fifty miles to get home after work, ran the same route, and repeated the routine every weekday. On Saturdays, I ran twice a day, sometimes more, depending on social activities. Sunday morning was dedicated to Mass with my family. We usually enjoyed lunch together and I usually ran during the evening, giving myself a little breather before repeating this weekly cycle on Monday. I did that for four months and this time, at the ripe young age of twenty-eight, the Lazaro gene with bad knees finally caught up with me. I met my goal at the expense of crushing my poor knees. My aggressive routine was the most grueling when my weight was at its peak. I was over two hundred pounds, not good for my five-foot eight-inch frame. After four long months, I lost more than fifty pounds, bought a new wardrobe, and walked through my alma mater with pride.

"If you don't have your health, you've got nothin'." My dad's words of wisdom energized and helped me to go beyond my expectations. I set a goal to lose forty and I exceeded that.

Still sitting still, I rubbed my trim belly. I managed a smile and repeated dad's words out loud. "If you don't have your health, you've got nothin'. Ain't that the truth, Dad." A rookie relationship at the age of twenty, a second relationship and a broken engagement at twenty-eight, thirty years young with a trim belly and alone.

Erwin Lazaro

I barely had the will to move so I let my thoughts continue dwelling back in time; five years ago. Aside from my growing pains with my girlfriend's mother and sister, at that time, I began my professional career in architecture. From the kindness of an employer willing to take a chance on two rookies, my girlfriend first secured a position at an architectural firm in Puyallup. I had decided to pursue a second degree in building construction, but I realized the managerial side of construction was not my cup of tea. After three quarters of building construction, I decided to graduate with a bachelor of arts in architecture from the University of Washington. That was the spring of 1993. A few months later, my girlfriend offered me an interview at the firm where she worked. Her employer sought help for projects that were beginning to overwhelm their numbers. Her employer had asked her if she happened to know anyone who would be able to help them. I was very blessed.

I craned my neck and looked up at the second-floor window. I'll never forget that interview.

I clearly remember the first day I walked through the doors of R.D.A. I was terrified. Thankfully, my first impression couldn't have been any further from the truth. My initial fear was a reaction, in part, to the fact that it was my first professional interview. The owner of the firm greeted me and he had the sternest mien about him. I was clearly intimidated. Then, he spoke with the kindest, most gentle voice. I was confused. His presence didn't match his personality. He turned out to be a living example of the catch phrase: "Don't judge a book by its Cover." Ross Deckman is the man in charge as declared by the name of the firm, Ross Deckman Architect.

During the interview, I also met a man who immediately became my brother. His name is Jef. As I was introduced to Jef, all I saw was the top of his head. He meekly said, "hi." That's all he said. I didn't notice him looking up from his work. At the time, I thought THAT was the most bizarre greeting. But, that's exactly what makes Jef one in a trillion. He is the resident ninja. The second 'f' in his name is invisible to mere mortals. In addition to Ross and Jef, I also met Bill, an easy-going personality with a generous smile. Bill could effortlessly be the PR for the firm. Four people, including my girlfriend (at that time) comprised the firm of Ross Deckman Architect. I was so nervous, but my introductions with Jef and Bill distracted me enough to help me forget about those nerves and the interview was a success. Surprisingly, that interview turned into my first day at work.

During that first day, I also remember being told that my employment wasn't guaranteed, depending on the number of projects that came their way. It was a realistic approach. I respected that. Ross is always honest and straightforward. Later, Ross gestured that if the workload remained steady, then I was more than welcome to continue with them. I will always remember the warmth of that sentiment. Ross may not remember, but I always will.

So, here I am sitting in the parking lot below my boss' window, almost five years later. Knowing Ross, he is more concerned about my well-being than my tardy appearance through his doors. That's the kind of man Ross Deckman is and I greatly admire him for his kind nature.

"Sorry Ross, I'll be inside soon. Ouch." My seatbelt tightened after reaching for my briefcase. That was a rude way to realize I hadn't unstrapped yet. "How am I going to function today?" I'm so angry at myself. I finally moved, but I moved for the wrong reasons. I have a bad attitude this morning. I'm going to work shrouded in anger and disgust. I don't want to socialize. I'm not in the mood to speak to anyone. Within an open space office, having a small crew, all within earshot of one another, including my boss, is going to be a disaster. We're all friends here and I can't handle any comments or questions. Please guys. Just let me work silently. Don't say anything to me.

IV

Comfort Food

HERE I GO. I opened the door to the building and slowly walked up the flight of stairs leading to my workplace. I turned into the open doorway and ... "Good morning, Erwin. Are you doing okay?" I cringed and shrunk within myself as the rage grew within me. "Remember, Erwin ..." I thought to myself, "They haven't done anything wrong. Don't take anything out on them." I was lost in my thoughts as I silently and briskly walked to my seat without responding to the morning greeting ... from my boss. Unfortunately, my silence didn't go unnoticed and the work day at the office started in the worst possible way.

I placed my briefcase under my desk as I usually do, but I had hastily put it down in the wrong place. I pulled my chair out to sit down and saw that my briefcase was in my way. Instead of simply moving my briefcase out of my way, I saw red and kicked it to the side. It made a solid thud against the wall and I sat down huffing and puffing like a child not getting his way. I was embarrassed and doing exactly the opposite of what needed to happen so that no one would know anything was out of the ordinary.

If my ex-fiancée still worked here, between friends, she would not let me act the idiot, especially within the office. She would approach me directly and quietly talk to me about this obviously impolite behavior. But, she's not here. Thus, I'm an idiot. Anyhow, she's not here because my ego tells me that neither of us would work proficiently if we both remained at RDA. Awkwardness would sprout, grow, and potentially fester after our separation. Either, the guys would continually conspire to reunite us or when we stepped onto the dating scene neither of us would freely discuss the details without feeling sheepish about the matter. Regardless of those circumstances, I have faith her concern would come forth. That's the type of person she is. Her instinct to help would push her forward. The reality is that soon after we separated she found a great opportunity and moved on, though she remains close to the rest of the guys here. Good for her. She is much more adventurous than I am and she is a free spirit. She grew.

Me, on the other hand, I'm not sure what I've accomplished in the last two years. I regained my health for my ten-year reunion, but after that, I'm not sure. I had to learn to be alone again and being alone is not what I want to be. I turned thirty this year and it was the worst birthday of my life. The ache within grew more pronounced just thinking about it. I typically don't make a big deal about my birthday. It's an ordinary day. This year I felt like crying, but that would have been the worst response or would it have been the best? I'm not certain. I am certainly feeling twisted inside, coiled so tightly, I'm going to explode. Rage, fear, frustration, helplessness, this is not good.

I took several deep breaths to pacify myself, staring at my blank computer monitor. I dared not look at my colleagues in fear that I'd have to acknowledge them somehow. I know I'm being selfish, but I can't help it right now. I'm more afraid of doing something stupid and lash out. I should have just stayed home. Just don't talk to me and the day will move as smoothly as possible.

Within my peripheral vision, Bill stood up and took a few steps. He stopped and began chatting with Ross. Jef chimed in and chuckled. I briefly smiled with my head low. Jef has that effect on me. Thank you, Jef. Brian, who had joined the firm before my ex-fiancée exited, retorted with a comment. "Thanks, guys." I said in my mind. I should have said it out loud, but I knew that if I opened that door, other comments or questions of concern might follow. I reached down and started the computer. The motor whirred, the screen flickered, and the day moved forward whether I liked it or not. I wanted the work day to move as quickly as possible so I could leave and be alone. My friends kept their distance, except for the occasional instructions from Ross. I accepted

Erwin Lazaro

his directives with polite acknowledgement. Otherwise, I kept my head down and focused on my work.

The hours moved quickly. I purposefully didn't look at the time. Keeping tabs on time ticking will make work grueling and be too much of a distraction. Keep my nose down and I can walk out of that door without adding to my regrets. I looked up at the open door and I nearly bolted. Dammit. *Keep my nose down.* Regret is ahead if I don't stay focused. My anger fumed and the idle chatter blurred around me. I lost track of time.

I did start the work day roughly an hour late so when I saw Ross, Bill, and Brian get up to leave I knew it was time for lunch. I also had a hunch that Jef staying behind was a strategic move. They know that I adore Jef and if anybody could reach me this day, it would be Jef.

I prepared myself, though with Jef, I don't believe that anything he could do would ever get me angry. If anything, he has a calming effect. He is humorously tactful, engaging his prey, always diverting attention away from himself. That's our ninja, Jef. I consider him my big brother from another mother. He is my kuya. I'm the kuya in my family, but here, Jef is my kuya.

"Hey, you know the guys are worried about you, especially Ross." Jef was leaning back in his chair, hands extended on his desk, face turned towards me.

I also leaned back and let out a long, drawn, audible sigh. "Yeah, I know. This is just a bad day. I don't want to talk to anyone today."

"Dude, you've been acting this way for a while now. It's not just today. The guys will hear you out if you give them a chance. Don't you have someone you can talk to? Why don't you have a private discussion with Ross?" Jef remained in his position, giving me a reassuring smile.

I guess I have been rather aloof lately. I hadn't realized the office was aware of my condition, but it makes sense. I'm usually talkative and I get involved in the usual banter, but I haven't been doing that. I guess it is a no brainer that they'd be concerned. I do go into a few quiet spells occasionally, but never for a long period of time. That's what makes this situation out of the ordinary and more volatile.

I gave Jef a half-smile and sedately responded, "Tell the guys I just need some space. I'd really appreciate that. I'll come around on my own. Tell the guys not to worry. Thanks, Jef." I leaned forward and buried my face into the computer screen.

I had to stifle the tears. I'm such a fucking idiot. I should add an apology for making them worry, but I can't say anymore because it would become clear that I am not doing well and then they'd want to intervene. If I said any more, Jef would hear the tone of my voice as a plea for help and I won't do that. I won't. I just … won't. Keep my nose down and the day will pass quickly.

That's exactly what I did. I heard the guys eventually come back, but I refused to raise my head. Thankfully, I wasn't required to coordinate with anyone. Thankfully, my phone was silent. Thankfully, no one needed to talk to me. I stayed focused on my work before I noticed that it was nearly 5 p.m. A few minutes and I'd be able to leave for the weekend.

That's when my heart sank. Monday will restart a new week of woe. No. I can't repeat this again on Monday. I can't. What am I going to do? I can't continue this. It's not fair to the guys. I'm going to explode and I don't want to take this pent up malice and release it here in the office. I have to go somewhere else. I have to go some … where.

I closed my eyes and thought of my Jeep … I'm going to drive.

I opened my eyes and I read 5 p.m. on the monitor. I quickly shut down the computer, picked up my briefcase, stood up, and walked to Ross. In a quiet and calm manner, I leaned on the plotter stationed between us and addressed my boss. "Ross, I'm taking vacation next week. I'll be back in the office on the following Monday." I stated it calmly and it was not a request. If Ross wasn't the man that he is, he could easily deny me for demanding this action without prior notice, but Ross is a compassionate man, a blessing for his employees. I had every confidence he would accept my action and respect my privacy, as well.

"We'll see you on Monday. I mean …" Ross chuckled, "Two Mondays from now." His reassuring tone was accompanied by his beaming smile. He stopped what he was doing and focused on me.

Again, I was nearly in tears. "I'm sorry, Ross. I know we're busy, but …" I pursed my lips together. I couldn't say anymore.

Ross, recognizing his queue to intervene, reassured me. "Don't worry. We'll be fine. Do what you need to do and come back safely."

I nodded, didn't acknowledge anyone else, jetted out the door, and didn't look back. My heart raced because I had committed myself. No turning back now. The next order of business is to talk to my family, give my family confidence, especially my mom. Persuade them to believing that I'll be safe.

My commute home was another fifty-mile blur, but this time, I focused on my will to follow through and move forward. I had been on the verge of approaching Ross all week about taking a vacation, but we've been so busy. I didn't want to impose. I was antsy yesterday and had made up my mind, but I couldn't. Today was too much for me. The compounding emotions were driving me crazy and I couldn't continue this way anymore. Today is all I could handle. Right now, my heart is telling me I am making important progress, finally acting on impressions that have been continually nagging me. This is my first step forward in two years.

I arrived at home with purpose. I gripped my steering wheel and released my tension with a long exhale. No matter what they say, I cannot let them persuade me to change my mind. My poor mom, she already manages so much with her daily struggles and now I'm going to add to her troubles, again. Thinking about that alone is almost enough for me to alter my direction. No, I cannot. If I don't continue moving forward now, I may spiral downward even further. I'm going to do this. Now is the time.

I braced myself and opened the door, trying to act as normal as possible. I had already made the decision to bring up the matter during dinner while we are all together as a family. As usual, as soon as the front door opened, the delicious aroma of Mom's home-cooked Filipino food engulfed my senses, comforting me and making my stomach growl at the same time.

Smells like one of dad's favorites. Pork kilawin, though not one of my favorites, because of the pork liver. I'll still eat it. The vinegar with pork, garlic, onions, sliced radish, and bell pepper strips, are unmistakable. And, because Mom knows I'm not a big fan of kilawin, I also smell tortang talong. Now, the grilled and flattened eggplant, dipped in a batter of whisked eggs, sautéed ground pork with garlic, onions, and tomatoes, plus raisins, all pan fried together, that's making my mouth water. And my baby sis, though she'll eat eggplant, she prefers something a bit different. Mom saves some of the mixture excluding the eggplant and adds potatoes to make torta, a yummy Filipino omelet.

I walked in, hurriedly closing and locking the door behind me. I wanted to protect the deliciousness from escaping our home. Dad was sitting in his chair and reading the daily newspaper. "Hey, Pops." His attention remained on the paper as I walked passed.

"Mom, you're always spoiling us!" I exclaimed while striding towards the kitchen, passing my sister at the dining table "Hi, Tina-pa", and giving my mom a kiss on the cheek. My mom's presence always bestows upon me the love and serenity I'd imagine being in our Lord God's kingdom in Heaven. And, Mom's radiant smile is a gift every time.

"I wasn't that hungry before I walked through the front door, but now my stomach is growling." I grabbed my stomach and accentuated my feelings.

Mom slapped me gently on the arm, keeping her hand still, holding me in place. Her squinting eyes remained focused on the frying pan, "Be careful. The oil might splash on you. Go put away your things and wash your hands. Dinner will be ready in a few minutes." She gently released me, sliding her hand down my arm, and opened the lid for the saing to check if the steamed white rice was ready to serve.

I turned to face Tina-pa sitting at the dining table, sinister smile on my face, and I inhaled deeply. She wasn't where I thought she was. It was then I realized I had projected myself back in time, thinking of fond memories, my expectations of that past. I entertained the nostalgic feelings and let myself drift momentarily. I stood still, remembering ...

It looks like she's working on a project from school. She had moved aside her place setting to do her work. Her back is turned towards me. It's a perfect opportunity to cause some havoc. So, I quietly placed my belongings on the floor and crept up behind her, extending my index

Erwin Lazaro

fingers. I placed each finger to either side of my head and made a clicking sound for each finger with my tongue, declaring the intention of tickle missiles ready for launch.

Tina must not have heard my warning because she didn't react like she normally does. The hood vent is so loud and the frying food is camouflaging my preparations to attack. It's a perfect set up. Within three feet of my eleven-year-old sister, I launched my tickle missiles, creating exhaust sounds as I swerved them in flight. Within one foot, she finally reacted as she recognized my imminent attack, but it was too late. My two missiles propelled faster upon reaching their targets and with my vocal explosion, each index finger hit their marks and rested firmly in each of her armpits.

Tina squealed and dropped her pencil. She wriggled my fingers from her armpits, stood up, and launched her own hundred-slap counterattack with both of her hands. I lifted my arms to cover my face, hiding the mischievous grin she could obviously see through my shoddy defense. Her dimples were shining as she continued her retribution for another minute before finally being satisfied. Without a word, she turned back around, sat down, and continued working on her project.

"Hmmph! Erwin! Stop teasing your sister. Dinner is almost ready." The memory faded and reality refocused into place.

The reality is my baby sister is twenty-one years old now. Kristine, or as I affectionately refer to her as "Tina-pa" or "Tina" is most likely in her bedroom, but she is *not* sitting at the dining table getting tickled by her older brother.

Dinner time, Mom in the kitchen, the enticing meal, family gathering, all of it is precious to me, the comfort and the care. That nostalgia made me recall the joy I'm missing now. That memory also roused me and brought me back to my intentions for this evening. I'm not here to reminisce and dwell in the past. I need to stay focused and move forward.

Every time I consider my mom, I can't help but feel that everything will always be fine. My mom, my dad, my sister, our home ... this environment is my security blanket. I love them dearly and I love our home dearly, but I can't rely on my family forever. My senses keep telling me the same.

"Okay, come to the table. Dinner is ready! Son, please get your sister." Mom announced behind me.

I hadn't moved from my position in the kitchen and I was in the way. After Mom's instructions, I dashed into my room, dropped my belongings on the floor, and knocked on Tina's bedroom door. "Dinner's ready." I heard my sister's reply beyond the closed door and I turned back towards the dining room.

I walked slowly while running through my thoughts. I know what I'm going to say so I'll reassure my family that my choice is sound. I'll reassure them so they don't worry. I pulled my chair out from the dining table and admired Mom's nightly feast. The meticulously prepared meals were set on serving platters. Steam was rising from the kilawin, the tortang talong, the torta, and the steamed white rice. Four place settings were waiting. I sat down and continued my mental preparations before my family joined me.

"The food is getting cold." Mom called out as she placed serving spoons on the platters. She turned back to gather condiments.

Dad folded the newspaper and put it down. He walked over and yelled out to my sister from his seat at the head of the table. "Kristine! Come to the table now." He picked up the bowl of rice and served himself. The kilawin was next and he began eating.

I waited patiently as my sister and mom sat down at the same time, Mom in front of me and Tina to her left. This is our usual seating. Mom and Tina helped each other. Tina started with the rice and served herself. She passed the bowl to Mom as Mom handed Tina the platter of torta. I sat watching. Of course, Mom immediately noticed that I had not yet served myself and encouraged me to eat before the food became any colder.

Once they were finished serving each other, I scooped a generous serving of rice onto my plate and placed a tortang talong directly over my rice. This is comfort food. Thanks for these blessings.

I noticed that Dad was almost done with his dinner so I had to begin the conversation before anyone left the dining table. "Mom, Dad,

Tina … I have something important to share." I focused on my full plate of food. "I've decided to go on a road trip."

No one interjected and I continued, "I need time by myself so I'm going alone. I already spoke with my boss and he's fine with it. I'm planning on travelling for a week. It could be longer, but at least one week." I wavered because the next part is going to make Mom worry the most and it will be the hardest for her to accept. "While I'm gone I won't call home, unless it's an emergency, of course." I looked at Mom and fear was plastered all over her worried expression. "Mom, I'll be safe. I know you're going to worry. Just pray for me. I'll come back safely."

"I'm always praying for you and Kristine. Do you really have to go? Where are you going?" Mom was no longer eating. Her appetite certainly vanished after I dropped this bomb on our family.

My answer is not going to improve matters or give them reassurance either. "Actually, I don't know where I'm going. I haven't decided yet." Honesty is critical. I really don't know where I'm going. Something or someplace is calling me.

"Erwin, think about what you're doing. You need to stay home. Your mom and sister will worry about you while you're gone." Dad always excludes himself, but I know he's always included too. "Your mom's already having a hard time every day." Dad folded his arms and made his point clear.

My heart cringed. Being concerned about Mom's health is the most difficult part for me. Mom's daily challenges make me feel inexcusably selfish for having to do this. She is going to worry sick about me no matter what I say. Mom's been fighting for her life for nearly ten years and I'm adding to her burdens, again.

I couldn't look at my mom. "Mom, I need you to trust me. I'm sorry. I don't want you to suffer any more, but … I don't want to make your life any harder than it already is, but … this is an urgent matter, Mom. If I don't do this now, I'm never going to do it. Please, Mom. This is hard for me to say already knowing you're going to worry about me while I'm gone. I need you to understand."

I was doing my best to hold back a tearful delivery. I didn't want to add more to this situation and make it worse. "I promise you. I'll be fine."

"Why do you have to go in the first place?" Dad maintained his posture.

Tina was eating slowly, listening to our conversation. Her attention was devoted to her food. My little sister's remaining portion seemed to be relocated on her plate. I noticed her quickly taking small bites every so often. I intently observed Tina-pa and silently apologized for making her endure this. I know she'll worry about me too, but I also don't want to give the wrong impression to a twenty-one-year-old either. I don't want her to think I'm running away because I'm not. In fact, it's the opposite. I'm finally tackling this situation head on.

I picked up my spoon and started poking at my own plate. "I've been having a hard time lately."

"Your mom has been worried about you." Dad interrupted and confirmed their awareness of my bad moods around them.

"That's exactly why I have to do this. I need to figure things out for myself and I can't do it here. If you know that I'm having a hard time, then I need to solve my problems so you don't have to worry about me anymore. I'm hoping that my trip will help me figure out what I need to do for myself. That's the point of all of this. When I come back, I want to be satisfied knowing I did it. That's why I don't want any of you to worry about me. I'm doing this so I can move forward and not be a burden anymore."

"Son, you are never a burden … and we will always worry about you." Mom's fear turned to compassion, her tone also reassuring me that I am never a burden while expressing her worry at the same time. Well, it was more of her smile that evoked those emotions clearly. Mom's smile is her magic.

I tried to return a reassuring smile. "I know, Mom. You and Dad give me everything. I have everything here. We are so blessed." I want to tell them that that's another reason why I'm doing this, but those words will be confusing. I don't want Mom's compassion turning back to fear or turning into uncertainty. I am always safe here and if they had their way, I'd stay with them forever, but I know I can't do that. I'm also fighting for my independence and the ability to know we can love each other in the same way without living under the same roof.

After living with a woman for three years, I wondered whether it was the right choice to go back home. When they learned the engagement was broken, my family never discussed how they felt about the matter itself, but I know they were happy anticipating my return home. They happily anticipated our family living together again.

At first, the reunion was comforting. I truly needed it. The peace here is the stability I sought after six years of mitigating emotional instability. I had to regain a spiritual balance. But, at the same time, I gradually lost my independence. I slowly became complacent towards the future. I slowly lost myself. The gradual decline of my self-esteem over the last two years has brought me to this unbearable angst, the turbulence I'm confronting now.

That impactful dream kicked my ass this morning, enough for me to finally act. I'm going to get things in order so I no longer dwell in the past. I can't pretend anymore and facing my problems is the only way I'm going to figure things out. I'll make a plea to our strong bonds and maybe they will understand my point of view.

I placed my spoon down and gave my full attention to my beloved family. "I'm not a helpless child. You know I can't live here forever." I chuckled and made lite of the situation. With a warm smile, I pleaded to my family. "Well, if you had your way, you'd do everything for Kristine and me. We would always be together and I love that. I really do. I'll say it again. We are so blessed." I paused and changed my tone, emanating from deep within. "But, I need my family to understand that living apart doesn't mean I love any of you any less. I'm only going to travel for a few days. I know you are always praying for me. I'll be home before you know it. I need to learn to let go a bit. We all need to learn how to let go a bit. This is a good experience for our family."

I sat quietly and waited for their responses.

I looked at each of my loved ones and witnessed their downward glances. Tina remained silent. She was intently waiting for Mom and Dad to say something. Dad with his arms still folded also waited. I believe he knew this situation depended on Mom's feelings. I focused my attention on Mom. She had her lips pursed. I could see her gathering thoughts before she spoke.

It was Dad that broke the silence. "Where did you get this idea? We don't care what other people do. Something like this is not a big deal for them, but it's a big deal for us. We won't know where you're going. We won't know when you'll get back. What if something happens? What if your mother needs you?"

I had no certain answers for my family. I could not offer any guarantees. "The most I can do is promise that I'll be fine and that I will return safely. That's all I can offer. I promise." I don't like promises, but I couldn't think of anything more convincing.

My attention was fixed on Dad when Mom finally acknowledged and accepted my plea. "Okay son …" Mom exhaled. "Make sure you pack enough underwear. Do you need me to do laundry? Don't drive at night. Always keep your doors locked. Don't go too far. Don't talk to strangers. Come home safely."

I turned my attention to Mom and I melted. I understood she had bent her will to mine. Her furrowed brows and gently forced smile told me she didn't want me to go. Her eyes were averted from mine. Mom didn't want me to see her fears realized and my heart sank as I accepted her approval.

Dad left the table and went back to his paper. Tina quickly finished eating and went back to her bedroom, closing the door behind her. Mom stood up and started clearing the table. The discussion was over. I made the sign of the cross, picked up my spoon and fork, and solemnly finished my dinner alone.

I didn't take long at the table and took care of my empty plate, setting it in the kitchen sink. I stared out the window and considered the rest of my evening. I already had plans to go out so I switched gears and hurried out the door. I didn't cancel and tried to enjoy a few hours with a friend knowing I still had to prepare for my departure in the morning. My home was still by the time I returned. It was finally time to work on tomorrow.

What was left of the evening was muted as I prepared for my journey. Silence allowed me to revisit the unsettled feelings I revealed amid dinner. My family reluctantly accepted my terms, but at a cost. I numbed my senses trying to convince myself I am doing what I must. Is my choice worth the additional suffering my mom will endure? I shook my head and stalled. I'm going to worry about Mom. She has overcome so much and the last thing I want to do is add to her burdens, but that's exactly what I'm doing. I keep telling myself that and here I am on the eve of uncertainty.

My sight was cast downward as I sat on my bed, contemplating my selfish intentions. I remained still for a long period of time. It was getting late and I still had to pack for my departure in the morning. I slowly stood up and opened my drawers, moving forward. "If I don't do this now, I'm never going to do it. I've already excused myself from work, too." I muttered to myself as I started choosing my clothes. "I'll pack enough clothes for a few days, clothes for dry and wet weather. It's been nice out. It's August. It should be warm and dry, but I should also be prepared for rain, just in case." I nodded to myself and stalled again. "I can't see any other way around this." I sighed to myself.

Trying to minimize my baggage, I reviewed my clothing laid out on my bed. Feeling comfortable with my choices, I sat down next to my collection of compact discs neatly alphabetized within the rack next to my desk. Packing clothes was easy, but now it was time to choose music. I glanced over the thousand cases I had carefully dated and identified by number after each purchase. "This is going to take me a while." Instead of searching by case, I picked up the binder where I had cataloged the music and film titles I collected so far. I immediately pulled out my favorites, but I used the binder to choose enough discs to fill the time along my way. I fondly studied the album covers as I took the discs from their cases and carefully placed each one within a sleeve of my travelling case.

Music is my lifeblood. It's the one thing no one can take away from me. Happy, frustrated, sad, and everything in between, music is my haven and what better company than music to help me overcome myself.

I look at these artists I've chosen and wonder if they know that they are counselors. I wonder if some, or all of them, had the intention of sharing their wisdom through music so people like me would take their efforts to heart and learn from their experiences. I certainly have. "Dan. I'm gonna need your help ... again." I turned back to the cover of my favorite album so very precious and dear to me. I placed my palm over the cover. Mom is probably the only one who knows how many times I've played *The Innocent Age* over and over and over again. The noticeably worn double vinyl album that I have is now kept safe and secure for me to preserve as best as I can. Lifting the needle thousands of times has given the music even greater character. These compact discs are a handy replacement for those delicate time pieces.

"Well, it definitely depends on the artist. Dan Fogelberg, yes, an artist with wisdom to share. "Weird Al" Yankovic, no, not on my list of musical philosophers, but definitely a mad genius who discovered his own unique niche to succeed." I dove onto my bed face down. "It sounds like I'm lecturing myself." My words were muffled by the face plant into my comforter. I giggled softly and my laughter turned into snoring.

V

Departure

I AWOKE AND turned onto my back. Feeling uncomfortable, I quickly realized I had fallen asleep on my neatly placed clothes. I sighed and glanced over to my clock, confirming that I had slept through the darkness. It's August 8, 1998, 7 a.m. Okay. 7:01 a.m. Time is wasting away. I was hoping to leave early, but that won't be possible now.

I stood up and dropped my shoulders as I witnessed the mess I had made of what were neatly folded clothes. Nothing was packed yet. 7:02 a.m. "Time knows no mercy." Even so, this anxious feeling of anticipation is a good thing and it's a bit strange. For the first time in a while, I don't remember any dreams. Too exhausted to remember and that's okay with me.

I opened my closet door and pulled out my duffle bag. I turned back to my bed and started refolding my clothes. I quickly packed my bag, reviewed the musical counsel sessions selected for my therapy, and hurriedly dressed. As if queued, the delicious aroma of Saturday morning breakfast began filtering through the cracks of my bedroom door. Mom's intuition never fails to amaze me.

My belly reacted with an audible grumble. The day was moving on, but I won't leave until after enjoying Mom's breakfast. I opened the door. The delicious wave hit me and Mom immediately announced, "Breakfast will be ready in a few minutes. Go brush your teeth." The obedient child in me complied and I took care of my bathroom needs, not forgetting the toiletries for my road trip.

I didn't bother to shower because I didn't want to add to Mom's laundry. I grabbed what I needed and disappeared into my room. I quickly packed my toiletries and hurried to Mom's side, giving her a good morning kiss on the cheek. Mom turned to return my affection with her typical Filipino "sniff kiss". It never fails to crack me up because she always inhales my cheek as she kisses me with her nose.

All the while, the sinangag, Filipino fried rice, was making my mouth water. I drooled over the scrambled eggs with sautéed onions and tomatoes. The glistening fried bacon strips on the table were ready to devour. I noticed the daing na bangus still in the packaging next to the stove. I was grateful Mom hadn't cooked that yet, otherwise … "Aiya … oh no …"

As soon as I thought it, Mom pulled out another pan, turned on a burner, and opened the packaging for the butterflied milkfish marinated in vinegar. I was hoping to begin my journey not smelling like fried vinegary fish, but apparently, I'll be taking this part of home with me until the smell goes away. The thought of passersby reacting to my homey essence made me smile.

Mom's squinting eyes stayed focused on the stove as she placed one of the fish onto a hot pan. The violent sizzling made me stare, but Mom didn't flinch as oil splashed in her direction. While she cooked, Mom pleaded with me once more, "Do you really have to go, son?"

"Yes, Mom. I know you're going to worry, but please try not to worry so much while I'm gone." That was a stupid thing to say. Of course, Mom's going to worry. "I'll be careful and I'll be back soon. This is important to me. I'm worried about you worrying about me." I'm such an idiot, "Please, Mom. Pray for me as you always do. I'm always praying too. I'll be fine." My resolve wavered, but reassuring Mom was the best option to possibly ease her concern.

"I'm always worried about you and Kristine and your dad. That will never change, my son." Mom finished the sinangag and was almost done frying the daing too. "I can make you food. What would you like? I have some embutido in the freezer. I think I still have some lumpia shanghai, too. Pack some rice. Do you have a cooler?" Mom's forced smile made my heart melt again.

"Thanks Mom, but I'm not taking a cooler. I …" hesitated to say any more. I don't know where I'm going yet. I'm trying not to make my family more concerned than they already are. "I'm just going to buy food wherever I go. It's easier that way."

Mom turned off the stove and pulled plates from the upper cabinet. After setting them down next to the stove, she scooped a generous helping of sinangag onto one and handed it to me. "Open the lights, sit down now, and eat breakfast before the food gets cold. Make sure you eat well so you don't get hungry when you're driving and take some food with you for later. I'll give you plastic containers."

I smiled and whispered to myself, "Oh, Mom ... open the lights ... and after I said I'm not bringing a cooler ... you'll never change and I love you." Mom made plates for Dad, Tina, and herself. I sat down and helped myself to the eggs and bacon. The food looks yummy as I know it always is. "Bless us, O Lord, and these Thy gifts, which we are about to receive from Thy bounty, through Christ our Lord. Amen."

From his usual chair in the living room, dad's face was revealed as he placed the morning paper on the coffee table. He silently joined me at the table and began eating in silence. I know this is dad's way of concern and I let it be.

I'm assuming Tina-pa didn't join us because she's still sleeping, but Mom sat down with her plate. Dad continued eating and Mom covered Tina-pa's serving with a napkin. Mom dug into the bangus and began eating quietly.

I could tell Mom was thinking of something to say that might convince me to change my mind so I spoke for her. "Thanks for the yummy breakfast, Mom. I won't eat for a long time because my belly is going to be so full." I cherished a crunchy bite of fatty bacon, followed by a generous fork of scrambled eggs, and balanced the savory combo with a spoonful of sinangag. This is Saturday morning heaven. I chewed to my heart's content.

I stuffed my belly until it was uncomfortable. I had no idea what kind of food I would buy during the next week so treasuring these precious mouthfuls of homemade goodness is great while they last. My spirits dimmed with my last bite because I knew it was time to move forward again. Mom makes it so easy for me to stay within my cocoon.

It's so easy to settle even though I know settling is not the option I should take.

"Thanks for all that you do, Mom. That was delicious." I relished this contentment while standing and rubbing my protruding belly. With my plate in hand, I scooted over to Mom and kissed her on the cheek again. Mom reacted in kind with her sniff. Placing my plate in the sink, I didn't say another word and quickly disappeared into my room.

Mom and Dad finished eating in silence. It wasn't until Mom was at the kitchen sink did I hear any movement outside my bedroom door when Mom turned on the faucet. I was almost ready to leave when it finally dawned on me that I still don't know where I am going.

On my knees, at the side of my bed, I laid my head on my blankets. I wanted to go back to sleep instead of facing this position. With my head turned towards the window, looking north, I peered at the trees beyond and thought about my options.

If I go north, a passport is required. I'll be across the border in less than two hours and then where would I go? Silence filled my head. I thought of Vancouver, B.C. I thought of baked barbeque pork hum bows. I thought of steamed barbeque pork hum bows. I thought of barbeque pork. I thought of eating all that barbeque pork at Stanley Park. My belly rumbled even though I couldn't possibly consume any more food and silence filled my head again. My mind wandered and my gaze drifted beyond the trees.

I love what I know of Canada. Our Lazaro clan with three or four loaded vehicles used to enjoy annual trips into British Columbia with Grandma Betty's incredible picnics, eating all day long. The men and boys would sweat up a storm playing basketball and then play volleyball after refueling with more food and drinks. The women and girls watched the games, spending most of the day chatting, managing the food, and relaxing. The biggest event I remember was the 1986 Expo in Vancouver. That was a lot of fun because I had just graduated from Shoreline High School. So many people and driving around was a nightmare, but enduring was worth the effort. My dad rented a bedroom for our immediate family from homeowners making extra cash during the major event. Good memories.

The problem is that I don't want to rely on the familiar. I'm not going to continue relying on the familiar. I turned and buried my face into my blankets, face down. My mind remained blank. I could drive towards Alaska and see how far I go, but that doesn't sound appealing to me. I don't want to just drive. I'm not sure what I want, but research is required to drive towards Alaska and I don't have time for that, not on the spur of the moment. Alaska is more like an expedition. Am I overthinking this? I breathed deeply into my blankets.

And then I changed my point of view. I lifted my face not only to breathe freely, but to look west, beyond my bedroom wall, beyond my home. I visualized the Pacific Ocean, the entirety of it. The massive body of mysterious water that is close to where I live yet spans thousands of miles beyond my point of view, virtually one hundred eighty degrees from where I could stand. Well ... I smiled in thought ... I'd peer over the Washington peninsula and the Olympic Mountains, but the Pacific Ocean that frightens me to the core and yet entices with its mysterious nature and awesome magnificence. Yes! But driving to the ocean would only take me one day going around Puget Sound. That's a dead end.

I continued visualizing the Pacific Ocean and changed my perspective once again. I looked over my left shoulder, turning to face southward, and imagined my way along the coastline. I thought of Ocean Shores and the Washington coastline. I thought of Cape Disappointment at the Washington-Oregon border. I thought of crossing near the mouth of the Columbia River. I thought of highway 101 and the Oregon Coast. I thought of great redwoods in Northern California and then I wondered how far could I go?

I thought of San Francisco and it dawned on me. I have a friend living in San Fran. I crawled over to my desk and grabbed my phone book. Unzipping the red leather casing, I found the number for my friend, Patricia. I just hope she's home, otherwise I'll need to stop along my way having to call from pay phones.

I dialed her number and prayed. "Hello?" Patricia's familiar voice answered my prayer.

"Patricia? Hi! This is awesome! I mean, this is Erwin! I'm so happy you answered the phone." I'm certain I sounded desperate and relieved at the same time. "How are you doing?"

Patricia laughed. "Hey, Erwin. It's been a while. I'm doing well and, how are you?" She paused giving me the chance to get right to the point.

"Well, this is sudden but I'm going on a road trip and I was thinking of driving to San Francisco. I was wondering if it would it be alright for me to visit you in the next few days?" I held my breath with anticipation.

"Oh my God. That's so cool. Yeah, of course. Actually, my roommate is out of town this week and she won't return until next weekend. Do you have a place to stay while you're in San Francisco?"

"No, not yet, this is all sudden. No plans. I'm thinking of staying just one night in San Francisco. I don't know how far I'm going, whether I'll be passing through or headed back to Seattle at that point." I pondered my options with those words.

"How much time are you planning for your road trip?" I immediately understood the direction of her question.

"Oh, yeah. Good point. I told my boss that I'd be back at work by next Monday, but I also kind of left it open-ended, just in case I need more time."

"I'll warn you already that unless you're driving straight here, it'll take you several days. You could easily spend a week or more just sightseeing through Oregon. I'd imagine that you plan to do some sightseeing along the way?"

Patricia is always a smart and matter-of-fact one and I'm so glad she's willing to help me. "Obviously, I'm not well-travelled like you are, though Oregon is similar to Washington in many ways. I've never planned a trip for myself so thanks for the advice, Patricia. Yup. I'm planning on making random stops along the way. I'm not sure yet about where and when. I'm just going to follow my nose and see where my travels take me."

"That's great. Would you like some advice?" Patricia has always been a free spirit and always so polite.

"Yes, of course. Please." I was getting more and more excited about my prospects.

"If you're planning for one week, I'd suggest you travel down the

Oregon Coast and pick a few beaches and caves and other natural sites. Check out some redwood forests in Northern California too. I'd say … try to make it here by Wednesday or Thursday. That'll give you five or six days to drive down and three or four days to drive back. That is, if you're leaving today. On your way back, you can visit some wineries."

"Nice. I like that advice." It was settled. "How about I give you a call when I'm within a day of San Francisco? I'll let you know then if I haven't found a place to stay for the night."

"Sure, that sounds good. I can meet you after work and we can go out for dinner. I want to hear all about your trip!" Patricia genuinely sounded pleased and abruptly changed her tone. "I hope you're going to be okay driving around San Francisco. I'll warn you now that the hills are steep. You're not driving a stick, are you?"

"I have no problems driving up and down pill hill and no, I drive an automatic SUV." It won't be so bad.

"Seattle hills are nothing compared to the hills here in San Francisco. Wait till you get here and you'll find out for yourself." She laughed loudly.

"Alright, thanks for the warning. I'll see you in a few days then and thanks for letting me visit." My excitement began to swell.

"Okay. Bye." Patricia hung up as I sat down on my bed.

Having a place to go is giving me a purpose. I just hope that I'm not a mess by the time I visit Patricia. That'd be a real bummer. I'm not planning on weighing her down with my problems so I'll do my best to keep things light, a simple visit from a friend. I looked at my clock again and it read 10:15 a.m. It was almost time to load up my Jeep, affectionately referred to as "my baby", but I had to do a few more things before doing so.

I went back to my closet and pulled out my Spanish guitar. I had recently walked into a music store trying to find inspiration. That was when my feelings of dissatisfaction were rising and I actively sought something to help. A place of music was a natural choice for me to begin seeking. I found myself standing in front of a massive wall of guitars hanging in place. Before reason took over I became attached to this one in my hand thinking we'd become partners in music one day.

I've strummed it a few times, but with my current state of mind the inspiration to learn has been low. I'm also hoping that inspiration to play will strike me along my journey. "You're coming with me." I smiled and leaned the case up against the wall next to my bedroom door.

Finally, my mountain bike came to mind. Dad and the Saturday morning paper were in the usual place as I hurried by. Mom had moved on from the kitchen to the rec room retrieving laundry. I excused myself and carefully moved around her activity as Mom moved her basket away from my path. I hadn't used my mountain bike in a long time and as I pulled it out of the closet I could already tell it needed some maintenance. The day was quickly moving on as I started working on my bike. I could tell Mom was hovering close by simply to be near me. As I worked in the rec room Mom occasionally broke the silence with some motherly advice and warnings.

"Don't pick up hitchhikers even if they are beautiful women." Her tone was serious and I was basically quiet while listening to her concerns for me. I smiled and focused on my tasks at hand, occasionally acknowledging Mom to let her know I was intently listening. Normally, I'd give Mom my undivided attention, but I'm in a hurry so I continued what I was doing.

It didn't seem like much, but after tinkering with my bike I loaded it in my baby, along with my guitar, bag, and a few miscellaneous items. My clock read 11:41 a.m. upon reentering my room.

After packing a few more items, I was just about ready. The last two things I grabbed were a notebook and my sketch pad. I saw Tina pass my bedroom door and she joined Mom in the kitchen. I called out to my family, "I'm ready to go." I had a big smile on my face, trying not to make this situation a big deal. I headed straight for the front door.

Dad put his paper down. Mom and Tina followed me. The three of them stepped onto the front porch while I placed the last of my belongings within my baby. I made my way back to the porch giving Mom a kiss and a big hug as she grabbed my cheeks with her two hands before letting go. I also hugged Tina. Dad was behind them. "Don't do anything stupid." Dad's stern warning was marked with his concern.

"Yes, Dad. I'll be careful. I should be back by next Sunday. If I plan to stay longer I will call home, but until then just pray that everything will be fine." That's when I looked straight into my mom's eyes and almost buckled where I stood.

Mom was silent, but her eyes spoke the entire truth. I saw the desperation deep within that she could not find in words. I saw the fear Mom's determination held back through welling tears. Mom's pursed lips imprisoned the feelings she kept from burdening me. As always, Mom continued to be the martyr that placed me ahead of her own needs. Mom's strength is astounding and my weakness for doing this to my mom is horrendous.

Maybe, I shouldn't have left them that way, but I selfishly turned my back on my family and moved forward. I am unable to be as strong as my mom. I don't know how I should comfort her because I don't have any answers yet. I am not taking time off for leisure. I am not going to San Francisco for the purpose of visiting Patricia. I don't know what the hell I'm doing … yet. I would have made things worse if I had started speaking so I just left.

I got into my baby, started the motor, and backed up. My family remained still on the porch as I shifted into drive. I waved as my baby slowly inched ahead and my family disappeared behind the trees. I said a prayer and silently told my family I loved them. I didn't consider this moment of departure, but now all I'm thinking about is how can a son who truly adores his mom do this to an angel on earth? My heart ached as I crawled my way up the hill. I couldn't have imagined a more painful departure. This is it.

VI

The First Day Of Tomorrow

NOT UNTIL I rounded the corner at the top of our hill, heading south, did I realize how beautiful it is today. Sunlight playing amongst the trees made me take notice. I was so focused on getting ready that I didn't acknowledge the vibrant sky welcoming travelers like myself to enjoy the outdoors. I finally looked up and admired the day. Colors are a powerful medium for evoking emotions and daylight radiating the entire light spectrum is a natural booster that can't be ignored. The energy of the sun is warmth felt through the air, through the ground, and everything it touches. This is the comfortable range of energy that supports life. No matter how I'm feeling, sunny days always manage to brighten my perspective.

It's good feeling the sensation of being alive. The warmth on my face, warmth on my arms, the warmth that comforts. I must pay more attention because I'm desensitized, so much so that I'm struggling to act. Fortunately, I'm not too far gone to be apathetic. My optimistic nature won't let me fall too far, always reaching out for help before I can't help myself any longer. At least, I've never reached those depths because I'm blessed to live with an angel who relentlessly cares for me. I've also witnessed apathy from others and I'm sorry to admit that I've learned from them, doing what I must not to follow suit. I also have Randy and Patrick that are always with me. Their tragic situations are embedded within my soul.

Even so, I'm an idiot for entertaining apathy and it's scaring me so much that I'm being selfish for what I am doing now. I'm trying to free my mind so I can notice the things I'm doing wrong. I'm not sure if there is even a right or wrong, but I know *things* are just not right, whatever those *things* are. Taking my right hand off the steering wheel, I reached towards the windshield and turned my palm upward. My hand felt cool, due to the air conditioning blowing directly at my arm. An artificial source counteracting a natural source. That's how I feel in a certain way. I moved my arm directly up to the vent obstructing the brisk air conditioning. I don't know if I'm supposed to feel discomfort by doing this. I suppose if I held my arm in this position for a long period of time the unnatural condition would cause suffering. I retracted my arm and took hold of the wheel again.

I've always cared, but I don't feel that I should care any longer. When I delve even closer to apathy that's when I physically pound my head and punish myself for going that far. I believe that just about everybody has bigger problems to face. Here I am wasting my time pondering apathy and everything else spinning in my head.

I looked through the rearview mirror, trying to abandon my guilt. My mind says I shouldn't feel guilty. Common sense says that I'm taking necessary steps. Unfortunately, pain is oftentimes required to grow. That's the part that's difficult to handle, not the physical kind, the pain inside that hides. It's never easy. My actions are currently following the practical approach, but my heart demands otherwise. And my actions don't simply affect myself, my actions are affecting my world, especially those most dear to me. I'm having a difficult time balancing my sensitivity. And even worse, I haven't been able to identify my problems yet. It's so frustrating.

I was such a happy person. My resilience was immeasurable. The bullying, the name calling, and even through the tears, I knew everything was going to be fine, because I have an angel's vigilant care. I smiled when my classmates teased me for being a rotund kid. I laughed with them, laughing at myself. I cried in the classroom for being afraid of the next time I'd get hit with objects from my second-grade teacher. I learned to fight my battles in my own way only because of the innate source of strength that is my mom. I smiled and laughed through the pain I felt within my chest, but those were simpler times because I always depended on my family. I will always be grateful for my loving family. That situation alone is my heaven on earth.

Adults always complicate everything and I seriously tried to prevent myself from falling into that complicated trap. I raised my right hand in the manner that a shy child in the back of a classroom would, "Congratulations, I'm a complicated adult. I'm such an idiot."

I am a problem solver though. I have always been a problem solver. I'm going to get through this and maybe I'm not the smartest cookie for trying to resolve this on my own or maybe I am depending on how everything works out. I do know that when I figure this out it will be on my own terms with no excuses. I am going to conquer this.

"Experience is always the best teacher." I looked up and saw the signage for Northgate. "When the fuck did I get onto the freeway!?" Spacing out while driving has to stop. Driving on autopilot is too risky especially on a road trip without any destinations. That's an excellent way to get lost quickly and I don't have time to get lost. "Or, do I?" I passed the nation's first suburban shopping center that, I think, opened in 1950.

It's strange when clarity strikes. It seems unreal. In my short-lived clearness, the silence irritated me. I had yet to choose music to begin this trek. "Who am I gonna pick first? Hmmm ... Well, I say. Fuck the counseling for now." It was decided. I used my left knee to steer and grabbed my binder. It was kismet that in my alphabetically ordered discs, Cake was first. "I'm feeling like ... Reluctantly crouched at the ... Oh YEAH! Let's start this one-man party with some Cake!"

Still driving with my knee, left hand under the binder opened on my lap, I slipped the first disc in and when the music started I cranked up the volume. My windows were rolled up with the air conditioning blasting. The music was blasting. The lyrics began and then I lost it. I don't really think I was singing as much as I was screaming. I screamed the lyrics. I screamed at the top of my lungs.

Tears started welling and I carefully closed the binder on my lap, placing it on the passenger seat. I grabbed hold of the steering wheel with a two-handed ferocity. I focused on the road and my path ahead. I wasn't out of control. These were tears of determination.

Erwin Lazaro

I looked down at my speedometer and confirmed I was maintaining the speed limit. The last thing I want is to be pulled over by police at the beginning of my journey. My emotions are through the roof, but my grip restrained my actions. My wits are intact. I held on tightly while my emotions continued erupting. This is my first step to learning. I feel the pain releasing. I hurried the pain to exit. With the last word of the first song, I roared in the confinement of my baby, a long and drawn out roar until I had no more breath.

"Shit … The first song, eh?" My throat was raw after that vocal explosion and especially after that last roar, but this is good. No holds barred. This is good. I cleared my throat. Blowing off steam is good. I didn't have anywhere or anytime I could really do this. This is confirmation that I'm doing the right thing … I think. "The Distance" by Cake. I would have never imagined "The Distance" to be first on my list of music counseling, but then again, that's why it's so effective. No matter how much I plan, God has a more effective plan.

My problems are far from solved with one song, but deflating my rage helps to alleviate a miniscule portion of the pressure. Some clarity of mind, a bout of controlled rage, and a hoarse voice. That sounds like a good prescription to me. I might do that again later.

My attention was drawn towards the sparkling waters connecting the Puget Sound to Lake Washington, this area known as Portage Bay. Crossing the Ship Canal Bridge always makes me feel like I'm going somewhere special. It's the approach. A sense of awe overcomes me whenever the iconic Space Needle and high-rise towers of downtown Seattle come into view.

"I *need* to write down or somehow record everything going through my mind … while I'm driving. Fuck!" Valuable thoughts are rushing to me when inspiration strikes. I don't have a chance of remembering even a small fraction of them. "I need a video camera is what I need."

I never take for granted crossing this magnificent bridge, the largest of its kind in the Pacific Northwest when it first opened to traffic in 1962. The upper deck stands roughly 182 feet above the canal and being stuck in traffic on this bridge makes me feel uneasy. Too many movies and my fear of heights crushes my sense of security, but even then, I can't help but take in the scenery, especially the waters below. My fear strayed. Even on solid ground, roadways are not "really" solid with the infrastructure and work underneath. A pothole could emerge at any time and that's not good travelling at freeway speeds. "I am a basket case!" Architecture, civil engineering, structural engineering, the Environmental Control Act! Paranoia ... This is kind of hilarious.

Exiting the nearly 4,500-foot span bridge feels like a triumph every time. I do love this part of the city though. The interstate curves in mesmerizing fashion upon the approach to downtown Seattle. The waters of Puget Sound, the boats, and the ships to the west, the homes above the interstate to the east. I-5 widens as traffic merges from the floating SR520 bridge and the huddle of giants become clear to see. I always pay special attention to the high-rise towers as their massive stature looms over drivers and we are swallowed by the shadows of the Convention Center before exiting the downtown area. I imagine a portal as I traditionally hold my breath travelling through this gateway and emerge on the other side, a child's game. Though it's more entertaining holding my breath while travelling through the express lanes since the tunnels beneath the interstate are much longer and depending on the traffic lights at the end, the vehicle could remain within the tunnel and I'm forced to hold my breath until the traffic light turns green.

"Oh, the things I do to entertain myself." I looked through the rearview mirror and witnessed the giants standing firm, but fading from view. The modest haze in the air, an industrial remnant shrouding the towers as castles of modern day, obscuring details just enough to bring most of my attention to each unique form, the Columbia Tower being the most impressive, head and shoulders above the rest.

Impressive for enjoying the skyline, but another matter understanding the plan. I shook my head while passing the industrial center south of downtown. Seattle is the port town that didn't know any better. As wonderful as the Emerald City is, the pioneers that planned the modern metropolis messed up so badly that the neighboring urban centers of Portland and Vancouver B.C. knew exactly what not to do. Highway 99 dividing *potentially* beautiful shores from the rest of the city will plague Seattle until rectified. Of course, hindsight is 20/20.

I'm dwelling on architecture and planning and as much as I enjoy the built environment, the discovery of a natural scape that inspires me is what I'm looking forward to the most on this road trip. I'm sure I'll discover many along the way. I'm so excited to take it all in … as much as I can, anyway.

A video camera would be useful. I'm approaching Southcenter. I'll stop at one of the electronic stores and find out how much a camcorder will set me back. A quick diversion and I should be good to go.

Two hours later, I became so frustrated finding outrageous price tags at several competing stores and getting sticker shocked at every stop. I wanted to yell at every sales rep. I was so pissed I stormed out of the area, refusing to look back, and I was still stuck with the dilemma of how to record my road trip.

Should I fork out all that money? My brain's hurting trying to decide how much I'm willing to spend as I entered the City of Federal Way. "I can't believe this." I'm wasting so much time. It's already past 2 p.m. and I'm still in Federal Way. I saw the next strip mall and out of convenience I exited the freeway.

As soon as I entered the building, as with the previous stores, I was seized by the nearest sales rep, but this time I smiled and didn't struggle to browse freely. Of course, my show of pearly whites was a green light for the pounce. In the blur of a few minutes I pulled out my credit card and walked out of the store with a new camcorder, a new camera, and a few accessories in my possession.

I was excited and dismayed at the same time. I had spent a couple of hours being careful and out of frustration I threw caution to the wind. I hurried to my baby and relaxed in the driver's seat with my eyes closed. Reaching into the bag I pulled out the receipt. I had to confirm that I had just spent a lot of money. I opened my eyes and saw that it was true. It was a penny less than a grand for the camcorder itself. Add the camera, 35mm film, VHS-C tapes, a fancy portable charger, tax, and my brain started hurting again, but this time it hurt because of how much money I had spent. "Ouch." I think it was the penny less than a grand price tag plus the complimentary carrying case for the camcorder that made me pull out my credit card.

"This is the price for therapy. That's the ticket. Yah." I hid the receipt in my glove compartment for safe keeping and quickly unraveled the packaging. My new toy was ready to go within a few minutes. I dashed onto the freeway, adjusted the camcorder in my right hand, and steered with my left, alternating with my left knee when I adjusted something on my new toy.

I got over the cost with the receipt out of sight and accepted the value of recording my travels being worth the price. That's the bottom line. I pressed the record button and focused on the time. The display read 2:46 PM, SAT AUG 8. "That's the time that Erwin Lazaro … is leaving … Seattle. It's a little late in the afternoon, but … you know what? Who gives a FUCK because I've got all week! Woohoo! I can't believe it. I'm actually leaving. Yah. I've got uh "Race Car Ya-Yas" goin' on from uh … Cake!" I turned the camcorder towards the road and panned across the view. "On the freeway. You can see that. Oh! Look at that. Freeway. Freeway." Swinging the camcorder around while keeping my eyes on the road, I tried to capture my belongings stowed away in the rear. "There's all my stuff. Look at that. Oh. Am I getting everything there? I have no idea. I gotta keep my eye on the road, but there's all my crap. Yup."

I turned the camcorder to face forward again. "As you can see, I've got this new toy. And, uh … Let's see. Where am I? I'm in Fife right now. I had to get all this craps, I mean CRAP, together before I had to head out. But HEY, wait a minute … I'm almost at Selden's, aren't I? Cool, cool. Okay, what's that? Ooh. Ooh! I'm there … Oh." I nearly dropped the camcorder in my excitement to try and video tape one of my latest built designs, Selden's Furniture Store, but thankfully I wasn't quite there yet. "Yah, I gotta be careful cause I'm driving while I'm doing this. But, uh … Let's listen to "Race Car Ya-Yas" for a second …"

"Now, I wonder if these people think I'm psycho doing this. Yah know. It's like, well … Okay …" I wanted to turn to the vehicles next to me with the camcorder up against the window and laugh out loud with my own madman's face pressed on the glass, one eye bulging at spectators. Instead, I nixed that whim and got serious.

I let out a loud, long sigh. "I guess ... Let's see ... Why am I taking this trip? Well, time to myself ... and I guess uh ... I bought a video camera. Just decided to stop by somewhere and pick one up. Spent another FRICKIN' ... uhhh ... Huh uh, I'm not gonna say how much money. Cool camera though! Umm, I doubt I'll be able to keep it later. Ah ... let's see."

I worked on gathering more meaningful thoughts. "About myself ... Well? ... I guess I gotta figure out what the, oh. Oh! Wait! Wait!" Distraction. "Now. I'm stuck in traffic right now so, maybe it doesn't count, but let's see if I can get my speedometer there. Uhhh ..." I tried to zoom in and focus on my gauges without looking down carelessly. I could partially see the gauges on the screen with my quick glances. "You can see that I'm not speeding. This is for my parent's sake and for my friends' sake to remind me that ... uh ... there's no rush. That I gotta take my time. I gotta take it easy."

I was carefully paying attention not to miss Selden's Furniture Store. "Oppp. Anyway. Anyway. Selden's is coming up. Oppp. It's coming up on the side there. Oppp. See if I can get a picture of that. Yup. Let's have a moment of silence. See if I can pick that up pretty well." Again, without being too distracted from driving, I aimed the camera in the direction of the store, southwest of the interstate across northbound traffic.

I tried zooming in, but failed miserably because I couldn't keep the camera steady. The image on the screen was blurred and bouncing all over the place. I fumbled with the zoom not knowing exactly which button to move and which direction to slide it. "Oh ohh, I'm gonna have a crash here or somethin'." I zoomed back out. "Is that good? I have no idea. That's okay."

"*Anyway* ... Picked up a new camera. I'm gonna turn this down." Cake's cover of "I Will Survive" was blaring too loudly for me to get serious. "A little excited. My first road trip ever. By myself. Anywhere. I have no idea what the fuck I'm gonna do. But, hell, that's okay, I guess too, huh? And, uh ... Well, I hope ... I know I'm not gonna find like all my answers. I've already been told that this isn't like a search for Nirvana or uh ... through Zen find peace and harmony here but ... I think uh … going down by the beaches and watching the ocean and goin' to places where I've never been before. That'll be fun."

"Already met a couple of weird peop … uh, cool people. Just on my way down here. Somehow, just wanted to talk. So, they started talking awhile. One of the guys who sold me this camera. He had just done something similar, but he was with a … a guy who went down to Ocean Shores and Oregon and all that stuff and ended up in Canada and had a blast, but … He said that uh … he did something similar to what I'm doing, but mine's a little different because … more of a soul search."

"Anyway, I'm rambling now, but … Okay … I don't know what … what I'm trying to find. But, I guess, the important thing is that … I'm trying for myself and …"

I glanced at the camcorder display and finally noticed. "Whoa, horrible zoom there. Gotta back this out a bit there. There you go. I know this is not the most uh … scenic … scenic drive, but … That's okay." I forced myself to stop yammering and tried to clear my head.

VII

This Is Not Depression

"OKAY. I GOTTA start out the trip with ... Here. Let's lower this some more." Cake was still too loud for my thoughts to come forward. With the camcorder fixed in my right hand, I reached over the steering wheel with my left hand and lowered the volume further. "I guess I gotta start the trip talking about what this ... what this is ... for me. And maybe it's not that serious. And maybe, it's not that critical. Maybe, it's not that big a deal, but ... Maybe, I'm just being overdramatic like I tend to do. I don't know what I'm ... I know already that I'm gonna be embarrassed when I play this back and I have no idea how far down the road ... whenever, I guess ... Hopefully, I'll have kids, and they'll have kids, and I'll be looking at this. And, by the end of this whole experience ... You know, I'll figure out what the hell's going on, but ... I'm *too young* to have a midlife crisis." I scoffed. "So, it can't be that!"

"I swear! I don't think I'm depressed? It *can't* be that. Though, I'm sure ..." Distraction. "Woah! Bug! You see that! Bug!" I turned the camera to focus on a shiny, white Volkswagen Beetle passing me by. "Okay. That's for the benefit of Jef and Bill and those guys ... if we ever ... if they ever see this ..." Speaking under my breath, "I don't know if I'll allow anyone to see this. I think I'll debate on that one too."

"But ... it could be a vision quest. It could be a soul search. Could be just spending time by myself. Never done that before. It's exciting. I don't know where I'm sleeping tonight. I guess it depends on how far I get on my trip." My mind wandered a bit. "Uh ... I hope I'm getting the road. I guess I am. This has a stabilizer so I hope it's steady."

The digital compass displayed a heading of due west between Fife and my approach to Tacoma, but the interstate veered southwest and revealed the largest arena with a wooden dome structure in the world. "The Aroma of Tacoma" from the Tacoma Tideflats and the Tacoma Dome are a tandem that will always go together. Rotten eggs and an arena. Somehow, that always makes me affectionately smile. It's kind of endearing.

"A lot of things have happened lately … and at the same time, nothing's happened. A lot of "catch 22" type things or just emotional upheavals, up and down and … I don't know if it's women? I don't know if it's my career? I don't know if it's … life? I don't know if it's a lack of peace? Because … I've been yearning for solitude. And … and … I guess, finding myself."

"The funny thing about all this is that I've never … I've never questioned that part of me … of what I am … and you know … of who I am. For some reason, I am right now. Maybe, it's because talking to some of my friends who have been more philosophical about the things they've done … parallels in my life and … meeting people."

"It's really interesting they've come into my life … uh find out we have a lot of parallels and a lot of things in common that we're trying to find ourselves and rediscover that part of our lives and … they're stumbling … well, stumbling? Not stumbling … they're on the right track with their careers, very confident in the things they are able to do."

"Me … I guess … since the 'frog … story' … maybe I'll be able to talk about that later … really kinda the milestone that's turned my life upside down for the last month-and-a-half. Um … it's kinda got me down about things … shattered my sanity, I guess … just because of a little frog. It just amazes me. I told that story three times and each time I've told that story … I've cried."

"I'm doing much better now, but … that's the reason why I'm taking this trip … because of the frog. Sounds so stupid too." I scrutinized memories from roughly forty-five days ago and fell silent at the wheel contemplating the gravity of that situation.

"I hope that … I learn to lighten up … to fuckin' lighten up. I know that's one of my problems. I'm too fuckin' overdramatic." I rolled my eyes at myself. "Please … if anyone sees this." I couldn't help but laugh at myself out loud. "And all I'm saying is the word, 'fuck', 'Fuck', FUCK' … and people don't know that." I mocked myself with more laughter. "I guess I'll shock a few people … whoever ends up seeing this. Hopefully, no one … or, I guess, maybe only the people that I trust who want to see this side of me."

"I uh, I bought a great camera, excited to use it later. *And*! And, buying this video camera is *so cool*! Oh, I brought a journal too. I'm gonna write in that … but this is … this is the moment. This is … you're seein' a bunch of cars passing … look at … Oh, oh, sorry. Sorry."

The speedometer read 70 m.p.h. and I displayed the reading on the camcorder. "Gotta turn to the speedometer. Looks like I've screwed up a little bit. I'm speeding. I'm gonna try and slow down here. I'll switch lanes. Sorry there. I'm talking and videotaping and driving at the same time. You know I'm a multitasker. So, I gotta keep up that uh … that whole part of my life, I guess. Can't get too simple on me now."

"That's what this is …" Another realization dawned on me as my voice trailed momentarily. "That's another *thing* this is about … is getting back to the simple *things* in life and learning to appreciate *things* again."

"There's a lot of *things* to go for … a lot of wonderful *things* to experience. But, if I can't take care of myself first, I'm not gonna move anywhere very quickly."

"You know, sometimes I wish that I *wasn't* so dependent on everybody around me. And, I know it can get me into trouble." Distraction. A business van passed me in the slow lane. "Reliable Locksmiths. You see that?" Yah, anyway, sorry."

"Um … What was I saying? … I wish that I wasn't so dependent on other people … and yes, it does make a difference what people say and how people perceive me. I know it shouldn't. I always thought I was good on my own. Maybe, the reality is that I'm not. And that reality is kind of … also … scaring me … the things I have prided myself in being … maybe I was that way or I am that way? I don't know … right now is just a little earthquake in my life … a little tremor. My world's a bit shaken to make me remember how I got to where I am and/or the person I am now ... to not forget what that really means ... maybe that's what this is about."

"See, this is cool! This is cool! Because, if I was writing this down, I wouldn't be able to talk about this stuff. I'd be tryin' to compose what I'm sayin' and making sure that it's all grammatically correct and ... Aww, I know. I know that's not what a journal's about but ..."

Cake caught my attention with the 'F' word. "Oh, here you go. Fashion Nugget." I reached over with my left hand to turn the volume up. "Shut the ... up! Learn to ... BUCK! Shut ... FUCK UP! WOOOO!" I roared with laughter. "Alright!" My fingers were still on the knob and I lowered the volume. "Ah ... okay ... yah. Yah. Okay. Break time here."

I took this chance and glanced at my watch. It's a little past 3 p.m. I've been holding the camcorder in this position for about fifteen minutes, but because the best perspective is directly in front of the central vents, the air conditioning is continually blasting on my hand. My hand is starting to freeze.

The lyrics subsided, giving time for some electric guitar riffs. "Learn to ..." The timing was good. "... to *buck up*. Hey, that's appropriate."

"The other thing is that I ... I fuckin' think too much. I think too much! Way too much and that really ..." Long pause. "Sometimes you can think too much." Period. "And, I notice that ... I ... well ... hell, everybody notices ..." I shook my head. I mean, "knows this ... The less that you think about things the more that life is ... I guess ... agreeable."

Images of my friends, Nick and Brian, filtered through my contemplation. "Start the ... what is it ... Nick's famous line in uh ... Nick's and uh ... Brian's famous line in uh ... from ... from 'Kim Phom' ... 'Think too much you fuck it up. Yah. *Fuck it up!*'" Spoken in Nick and Brian fashion. "That's right. Oh. Yup. That's right. Okay."

"Maybe the uh ... maybe the word of the day ... or it could last, we'll find out later down the road, but ... for the entire trip ... Let's, let's make ..."

Totally going on a wiseass tangent. "Children! Today, children, let us ... let us make the word ... of the day: FUCK."

"Okay. FUCK. Fuck. Fuck. Fuck. Fuck. Fuck. Fuck. Fuck-ACKKKK!!! FUCK! There you go. Okay."

I absorbed a few measures of Cake in silence to sense whether I got all the *Fucks* out. Of course, the answer was clear with a sigh. "Eh ... It's still not out of my system, but ... anyway."

"So, I've rambled on ... I wanted to start the trip with this little ... I guess, my first entry. Let's see. It's uh ... 3:04 now. Uh ... August 8, still. Same day." I cackled at the length of my long-winded banter. "I feel like I've been talking for a while here, wasting my tape. Hope people aren't like, looking at me, and thinking I'm strange, but ... You know what? Who the fuck cares, right? Yah?" I pivoted the camcorder up and down with my wrist to represent a collective head nod for everyone's sake and I answered myself. "Okay. Very good. Very good! You're a good audience. You're good listeners. Now that I have your undivided attention. I guess there's always the fast forward button, but ..."

It feels good letting out this steam. I'm anticipating a lot of rants and sighs as I acknowledged my prediction with another long sigh. In the normal case of sighing, I think of Eeyore and his doldrums, his physical form with head drooping and body language of depression. But, I sigh to clear the negativity within as a cleansing exercise. The effort brings awareness, as well. For instance, my right hand is feeling more and more uncomfortable because of the air conditioning, but I'm choosing to ignore it with a sigh.

"We shall see what happens ... Galvatron. The important thing is to find peace. There's no rush." Distraction check as I focused on the gauges. "Look at that. Look at that. I'm going to continually check my speedometer. I'm doin' pretty well. See that? I'm talking and I just noticed that I'm still maintaining the sixtyish mark. Now, when I get down to Olympia and the speed limit goes up, I probably will go up to seventy, but that's okay. Is that okay with you?" I used the collective head nod move again with the camcorder. "Okay!"

I'm very comfortable talking to my new toy. "I'm going psycho now. You're all probably thinkin' I'm nuts." Sighing again, "Oh ... maybe I am. I don't know." But, I switched gears and considered a different perspective. "This is a memory. I spent a lot of fuckin' money for this camcorder." More mocking laughter for myself. "I got a new camera at my side here. I didn't need to buy either ... or both. I could have bought one or the other, but I bought both. I don't know any other *fuckin'* better way."

"I set standards high for myself and I expect myself to do the best that I can. Not only for myself, but for others. I expect the best out of myself, so ... hell, why not reward myself with the best right?" Trying to justify my purchases. "I can't afford it, but ... who ... gives ... I guess I'm having fun. That's the important thing."

Distraction. A small carload of people passed me on the far-left lane and I focused on them. "See, look at that. There's a group of people going on a trip. I don't know if I have them in the car ... in the image or not, but ... this is kinda cool ..." A sharp pang bursts from my chest with an apprehension. "Uh ... little scared ... because this is the very first time I've ever done this. Like I haven't mentioned that twenty times already."

I couldn't withstand the air conditioning blasting on my hand any longer. "My hand is freezing. I'm gonna move this vent away." I lifted my knee to steer, but didn't transition between my hand and knee very well. "I'm veering off the road a little bit, but that's okay." I maintained the position of the camcorder as I turned the vents and quickly returned my left hand to steer. "My hand is *cold*. My God. Um ..." I couldn't help but laugh because my right hand is numb.

"What was I saying? Tangent Boy. I go off on tangents. That's what a friend calls me. Tangent Boy. I start on one conversation and I always end up somewhere else. I forget what the hell I was saying beforehand." Long pause.

"OH! This is cool!" I turned the camcorder to focus on the passenger side floor. "See that there? I bought that adapter and the plug. So, it's like, if I want to bring a microwave in here." I focused on the front panel. "I have it hooked up to my ... uh ... my uh ..." I couldn't pull the word out of my ... "Mm, okay. Charades ... What is that? Two words ... No. One word. One word. What is that? That is uh ... lighter! Lighter. Yah. Eh ... whatever that is. Anyway ..." I refocused on the floor. "It plugs into there and I can plug in a microwave here ...

a refrigerator ... a VCR. I can do my whole home theater system in here if I wanted to." I speculated on that possibility and believed it so I rolled with it. "But, this way, this allows me to talk like this ... like everybody's fuckin' hating already and um ..."

"I'm gonna; I'm gonna; Okay. I'm gonna pick the; Oka; Oka; Okay; Oka; Okay. Okay. Okay. Okay. Sorry, that's a bad Joe Pesci, but I tried. Anyway ... Where was I? Oh yah, I got that so I won't deplete my battery and I can talk endlessly. Of course, I am limited to a ninety-minute tape. So ... my first entry could be ninety minutes. Then I'm in real trouble because I only have three tapes. So, I better stop at a store and get more tapes. That's my problem."

I passed what looked like a two-story community college with a faux brick façade. "Look at that building. Gotta do architecture. That's another cool thing about this. Architecture. Hope I find some cool architecture, maybe some churches, dilapidated barns, or craftsman-style single-family dwellings. I can't wait until the bed-and-breakfasts. Check that out. Never done that before. Of course, I'd love to be there with a lover. Someone that I'm intimate with and share that with. There's always time for that later, I guess."

My thoughts drifted towards the possibility. The background came to the forefront and the lyrics from Cake's "Italian Leather Sofa" hit home hard. Entertaining the idea is wrong, but still enticing. Well, the possibility is only a fantasy now so I got irritated and noticed my speedometer. "Hey, this guy's going fifty-five. So, I should pass this guy. Hope you guys don't mind?"

"Um ... oh, gonna have ... gotta correct, correct my English, my grammar. Grammar? Grammar ... not grammar. Whatever ... Okay. Anyway ... now I'm gonna crack myself up! I'm sure I'm cracking somebody up right now ..." Thinking out loud is what Erwins do best.

"I don't *sound* depressed, do I? *See*!? I'm talking *and* I think my tone of voice is pretty good." I smiled at myself in the rearview mirror. "And, maybe it's becausssse ... I'm excited!? And, maybe becausssse ... this is newww? Maybe because I'm by myself? Maybe because I have a whole *fucking week to myself*!! See how far I get ... see if I get laid." I couldn't help but laugh. "No ... that's not the purpose, but ... it'd be a kinda nice benefit." Joking aside, some hope creeped into my thoughts. Hoping is what Erwins do best.

"Okay. But, you see? That's why I don't think I'm depressed. You know? It's more of a vision quest. You know, trying to figure out ... well, I'm a problem solver and ... I've always prided myself in being that, in being able to find solutions and always having a solution for ... difficulties and ... problems and ... everything, whether it's personal or professional. I've always prided myself in being able to do well. Now ... as that cliché of a quote suggests, something to the effect of ... It's always easy to give advice and it's always hard to follow your own advice."

Distraction. A white minivan suddenly cuts me off. Travelling in the left lane with no one in front of the minivan, this idiot decides to slide between me and the truck I was safely following in the center lane, braking harshly after tailgating the truck, and forces me to slow down so I don't rear-end this moron. "What is this guy doing?" The steam inside rose quickly and I spoke to the idiot-moron. "Okay. You merge with no one in front of you ... and you decide to cut me off?" I was exacerbated.

I grabbed my collar and shifted it left and right a few times as the idiot-moron merged to the right lane. "You're lucky I'm a good guy. I'll take you out ... with my bazooka. Yah. You guys don't know that, do yah? I've got a bazooka at the end of this camcorder. It was like ... uh ... *free*! *Yah*! A little benefit for bein' such a *Good Guy*!"

Unfortunately, the idiot-moron didn't stop the stupid there. "Look at that *asshole*." After passing the truck in the right lane, the idiot-moron-stupid cuts off the truck by merging into the center lane without signaling. How does any of that make any sense?

"Stupid is as ... *ugh*" As the famous Forrest would say.

"Oh yah, that's another thing. There's gonna be *assholes* on the road. I've gotta remember that they're not worth it because I'm going sixty-miles-an-hour." Instantly panning to the speedometer, "Look at *that*! I'm still going sixty! You see *that*! I'm still going sixty!"

"And ... uh ... been talking nonstop for ... who the hell knows." I focused the camcorder on the digital clock. "It's 3 ... 3:12 now ...

so, maybe half-an-hour?" Since this is a new toy, I don't think thirty minutes is that bad.

"I bet I sound like a goofball too. I've heard my voice on a camcorder before … Now singing, singing is different. I'm good. There's no doubt about that." Uh … yah. "Maybe I'll sing a song for everybody later when I feel like it. But, uh … talking is a different issue." Boy, that sounds pompous, doesn't it? It's more reasonable to say that sometimes I have enough confidence to tell myself I sing well. I know I have a good voice, but I often forget to sing from my heart. I tend to overthink and that's the root of my insecurities, not just about singing either.

Images of Nick and Brian appeared above me chanting, "*Think too much you fuck it up. Think too much you fuck it up. Think too much you fuck it up.*"

I *am* amid an internal struggle so I must encourage myself, even though sounding confident is different than being confident. I'm trying though, otherwise life becomes more and more complicated. I don't like complicated.

"I hope the mic is really good on this thing. Of course, I also hope the record button is really working because I'm trying this out for the first time and I have no idea if … That's a good point!" I laughed at the idea that I had just rambled for almost thirty minutes with nothing to show for it so I glimpsed at the screen. "Nah, it's saying record. Okay. That's cool." Whew …

Distraction. A red, compact sedan passed me in the slow lane. "Oh, look at that. There's a cute family. Mommy and child in the backseat being chauffeured by Pops … That's sweet." I have mixed feelings about this scene.

"I thought that'd be me a while ago, but … I guess … it's not meant to be at this time in my life for whatever reason that may be … I've been trying to figure that out." Now, here's a subject that's weighed heavily on me for years, but I'm not sure if I want to talk about it during my first entry. I have less than sixty minutes remaining on this tape. I doubt that's enough time.

Distraction. I've been following one vehicle for some time now and the velocity is unwavering. "This Accord … must be on cruise control. I should be on mine I guess …"

Distraction. A motorcycle passed me in the slow lane. "Oh! Biker dudes. Look at that. Biker chick and biker dude. Studs and everything …"

Distraction. A large sign advertising food caught my attention and my tummy responded. "Oh! Look at that. Food! Food! I should probably eat in a while. Maybe I'll videotape my first meal. I'm sure everyone will enjoy that."

"I'm approaching Yelm. I'm still going sixty. I'm getting impatient. So, I'm gonna figure this out." I'm amused that my diligence is making it seem I'm moving at a snail's pace. "I do want to get, eventually, out of Washington. So … going sixty seems like it's inhibiting that, but …" I changed my tone to match the courtesy of my plea. "For the sake of everybody out there …" I snickered and spoke under my breath. "… Or at least while I have the video camera on …" I jerked the camera to focus on the speedometer again and rapidly blurted, "I'm going sixty! See that!? I'm still going sixty." The camcorder's view rebalanced onto the freeway once more. "Okay. Got that straight."

To reassure my audience and help motivate me to stay true to my intention, I jerked back to the speedometer. "I'm … I'm gonna be good. I'm going sixty. Okay. I wonder if I should play this back later …" to serve as a reminder for me if I go astray.

It seems I'm easily adapting to this camcorder as a third eye. Yah, baby. Twisting and turning it to focus is a piece of cake without my need to avert attention away from driving. I just give a quick sidelong glance to confirm the image and I can add to my multitasking checklist. Check. "Cake's almost done … so, when that finishes … I'll end this … this entry." The camcorder showed the digital display reading track fourteen as well as the time elapsing on the disc player. This cover of "Sad Songs and Waltzes" written by Willie Nelson is winding down the final track of the first disc of my journey. "First video journal entry, Saturday afternoon … first day towards my quest … for peace … personal peace, that is …"

I refocused by thinking out loud, searching within for clues. A recent conversation came to mind. *"I'm not cocky!"* I just blurted it out. "At least, I don't think I am. I love to write and I wrote about this once before ... about the difference between cockiness and confidence ... how it's like walking a tightrope. It's always a continual game, so to speak, in trying to maintain that confidence, to know you're doing the right thing, being confident in your abilities to be successful and move in the direction you want to go. And sometimes you can step over that and you can end up hurting somebody. That is definitely not my intention."

"As far as I know I haven't hurt anyone from being overconfident. I tend to joke about being cocky, especially at work. I know the guys at work probably think I am, but I just play with them. It's so funny. I don't know if they believe me or if they're playing the game too, but ... Yeah, it's always good to have a little attitude. I know that."

But, recent conversations have added to my introspective complexity, making me more vulnerable. I'm hoping, unnecessarily. Still, I can't help falling into the trap of relying on what others say about me even though I know better. This is a fine line also. Accepting constructive criticism depends on emotional conditions. Take these recent times. I'm hypersensitive and conscious of my sensitivity. "A friend told me last night that I am arrogant. I understand what that perception is, what that means, and why I'm described as being arrogant."

"I was told I am beating myself up and that I have been doing so for a long time. I set myself to standards that are too great for anybody. That I expect myself to be better ... not than anybody ... but *for* everybody." My arrogance is defined by the perception that I think so highly of myself ... that I believe I have a profound impact on everybody around me? Is that it?

"But, you know what? My response was that not enough people try to do that. And, I'm not just anybody. I know I am a special person just like everybody should feel about themselves. I'm grateful to understand I'm always trying to move in a direction to improve myself, to always be better than I am right now."

"My friend's response was that maybe I set my standards too high. I beat myself up for every little mistake that I ever do. Now, there's a difference between making stupid mistakes and just making mistakes that are … expected … that everybody will make. But, I beat myself up about those things, too." I'm starting to sound like a perfectionist by this line of thinking. I honestly believe I am nowhere near trying to be perfect in anything. It's not possible.

"Yet another friend got on my case recently and called me arrogant too. I wonder if it means the same thing. Maybe it does, but …" Two close friends who have no relationship with each other, describing me in similar fashion, is a bit too coincidental. That's why I'm scrutinizing these conversations.

"I've always wanted to be strong for everybody around me because it makes me happy to know that people rely on me and that people want to come to me for advice or know that I'll listen and I love to listen. I'm lucky to know that." People are social creatures and being reliable for others is gratifying. I'm grateful when people rely on me.

"But is … is that wrong? What's wrong with that? You're telling me … people are telling me …" I feel like two of me are in my baby having a debate. I stroked the wheel. "Look at this. Like there's another me sitting right here." The camcorder focused on the front passenger seat. "Right … There's only one me. I'm not gonna point the camcorder at myself either." I'll take being psychotic only so far.

Realization. "Wow! You know what? I've had the camcorder focused on my rosary the whole time, haven't I? Interesting … Maybe this is a heart-to-heart with God." Other than the fact that I have the lens focused on the center of the windshield where the rosary is hung from the rearview mirror, it's still enlightening for me.

"Nyah! Nyah. Yat's the ticket … God has a sense of humor. I think we're all lucky for that." Joking with God is a good thing. It's obvious that God has a lot to laugh about witnessing the follies of mankind. I'm not even going to venture into the overall stupidity of mankind. Instead, I'll consider my own frustrations about what people lack in general, especially within myself. The shortcoming of learning anything and forgetting or losing that skill without practice. That is excruciating on so many levels. I work so hard to become better at something and as soon as I let up, I have to retrain. How about being my own worst enemy? Why should I worry about other people when I battle myself relentlessly? Isn't that right, Randy? How about doing something that common sense is warning not to do and it's done anyway? Those are situations I have control of, but fail often. How about the ones that I seemingly have no control over? How about hitting all the red traffic lights when nobody's around? Or getting sick the day before leaving for the only big vacation of the year? Or being prepared for every meeting and not requiring the preparation, except for a harried state one time and, of course, that's the one time I wasn't prepared. It goes on and on. I raised my left hand to each situation and slowly veered from my driving lane a smidge before re-centering with my knee. The examples are endless. I do have a theory about those situations without seemingly having no control, but I'll get back to that later.

God has a lot to laugh about and laughing at myself is the best consolation for my own idiocies … or mistakes. Am I being overcritical? It's not that I'm trying to be perfect. I just want to do well in everything. Isn't that different than being a perfectionist?

I notice my rosary swaying thus bringing my attention to God. Of course, I'm having a conversation with God. Thoughts are prayers. God is omnipresent. God is omnipresent and gets the giggles all the time. In general, I think too seriously of God. It's mostly about damnation, apathy, or salvation. Come on, man! Under these circumstances, I'm bringing attention to God's sense of humor.

"Um …" I couldn't help repeating, "The Distance." Such a great tune. I love it.

VIII

Arrogance

THE DISC FINISHED. I turned off the camcorder and set it on the passenger seat. I also turned off the receiver/cd player. Ambient freeway noise took over the soundtrack for the time being while I drove in relative silence.

I was fixated on the perception of me being arrogant. It fascinated me. I had no choice but to scrutinize these opinions because of the primary intentions that guide my daily prayers, and thus my life: gratitude and humility. Obviously, some close friends and their impressions of me are contrary to my intended lifestyle and I have no intention of being a hypocrite. Though, that is impossible to avoid entirely. All people are occasionally hypocrites. Just like all people are occasionally idiots. All one can do is try to minimize their own idiot factor. My factor fluctuates constantly no matter how hard I try. I cross the arrogance line too. That's why I pray so intently to minimize the need to apologize for my sometimes-callous nature.

Now, as I mentioned on the recording. I understand very clearly why I am considered as such. In some instances, I'm not helping disapprove the notion either. My workplace. The poor guys. I learned to play the game from the master himself.

Jef is the opposite of arrogant, but he is a master of deception. My colleague, mentor, and dear friend is a very humble man. I mostly jest about the master of deception part because of his ninja status. It's not his apparent physical presence that calls for the ninja status. Jef is real. Jef is very real. Jef creates an aura of a man of mystery, able to divert attention away from himself with seemingly little effort. Jef only shares what he is willing to share. When asked questions or asked to expound on scenarios he wishes to remain private, Jef conveniently turns the table and redirects the conversation that makes the one inquiring feel like the life of the party. He does it with a smile and his jovial behavior. Everybody is happy to agree with Jef and life moves forward in an undisturbed fashion.

That's why Jef is spelled with one 'f'. The second 'f' is *actually* next to the first. Normal people cannot see the second 'f', but I can. It's as clear as day to me, just as he is. Jef, the ninja man of mystery. I admire him greatly. He is my brother from another mother.

A smile is always plastered across my face when I think of Jef. I'm probably making him sneeze or making him sweat under the collar from this attention right now. I'm sure he can sense my focus on him. He has uncanny abilities. I swear I've witnessed him catch a fly with chopsticks. Jef is that kind of man. I nodded my head and pictured a bonsai tree.

With regards to my nature at work, when I have a chance to play along with my colleagues, I'll play the opposite game and I play mostly with Bill and Jef. I don't tend to mess with Ross strictly because he's the boss though I slip here and there, especially during frenzied storytelling when I exaggerate a bit. I don't like to tease Brian because he's like a little brother to the office and I want to protect him. I'm pretty good there, but Brian's a good listener and I rile him up as a third party. I don't let the chitchat adversely affect my work either. I'm probably the one that takes work way too seriously because when the workload is thick I'm ferocious and focused.

The others like to blow off steam with casual conversation, but I don't do that. I can't relax until I've completed pressing tasks. Leave me alone when I'm busy unless the interruption is work-related, of course. I keep my nose to the grindstone until I'm able to breathe again.

Between deadlines though I loosen up a bit and let myself mess with my peers. And, I only do so to play along. The conversations are typically so random it's difficult to pinpoint anything that exemplifies my cockiness at work. In general, if the guys will scoff at a response I make during a conversation, I'll cross that line to make their eyes roll. It's not like I'm doing it all the time, only when the impact is the greatest. That way my action is marked by an exclamation point. I try not to do this anywhere else. I consider these actions as part of my workplace culture.

There's always a danger of hurting feelings during these verbal bouts. I can't remember the specifics of the situation, but I did make Jef's blood boil over once. I was exiting the office one afternoon and the conversation was mostly about invincibility so to speak, about having everything and lacking nothing, something of that nature. I can't remember if it was about growing up, about our current lives, or regarding the future. I basically commented as a spoiled brat with a smug attitude and I remember Jef snapping at me not as a peer, but as a parent scolding his child.

It was so uncharacteristic of Jef that his admonishment obviously had a profound effect on me. I had overstepped the line way too far. Maybe, Jef sensed that I was no longer joking and I had revealed a darkness that could not be left alone. He woke me up from my absurd rambling and knocked some sense back into me.

I apologized on the spot and I haven't crossed that line again as far as I know. I can be somewhat dense though. "So, guys, I'm sorry for my arrogant behavior at work. I have no excuse. I'm just an idiot."

But, who doesn't toot their own horn from time to time? I can think of a few people who are absolutely modest, including my mom and sister, but it's because they're discreet. Generalizing is always dangerous, but people are born with egos and that ego needs attention. Some are just more expressive than others. The quiet ones are smart. Being expressive is what gets people into trouble.

Unfortunately, my stupidity at work is nothing compared to the worst unparalleled egotism I possessed as a teenager. I'm not a stranger to arrogance, but that's why I mentioned the learning and forgetting scenario earlier being so excruciating. Being careful is not enough. Being vigilant is the only thing I can do, that and calling myself an idiot often. I continually squash my ego so I can continue to walk through doorways. The purpose for acknowledging my daily failures is so that

Erwin Lazaro

vigilant humility will continually teach me to do better. I learned the hard way and even then, it's still a daily struggle.

I remember the time well as an eighteen-year-old. My senior year was the culmination of four fairytale academic years in high school. Nothing could go wrong. The school year was wrapping up in June 1986. I was one of the top five percent graduating students. I was accepted into the university of my choice. I had received several awards throughout my junior and senior years. I was captain of the tennis team and voted most inspirational player two years in a row, playing varsity for all three years I was on the tennis team. I was class vice president for my junior and senior years. I sang solos at school assemblies and annual variety shows. The student body had voted me in as a prince for the homecoming court. During Spirit Week, I helped my class win another banner competition. Every year that I designed and painted the banner for Spirit Week our class won that competition. Seniors traditionally win every spirit keg, but during my junior year I helped my class take the spirit keg away from the seniors. The Shoreline Class of 1986 triumphed the following year and won a second spirit keg. Our class was amazing, but it wasn't just our class. Shoreline High School was amazing. Overall, I'd say class distinction was minor. The students didn't care about who was in what grade. The typical cliques existed but because students seemed to fit into more than one clique the lines were blurred and that's why those distinctions didn't matter as much. I was one of those that blurred the lines by being a school leader, playing sports, singing publicly, excelling in advance placement classes, entering art competitions and submitting personal writings for school literary publications. I had friends in every class and not just casual friends, friends that were valuable to me on many levels. If I had a chance to see them today, my grin would just be as wide as those days when we walked the halls of Shoreline High School together. That's how I treated almost everybody, or so I had thought.

I didn't toot my own horn for people to take notice even though I had a lot to toot about. I was a humble person on the outside. The real problem was how I perceived myself. I was genuine with my feelings towards the people around me as I am now. I wear my heart on my sleeve. That hasn't changed. The problem was that my idiot factor was so high that I felt invincible and on a level much worse than the incident with Jef more recently.

I remember the evening I was lying in bed with my arms folded beneath my head and I issued a personal challenge to God. I had boldly proclaimed that life was too easy and I pleaded with God to challenge me. I don't think I went so far as to dare God. I simply asked God to make my life more challenging.

Idiot factor: immeasurable.

I remember my complacent nature, the height of my conceited state of mind. Even now, the anger I feel towards myself swells considering that time in my life. It hurts so much, the growing pains I experienced thereafter. It still hurts. I'm still enduring that challenge. God has eternity, but I don't, not during this lifetime. I asked for a more challenging life and without question, God answered my call.

Maybe I'm also egotistical for believing that my selfish plea was the impetus for the hardships that followed. Maybe I haven't changed believing that I have any ability for God to answer me directly. That's just it though. I believe. God is omnipotent. God has no limitations. The problem isn't that I believe God answered me directly. More people need to believe their dialogue is personal with God every time and that every thought, every action, has a direct impact on the world. If everyone believes in their own importance for every fabric that is shaping this world, then that awareness would empower people to take their lives and this world more seriously all the time.

Along those lines of thinking though, the problem isn't having the ability or power to shape our world. The problem is that not enough people are willing to make the effort required to shape our world in the manner that needs to be done. Apathy is the true culprit. Doing nothing is also a choice. Always fight the compulsion to make the wrong choice because it will always be easier to choose poorly and always more difficult to choose wisely. It's not even about making the right choices and more about making choices that enable people to learn and evolve with each effort.

Somehow, I knowingly shove apathy away every time that useless

Erwin Lazaro

feeling surfaces. I can't stand sitting idly and waiting, unless wisdom unmistakably dictates so. Even then, I'll reinvestigate and dissect the options to make sure I've exhausted every opportunity. I may not know when to shut up during the initial steps, but I do eventually learn because I'm always seeking wisdom. Twelve years of agonizing has led me here. I feel like I'm on the verge of discovering ... something, unravelling ... something, within the next few days of my life.

I actively and boldly claim these actions to help me fight against apathy. That's another reason why I'm on this trip right now. A few days ago, I really did begin to feel I should give up. But instead of giving up, I got angry. I got angry at everything. On the surface, it's a horribly selfish reaction, potentially causing a lot of trouble for myself with other people who may not understand my actions. It's also uncharacteristic so I have a little leeway from the people who know me, but sympathy will only take me so far. That's my need for alone time. Push too many buttons and I may cause irreparable damage from idiotic choices. It's all justifiable. That's what I want to believe so I keep practicing. I keep fighting. I continue trying.

Whenever I look upon myself from the perspective of an outsider, doing my best to be objective, it is seemingly convenient to blame these growing pains as part of the normal process for being a twenty-something. It is unquestionably tough being a teenager without realizing what's in store for a life beyond a daily schedule. Adolescence, in general, introduces the complexity of possibility. But, life after high school is the outer space of time. Between preschool and high school, time is linear. The defined timeline is a security blanket for many children growing up in suburban America. Upon graduating from high school, I felt the sensation of blasting off to outer space. The security of gravity limiting my movement was more comforting than I realized and graduating from high school placed me in a world where no one really cares if I succeed or fail. I'm just a number until I can prove my worth and provide value for someone who needs me to do something for them. Of course, my mom and dad care, but I'm just trivia or gossip for everybody else. That's scary. I carried this sense very early in my life.

I wasn't one of those that couldn't wait to grow up. I treasured being a young child. I was always afraid of growing up. I still am. I want to be a child forever. Some teenagers couldn't wait to get jobs and gain their independence. I couldn't understand the idea of dropping out of school or skipping school just for a chance at "freedom". That way of thinking didn't make sense to me at all. I always knew that "freedom" required a price. I was happy living within my bubble because it was comfortable and I became good at making the most of my opportunities within that bubble. The success I achieved made it even more difficult to venture outside of my comfort zone and I didn't want my bubble to burst.

Time knows no mercy. I knew that pending "freedom" was imminent. I didn't want it.

I did have a very selfish perspective because of my secure family life. I have friends, even to this day, who love my home too. My mom's endless offerings of lumpia shanghai made certain of that. It obviously didn't make any sense to me because I loved and do love my home and my family life and that may not have been the case for those who wanted their adolescent independence. Maybe their homes and families didn't make a happy place for their hearts, for those who couldn't wait. On the other hand, I wasn't any better clutching to what I had and scared of letting go. We were just children with contrasting perspectives about the future.

But something doesn't add up. If it were truly the case that I didn't want to move forward and I truly wanted to protect everything I had accumulated up to that point in time when I laid in bed with my hands folded beneath my head, why did I issue that challenge to God?

I do have one dream that has fueled my feelings throughout the years because of my happy home. Is that the reason? Did I act because I knew I wouldn't have any chance of achieving that dream unless I burst out of the comfortable life I'm living thus far?

Time knows no mercy. I knew that pending "freedom" was imminent. Maybe I did want it.

Again, is this arrogance for being so self-confident that I innately propelled myself forward, moving in the direction of making my dream come true? I know people who sit on the fence and never take chances, perpetually considering possibilities as life passes by. I was always petrified, but am I fearless? No, that's not it. I was and I am petrified. That is not a question, but despite my fear, I take leaps forward not knowing what will happen. It's a dedicated leap. Some may call that stupid, but it's more stupid maintaining the status quo and calling others stupid. That's stupid.

It's not like I'm randomly taking chances based on whim or gambling with my life, closing my eyes in hopes for good results. Maybe the challenge was an effective means to make sure I don't let time slip by, wasting my life on daydreams knowing very well that I won't achieve anything being comfortable within the status quo.

I was comfortable within the status quo as a middle schooler. I was an average student and I didn't work for any future. I just went to class and did average work. I was a carefree preadolescent. I didn't discover my potential for singing until I was thirteen years old and that was just the beginning. I had only one thing that excited me at Cordell Hull Middle School. I lived for competitive ping pong with Patrick, Randy, and our friends. We competed for bragging rights and pepperoni sticks. Then Patrick died and that trauma woke me up from my passive existence.

The summer one of my best friends died was also a time of transition in my life. My baby sister was five years old and my dad was continually on my shoulders about doing everything I can for her. Kristine is my responsibility. I'm her big brother and I must set a good example for her. I must succeed for her sake. My dad was worried because of my lack of effort and lack of commitment at school. By eighth grade I was showing zero potential for excellence or inspiration. I wasn't a good role model for my sister. Patrick died and that changed everything for me.

Being a teen is tough. A best friend's death was my introduction to adolescence. When I turned fourteen in January 1982, I didn't care about much except for the happiness within my home. That tragic summer placed chains around my heart. I was no longer free to enjoy life without care. I had a best friend who challenged my nerves of steel in ping pong and then one day he was gone. I found purpose when I was fourteen years old and entered Shoreline High School with a chip on my shoulder. Instead of looking up with my nose in the air, I looked straight ahead, eye brows furrowed, and my nose to the grind stone.

I entered high school with vigor. Randy adapted to the untimely death of our friend Patrick with darkness shrouding his vision and we veered away from one another with our choices. Already coming from a darker place within himself, Patrick's departure fueled Randy's choices. I was the moronic friend who didn't clutch onto Randy and remind him how much potential he had. I had no purpose and when I finally found my purpose I developed tunnel vision. I didn't see beyond my own goals and Randy suffered quietly. I was too dense to hear what he was saying when he tried to communicate his pain. We started high school as best friends, but our friendship waned over time. I wouldn't say our friendship diminished. Our hearts were always linked by our strong bond, but our daily interaction was nonexistent during the weekdays because I was required to stay home, do homework, and always be productive.

Randy didn't sit idle. Randy developed new friendships and found new activities to share with other people. Music became Randy's passionate outlet and he found comfort with an electric guitar. Randy was genius-level in everything. Even his good looks were genius-level and he dove into the music culture without inhibitions.

Among the friendships Randy made at Cordell Hull Middle School and continued to nurture through high school and beyond, he found a kindred spirit in Jon. In fact, Jon "the stick" six-foot-something tower, ever-present smile and Def Leppard fanatic, became a dear friend and we naturally formed a new trio in high school. Jon has a warmth that naturally attracts people to him and I was one of them. Jon also played guitar and the two of them jammed as their friendship grew closer. Even though I considered us a trio, my lack of presence most of the week seemed otherwise. I just included myself because I wanted to belong.

Randy was a middle child and his dear baby sister Laura was close to Randy's friends like Jon and myself. Jon adored Randy as much as I did. Randy and Laura were close. So, when Jon and I were at their home, Laura would hang out with us and we'd enjoy a lot of time together.

Erwin Lazaro

Their mom Linda was also a delight. Her hospitality was wonderful and made us feel at home regardless of time.

Linda even hired me to mow their lawn so I could earn some money to buy vinyl records. Not only did I mow their lawn, but they had so many fruitful plum trees. During the summer months, the ground was littered with plums and I went around the yard eating as many of the good ones as I could. If the ripe plums didn't have insect holes, as far as I was concerned, they were ready to eat from the spot I picked them up. Yummy!

I keep diverging within these memories, but that's all I have left of that time. In my current struggles, these recollections keep me grounded. These memories keep me anchored. It's always a mixed bag. The fond memories and the not-so-fond memories go hand-in-hand. Thankfully, the not-so-fond memories are few for me. I look back with adoration. Those were my glory days.

My success through high school might exemplify a leisurely period, but it was no cakewalk. My determination was fierce. I'll always attribute the motivation for my efforts during high school to Patrick. My success was sparked by that tragic catalyst. Patrick's untimely death will always be a constant reminder for the lack of time I may have. Add Randy's influence during that time and the two of them were the constants that fueled my will.

Now, twelve years later, here I am, driving out of Washington. I'm experiencing a sense of desperation. I can barely breathe and constantly calming myself, feeling prone to acting rashly. The urgency is stifling.

I'm questioning everything I'm doing and putting myself down, dissecting myself into little pieces so I can put the pieces back together into an image I still cannot imagine with any sense of clarity. This is driving me crazy, but I won't relent. I can never give up.

As desperate as I am, I have hope.

As a preadolescent, I thought that being a teenager was going to be tough, but not in the manner that it became for me. I could never imagine that. I imagined social awkwardness, potential relationships with girls, and challenging courses in high school. Instead, Patrick vanishing from this world made me negate those concerns. I didn't ponder those typically youthful growing pains any longer. I just did what I needed to do and I didn't spend any time being awkward.

When I consider the round trip from that time when I found purpose and this moment when I'm questioning my own confidence because valued friends with valuable opinions consider me to be arrogant. I confidently declare I am arrogant.

I am arrogant.

I am careful not to be a vain and pompous person, but unfortunately, I make mistakes. I know I can cross a line that makes my friends consider poorly of me, but I also feel I make up for those, hopefully uncommon, indiscretions with my genuine nature. I will continue to declare that I wear my heart on my sleeve. I have nothing to hide, good and bad.

If I do not seek perfection, then I can remain confident in my actions. I will not tolerate preposterous ideals of perfection within any person. It doesn't exist. People are designed to be imperfect for the sole purpose of living. Without a doubt, I know this to be true.

Call me arrogant. I accept. I put myself down continuously so I can walk through doorways. I continue pushing the limits to go beyond my own feeble mind. I push my limits with the intention of growing, not with blind obsession. My heart is the gateway to the vision I have for a future I desire and arrogance is my will to see it through. I will keep searching and I will eventually realize my dream. It's just a matter of when. The how will be revealed at the destined time I seek for myself.

Of course, I can't do any of this alone. I rely on my experiences and build upon the foundations I've already established for myself. I nurture my life. I invite the future with open arms and can't fear delving into the unknown. The motivation for my effort here is to progress, bringing me to uncertain circumstances and through that uncertainty I'm forced to make choices, hoping that I'm choosing wisely along the way. It's guaranteed that I will stumble, fall hard, struggle to get on my feet again, brush off my knees, and progress once more. If I appreciate this tedious process, I'll make it through and I'm never alone while doing it.

Through it all, as I'm having this personal dialogue with God, I'm getting instruction. Thoughts are prayers. Thoughts are instructions,

Erwin Lazaro

too. Therefore, God is instructing me right now. If only every person understood this. Arrogance is not necessarily a negative attribute within the consideration of intention.

A wise priest from my childhood parish in which I have now served as a lay minister for ten years once told me something I live by daily. He said, "Ask everything of God for God already knows what you need before you seek it. You must figure out whether what you seek is really what you need. Your prayers will always be answered, but you may be surprised with the answer." He went on to say that, "I am a child of God and who else but a responsible parent, first and foremost, provides for their child's needs. Of course, you can't fool God, just as parents who are keen to the intentions of their child, whereas parents will err, God will not. A child pouts upon receiving an unprofitable result and God's wisdom will prevail. How many times have you shown anger to your parents when you didn't receive what you asked? And with your parents, how many times have you asked, 'why not'?"

I'm arrogant as a spoiled child of my Faith. Ask and ye shall receive. I ask and I receive, but I always conclude each prayer with "Your Will Be Done." So, I ask without expectation and I'm graciously humbled every time my prayers are answered in the manner I ask.

I receive without expectation. I do not lie to myself. I accept with humility. My heart tells me when I receive through prayers. Arrogance taken too far though … well, that's a deadly sin.

Maybe I'm facing troubled times because I'm overstepping with my arrogance. My prayers aren't being answered in the manner I seek. Maybe my intentions are misplaced. Maybe I'm no longer praying, instead I'm pining for selfish desires. The difference between desire and prayer is that desire is self-centered, while prayer radiates with open arms.

In my daily prayers, I ask for guidance and signs so that I may know I'm acting wisely, but more recently I lack patience and demand answers. I'm acting alone and I can't breathe freely. My heart hurts and I clutch my chest to try to stop the pain from bursting out. I'm desperate and my fuse is short.

I inhaled deeply and exhaled deeply. I didn't realize I was clutching at my chest trying to make the physical pain counteract the pain I couldn't reach. Then, the physical pain forced me to react. My thoughts quickly transformed into something very dark. I forcefully regained control and focused on breathing. Is this an anxiety attack? I've never had one before, but if that was the beginning of one, I don't want them. I lost control so easily. I'm such an arrogant idiot. Idiot.

Erwin Lazaro

IX

Westport Motel

I THINK I finally blinked. What a horrible feeling. Somehow, I'm maintaining the speed limit even though I spaced out while driving ... again. My heart continued racing as I drew longer and deeper breaths to calm my nerves. My emotions were stable and one dark thought turned my nerves into a frazzled mess. I need to remember how fragile I am right now and guard against this in the future. "Remember." I tapped my forehead. "Remember."

My mind settled on the landscape, adapting my mood by looking around. It's no wonder I got lost in thought ... again. This stretch of driving is perfect for deep reflection. No sight-seeing between Olympia and Longview, and I'm approaching Longview. If I maintain seventy-miles-per-hour, I'm doing well. It's a bit of a relief with the speed limit increasing south of Olympia. The sky continues moving past the sun and I'm still in Washington State. I'm staying true to my intentions of maintaining the speed limit. It's another detail that's helping me be the person I'm working on becoming. Lying to myself would only detract from my precious efforts here. So, as best as I can, I am not going to rush.

"Yes, no rushing." Since I'm travelling alone I'm speaking to myself. "I think it would be weirder for me to be silent the entire time I drove." I looked into the rearview mirror and nodded to myself. I took this opportunity to look at my teeth. All clear. Random thoughts filled my head. Then, my brows furrowed. "Actually, the camcorder gives me an excuse to speak out loud, but this is kind of ... weird ... speaking to myself ... out loud."

Okay. I concluded it is weird speaking to myself, out loud, on a regular basis. It would be okay for practicing a speech or for figuring out how to say something important by formulating thoughts out loud. Thoughts within my head are only good for planning to a certain level, but not good for thorough rehearsing. When I'm learning a new song, I can read the lyrics and try to remember just by recalling, but that method is not nearly as effective as actually singing the lyrics with the music. That's an obvious one in my opinion.

Thinking of music … it's time to put in the next disc. "Hmm, who should I pick?" I reached over to the passenger seat and flipped open the cover to my binder. I browsed over a few discs and decided I wanted something with similar energy to Cake. "Oh, yah. This is perfect." I saw *Before These Crowded Streets*, the third studio album by Dave Matthews Band and it was settled.

I popped it in and as "Pantala Naga Pampa" began, my head bobbed up and down in rhythm. Dave sang knowingly with one verse. Their music sings directly to me. Those words and that music are impactful during this wavering time. And what a teaser it is. The first track is just about forty seconds. It segued too quickly into the second track, "Rapunzel".

I see signs for the Lewis and Clark Bridge. I'm quickly driving through Longview, where my boss grew up, and finally about to drive into Oregon. Finally …

Fare well, Washington … 4:42 p.m.

The approach into Oregon is so cool. This is near the mouth of the Columbia River so the width of the river is incredible. I grabbed the camcorder. I want to capture the drive on the two-lane bridge. And, record. "Okay! We're about to drive onto this cool bridge. Thought I would film this baby. This is going into Oregon now. The Lewis and Clark Bridge. Is this the one you were talking about Jef? I think this is the one you've told me about before. Anyway, cool bridge. Entering Oregon. Thought I'd film this." Wait. I already said that. "Uh, it's about four … forty … three or so."

It amazes me that this is only a two-lane bridge, but it makes sense because the length of the bridge is so expansive. The cost to add one lane

104   Erwin Lazaro

in each direction, more than doubling the materials and labor, would *definitely* be more than twice the existing cost. Add maintenance to the equation, as well.

I drove onto the bridge. It inclined upward upon approaching the north bank of the Columbia River. The rise appears to be a long distance at the speed I'm travelling. I feel like I'm ascending a rollercoaster. I started feeling a bit nervous. "Uh, let's see … Cool. Cool. This is Longview. And … we're leaving Longview." I panned across the bridge deck from east to west over the industrial portion of Longview adjacent to the river bank. As the bridge leveled at its highest elevation above the river, six-foot wire mesh fences lined the east and west sides of the bridge. Drivers, bicyclists, and pedestrians, are secured for good reason. "Secured", that's kind of funny. I let out a timid laugh.

It appears I'm rapidly approaching mid span because I can see the above deck bridge structure ahead. I'm always fascinated by bridges because of the engineering prowess required to design and build structures of this nature. I'm even more fascinated by the laborers who build them, like the people who construct high rise towers. I assume that heights are mesmerizing for these people. I think of the distance to the surface below, of course. But, not only is that the concern. Adding Mother Nature's unpredictable conditions to the danger of working at dizzying heights makes me nauseous, especially considering winds and rain. The Tacoma Narrows Bridge and the 76-story Columbia Tower immediately come to mind.

I focused the camcorder on the upcoming overhead bridge structure. "Look at the perspective. Is that cool or what? Ooooooo …" The stout metal girders and trusses that help maintain stability of the bridge structure is beautiful to me. X-bracing, horizontally and vertically, framed the entirety of this above-deck portion of the bridge. Light filtered between the supports and the shadows being cast, formed repeating patterns while passing through. It didn't count as an enclosure. So, I didn't hold my breath.

"Cool bridge. Crossing into Oregon." I peered ahead to the Oregon side of the bridge. I see the freeway turning westward up a massive hill parallel to the river. It's really the highway cut from the side of a cliff face. "Looks like I'm going to go up this big hill. Is that right? I have no idea where I'm going. But that's okay. Just follow the signs. Highway 30. Take me to 101. That's all I need to know."

"Isn't this gorgeous?" The road surface dipped upon a mismatched transition to exit the bridge. "Whoa." A posted sign specified my intended destination. "Astoria! That's where I want to go, next right. Looks like I'm going up that big hill." I exited the freeway and transitioned onto Highway 30.

I gunned the engine to gain speed for the upcoming climb. The roadway continued turning and I continued accelerating. "Keep her steady! Got a little Dave Matthews to keep me going." A sign stunned me as I passed it by. "Bike Route? Who's going to bike up this fucking hill?" I laughed in disbelief! My baby is struggling to climb with the RPMs pushing hard. The shoulder is barely wide enough for one bicycle. I can't imagine sane bicyclists peddling up that distance amongst vehicles moving at freeway speeds. The road does ascend a cliff via a manmade highway.

Okay. I just imagined insane bicyclists on first gear, feet whirring within The Road Runner veil of dust screaming at the top of their lungs, "BRING IT ON!!!" Crazy people are being challenged by that sign. The sign reads "BIKE ROUTE" and in small print below that announcement is "I dare you."

After a few minutes, I finally ascended the mountain and another sign announced, "Viewpoints for Mt. St. Helens". I swear I saw another sign leaning against the rail declaring "You blooming idiot on the bicycle. Why?" I couldn't help but burst into laughter with the thought of it.

As I passed the viewpoints I turned the camcorder and captured the view back across the Columbia River into Washington. I don't know what altitude I am at now but it's a magnificent view for many miles on this clear sunny day. I remained silent and peered northward as best as I could while driving west. "Rapunzel" ended and as "The Last Stop" came on, lines of trees barricaded any further appreciation of the panoramic view. Highway 30 turned southward and away from the mouth of the river. The enchanting melody triggered a passionate response from me. I pointed the camcorder forward and soaked in the music. Track 3. I was captivated for 6 minutes 57 seconds.

I decided to just record the scenery along with the music until the fifth track "Stay (Wasting Time)" ended. "Okay. I am about twenty-five miles from Astoria. I could go forty-three miles to Seaside. Haven't decided yet. It's about 5:07 right now and I'm not that hungry. I kinda want to enjoy Astoria … Should I drive to Seaside first to find lodging and then work my way back to Astoria? … End up in Seaside for the night?"

A posted sign read "ASTORIA 26 MILES." The landscape is expansive here. Grasslands and trees as far as the eye can see. "Isn't this beautiful?" Another sign read "PLEASE NO DRINK AND DRIVE." Okay? I shook my head with that one. I understood it, but … "The Scenery is just gorgeous, isn't it?" I can't wait to drive along the coast. I'll play music and capture more awesome views.

"I've probably done about fifty minutes … yah, fifty minutes-worth of taping now. So, hopefully when I review this I won't get bored with what I've done. As you can see, my windshield is slowly getting caked with mushed insects. May God bless all life."

Beyond the insects though, I focused on the highway bisecting a grove of lush deciduous trees. I came upon the grove in no time. "This is beautiful!" My eyes widened, imprinting this fleeting scene for future recollection. "This is gorgeous!!" The grove appears to cover a large area, but I was through and passed in a mere minute.

I felt a pang of loneliness. "See, my first thought is I wish I was here with someone special. I would hold her hand, lean over and give her a kiss, and things would be good, but … that is *not* the case. So, I guess I can't be thinking that."

Distraction. A hitchhiker. "Whoa! Look at this guy. He's making his way to the same place I am except I'll probably get there much more quickly than he will. Oh! He's got a big smile on his face!" That's suspicious. "My mom told me not to stop and pull over to pick up any hitchhikers … no matter how good looking they are." I thought of an exception. "Now, it'd be a different case if it happened to be somebody who looked *exactly* like me. If *that* were true, then I'd have no choice *but* to stop because *that guy* would be an awesome person besides … how good looking he would be. So, *that's* the only exception." Back to reality. I cleared my throat. "Mom said don't stop for beautiful women or anybody, otherwise. *But*, there's always an exception to every rule."

"I'm just blabbering, but I'm enjoying the view. I love the colors … and the trees and the …" I exhaled deeply. "Too bad I just can't go around the country this way. Too bad that this is just a nine-day journey. Oh, sorry. It's not a glass-half-empty thing, okay?" I gave myself a big smile and chuckled. "But, this is cool. No, I'm not thinking about the end of the journey. I'm just beginning. So, I'll keep it positive. How about that?"

"I have travelling music. Dave Matthews. Dave Matthews is more for energy to make sure I'm okay and everything like that. I'm a little tired." I yawned and shook my head a bit. Apparently, I just crested this massive hill and started heading back down again. "Clatsop Crest … I think I'm gonna stop recording for now. I need a little break." I set the camcorder back on the passenger seat after turning it off and yawned again.

My energy suddenly took a nosedive and nearly sank to zero. I wasn't hungry a little while ago, but I'm hungry now. It is getting closer to dinner time. I'm almost in Astoria. That's where I'll refuel my belly. I braced the wheel and concentrated on driving. A few more miles.

I'll focus on Dave Matthews as my travelling companion for the next twenty miles. I'm hungry, but I think it's more about the monotony of sitting on my butt for this long period of time. I made a few stops early on, until eleven this morning, but now it's after 5 pm. Walking around or doing something different would do me good. I don't know how truck drivers do this. Hats off to them, for sure.

I don't have energy to think too deeply so I'll just listen to Dave chant wisdom through lyrics and embrace the music. I'm relying on these compact counselors to help me comprehend what I seek. Words are great for communicating thoughts, but weaved within music the poignant expression becomes amplified. That's what I truly consider so inspirational about musicians. They share their philosophies through music. Well … I should narrow that consideration to artists who have passionate messages to share. Sometimes it's just one line or verse, here and there, as Dave Matthews Band does for me. Sometimes it's an entire album such as *The Innocent Age* by Dan Fogelberg ... the heart of all music for me.

Dan Fogelberg ... *The Innocent Age* ... the top of my list for the most impactful album in my life. Tied at the top with Barry Manilow's *2:00 AM Paradise Café* for favorite album in my life, thus far. Thinking of Barry ... Barry's music overall encapsulates the essence of loneliness for me. In addition to the broken hearts he serenades, Barry does write and sing about hopes and dreams. He sings with the passion to inspire lovers and relationships, but even through those songs, a sense of melancholy permeates his music. I sense a pensive nature from his voice and the tone of the melodies he chooses. Maybe it's me and that's how I feel and that's what I draw from his music.

Dan Fogelberg is a poet and philosopher from a distant past that successfully breached the gates of popular music and found the way to reach millions of people. I imagine something like, but not necessarily, a stone tablet in his hand as he walks amongst the people. I have a reverence for his teachings as I would for a pastor. Again, that's how I feel about his music.

I devotedly empathize with both artists. That's the power of music. Even though the chances are almost zero that I'd ever meet either person, music is a medium that connects feelings between people without personal contact.

My mom and dad's love for music inspired my early appreciation for a wide variety of genres. Singing with the radio became my life. I sang the tunes by both, male and female artists. I enjoy most pop songs prior to the nineties because the variety is diverse. The genre of popular songs was expansive back then. As time has passed, the people with money have allowed fear to *severely* narrow what *they* define as "popular". It's a shame.

Of the pop artists in the seventies, I found an affinity for the tunes by Barry Manilow. Even now, the songs made popular by Barry are closest to my heart. I laughed, "I like that ... great song." Closest? Hmm ... Dan Fogelberg is equal for different reasons like brothers from different mothers. Not quite as good with that one since the album title is *Twin Sons of Different Mothers*, Dan's collaboration with jazz flautist Tim Weisberg. And, the time frame is teetering on the edge since my deepest appreciation for Dan's music didn't really begin until his *Phoenix* album release in 1979.

Anyway, I stayed in my bedroom and sang endlessly. Music shaped my emotions and the nurturing love I enjoyed at home transformed into a deep desire to discover that love for myself. I honed my imagination. I envisioned a life with the woman of my dreams, getting married, having children, and nurturing my own family in the manner my own family loves me.

What was I thinking earlier? Oh, yah. I admire philosophical musicians. Well, I wouldn't place Barry's music in that category, but Barry does something equally powerful. A simple reason why millions and millions of fans adore the songs he produces. His music connects hearts. Obviously, Barry got me tangled within his web of magic and I'm tangled for life.

Through my own reflection, Dan Fogelberg not only connects hearts, his music connects minds and spirits, as well. I'll admit that not the entirety of his music is impactful for me, but however he conceived *The Innocent Age* was masterful. Every note and every lyric within that album has become dear to me. I believe that he was inspired by Thomas Wolfe's novel *Of Time and the River*. I swoon from just contemplating the impact that every note and every lyric has had on my life since the first song I had heard from that album, "Same Old Lang Syne," timely released during the 1980 Christmas season.

And going back one year earlier, I recall the first Fogelberg song I recognized. I was eleven years old. "Longer" was released right after Christmas Day 1979 and it immediately drew me in. Mom always has music playing. I pay attention to every song. I heard "Longer" for the first time and learned the lyrics from the radio. I waited intently. Placing a cassette player-recorder next to the radio, I pressed the red button when the new hit played. I repeated this for every song I wanted to learn. I'd use a sheet of college-ruled paper and a No. 2 pencil, sit at my desk, play one line at a time, and quickly write down the lyrics before I forgot. And when I couldn't understand the words, I'd have to rewind and replay. I rewound a lot. It was worth it though. I have a collection of hand-written lyrics stored away in a memory box. The funny thing is that some of the lyrics I wrote down didn't quite make sense. I'd try to decipher the artist's intentions, but when my limited vocabulary and the dictionary weren't enough, I'd pick a word that sounded like it could fit. That's called phonetic interpretation. I smiled to myself.

The incentives for me to buy 45 rpm and 33 rpm vinyl records was not only to be able to replay my favorite tunes, but also to possess the lyrics of my favorites. In fact, the first thing I still look for are lyrics being provided by artists whenever I buy new music. I was incredibly relieved when I pulled out the sleeves for the double vinyl album of *The Innocent Age* and discovered the lyrics to every exquisite song. The production team chose an elegant font too. Those printed words are an art form visually and lyrically. I remember thanking God that Dan Fogelberg is such a kind human being for providing those lyrics. Otherwise, I would have had to spend countless hours rewinding and replaying on the cassette player-recorder. I would have done so as a labor of love.

Those days of vinyl records from the perspective of a preadolescent … a fond reminiscence of innocence passed. In fact, compact discs were introduced when I was fourteen years old. Compact discs and disc players hit the market in the early 1980s and I already intended repurchasing most of the albums from my vinyl record collection over time.

I keep my vinyl records in a memory box for safe keeping. I still use a Technics audio-rack system that includes a turn table. Once in a long while, I open the box and pull out a few records to enjoy. Nothing like listening to the matured character of music through the years-old scratches. I do it because it's comforting.

"Oh, my goodness …" So much for having a still mind. I'm just not designed that way. It's "Tangent Boy" at it again! A nickname a friend has given me. *2:00 AM Paradise Café* and *The Innocent Age*. I am looking forward to playing both discs during appropriate times, maybe even more than once if time allows.

And, just like that, I'm in Astoria. Well, that's the way to get to my destination and not be aware of time. First thing first. My belly calls.

And … *Before These Crowded Streets* CD just finished, so my belly won't be first. Music comes first. "Who to play next …" I looked around Astoria and my first impression gave me inspiration. I flipped to Eagles and replaced Dave Matthews Band with *Eagles Their Greatest Hits (1971-1975)*.

"Take It Easy" started playing and I felt as if I was home. Perfect song to kick off their greatest hits album. The energy fits so well here. Now's the time to find a diner and have some good eats. It'll be a good change of activity too. I started singing with Glenn Frey and my spirit lifted. Thanks, Glenn and company.

Singing to my heart's content I observed the people and the buildings of this city. I seem to be driving into the heart of Astoria. This appears to be the business district and it was easy to spot the sign for Farrell's Burger Basket right away. Maybe I should have a burger for each hand … I smiled as I easily found street parking.

"Oooo … my first contact with Oregonians!" I secured my craft and cloaked my belongings with my jacket. The evening approaches and it's going to be a beautiful one at that, so no requirement for extra shielding. I practiced the Vulcan salute a few times so I'm ready to disembark. Nodding confirmation to myself, I opened the hatch, and stepped foot on Oregon soil. I let out a hearty laugh. A few Oregonians stopped and stared, but I focused on my mission: feed my belly.

Okay. I did everything except the hearty laugh part. I'm not used to eating in a diner or restaurant without company. I just hope I don't look awkward even though I'm feeling excruciatingly uncomfortable. Oh, well. I must eat. Nine days of meals without companionship … shivers ran up and down my spine as I walked across the street. I hope nobody noticed that. It probably looked like I had to pee.

I opened the door to the diner and immediately saw the sign: PLEASE WAIT TO BE SEATED. As if entering a restaurant alone isn't difficult enough, I'm standing amongst other parties with more than one person. I quickly glanced around and confirmed I was the only single person waiting. My eyes instantly focused on the décor. Looking at inanimate objects is always comforting.

"Party of one? Excuse me. Sir? Party of one?" My ears tingled as I turned to face a server. She wore a genuine smile and repeated her question a third time, "Party of one?" I felt eyes on me from the other guests and wanted to point to myself and confirm, yes, I am alone.

"Yes, unfortunately." I shrugged my shoulders and turned my palms upward.

Her smile grew wider in a reassuring manner, "I have a spot for you at the bar if you'd like? Don't worry. We'll take care of you. Follow me." She turned without waiting for my response, picked up a menu, and motioned for me to follow. I respectfully followed her. It seems this is a perk for dining alone. The wait is next to nothing. One burger for each hand?

I followed while looking at my hands, imagining one bacon cheeseburger in each. I don't think I can finish two. "Whoops!" I almost walked into the server, clearly distracted by my imagination.

"I think you're hungry! Here you go and here's your menu." The server had taken a step backward after turning to face me, aware of my distraction. Her smile never dimmed as she continued. "I told you. We'll take care of you. Someone will take your order shortly."

"Sorry, about that. I almost made a fool of myself. I was just considering whether I could eat two burgers. I don't want to look like a pig though." I finished with coy laughter and avoided eye contact.

"How about this? Order one burger basket and order something yummy from our dessert menu. Lots of delicious treats to choose from. I'll check on you later." And with that, she was off to attend to other customers.

I took my seat and browsed over the menu. A simple matter really. Bacon cheeseburger with all the fixings and fries with a side of tartar sauce. Oh, add a glass of root beer, unless they have orange soda. I'll take orange soda instead. Yes! They have orange soda.

"Good evening!" Another server greeted me from behind the bar. Big smiles for everyone! "What can I get started for you?"

"Good evening! I'll have a bacon cheeseburger with everything on it, minus onions. I'll have fries, orange soda, side of tartar sauce … actually, can I order onion rings instead of fries, please?" My eyes lit up with the realization. "Oh … I change my mind about the soda, too. May I have hot water?"

"Well, of course you can. It's a dollar fifty extra for the rings, if that's okay with you?" She was already writing down the revision before I replied. "Hot water?" She looked at me for confirmation.

"Yes, yes, please. This is my first meal in Oregon. I'm looking forward to it." I acknowledged with my own wide grin. "Yes, yes, hot water, please."

"Oh, wow! Are you here for the regatta?" She paused intently.

"No, sorry. I'm just passing through. I do have some questions for you when you have a chance though." I know she's busy so I hope she has time for me later.

"Sure. Let me take care of your order and help a few other customers and I'll be sure to answer your questions when I have the chance. I'll be back." She pressed her hand on the counter while engaging me directly and without waiting for my response she turned to take care of business. Her smile never dimmed.

The first two Oregonians I've greeted seem so friendly; friendly and busy. I haven't had a chance to present a Vulcan salute yet. I think I'll save it as a last resort, in case a situation calls for a recognizable interstellar greeting. In the meantime, I looked around and being the time that it is, it's good to see that business is doing well. People are enjoying the atmosphere and the servers are keeping things lively with their friendly banter and laughter.

It is nice to be within an uplifting environment. I get the feeling that many are regulars and they know each other within this small city. It's a modest space and that adds to the homey character of the setting. Of course, my stereotypical first impression of small communities might be a bit pretentious, but it's not condescending in any way. Being here makes me happy.

A whirlwind approached and rested directly in front of me. "Okay! You had some questions for me?"

I should have been aware of her, but I was still startled. "Oh, yes. Yes!

Please." I thought quickly and decided not to reveal any melodramatic stuff. I'll just keep it informational. "This is my first time in Astoria. I don't know anything about the city. Do you have any recommendations for sightseeing while I'm here?"

The server was very sweet. She spent a few minutes telling me about the history of the city and the local amenities I might be interested in seeing, but since the day was gone, most of the tourist spots are probably already winding down for the day. The most popular feature is still open though. During the summer months, extended hours allow visitors more flexibility with time. The Astoria Column.

The suggestion was perfect for me. "Nice! That's where I'm going then. It's starting to get late so I better visit soon. One more question for you." She nodded in anticipation. "I don't have any overnight reservations in the area yet. I was thinking of going to Seaside for the night. Do you have any other suggestions for lodging?"

This was the first time her smiled faded, but it was because she was thinking. "Ooooooo ... I thought you might be passing through because of the numerous events in the area, but ... this is not a good time to look for lodging if you don't already have reservations. The boat regatta is underway. There's a huge volleyball tournament in Seaside that always brings in a lot of people. This is the height of the tourist season too. I highly doubt anything will be available in Seaside or Cannon Beach or any city close by ... actually." I watched her dig deeper into options hoping she'd come up with something viable for me. I secretly crossed my fingers and toes.

"Are you headed south?" She focused on me honestly trying to be helpful with my obvious lack of preparation. I confirmed with a nod. "I'm assuming you're going down 101?" I nodded again. "Well, you might find something in Tillamook. If not, you'll definitely find something in Lincoln City, but that's more than ninety minutes past Seaside, especially with the large number of tourists now." My shoulders visibly slumped. "I'm assuming you don't want to bypass the beautiful ocean views and tourist locations between here and Tillamook or Lincoln City." I nodded, but with much less enthusiasm and it appeared that she was struggling for more options.

I reaffirmed to myself that rushing is not an option. I pursed my lips and waited for her to come up with anything else. The other server noticed and walked over to us. "It sure looks like you two are having some serious conversation while everyone else is enjoying their meals with light chitchat. What's going on? Can I help?"

My mood brightened and hope reasserted itself. I temporarily monopolized the help for the entire diner. The server originally helping me find lodging relayed the gist of the situation. Meanwhile, I could see the server who had originally seated me thinking about more options. My mind was unusually empty as I waited for a good reply and thankfully a good reply came.

"This is not the best alternative, but it may be the only option you have." The server behind the bar quickly left and returned with my meal. She motioned towards the rest of the customers and I knew she was needed. I smiled and mouthed a 'thank you' as she returned my smile. The server taking over the conversation continued. "Your food is here so I won't take much more of your time before it gets cold. I'm assuming you came down from Washington?" I nodded. "Well, I know the person who runs a motel nearby and I'd bet that there's a room available there. The bad news is that it's on the Washington side of the border." She paused for my reaction.

I smiled and gave her my most sincere expression. "Thanks to the both of you for taking the time to help me. I truly appreciate your efforts especially with it being so busy. I won't waste any more of your time. Yes, I'll go for it if a room's available. Please."

She pointed a finger at the ceiling and winked. "Before we count the chickens before they're hatched, I'll make a phone call for you and find out if there's a vacancy. Okay?"

"Oh my gosh, yes! Would you please find out for me? I am really so grateful." I made a prayer sign with my two hands, palms together.

She hurried off to a phone and I imagined myself sleeping within my baby for the night. I wasn't thrilled by the prospect so I placed my hopes on the kindness of a stranger going out of her way to help a Washingtonian in need.

My food was getting cold so I took this opportunity to say a quiet

Erwin Lazaro

prayer of thanks for this meal and started eating. I chewed intently and savored my first mouthful. This is my first meal on my own and though it's sobering to a certain degree, I'm amongst people who are sharing good energy with me. Being here is pleasant and I'll be even happier with good news about a place to sleep tonight.

I quietly ate my meal at the counter and browsed casually around the diner. Empty stools to one side. A couple sitting two stools from me on the other side. The tables were filled with young families, older couples, and teenage groups hanging out to begin their Saturday night.

"Good news!" An excited voice brought my attention back to the counter. "There's one vacancy left and your information is required to reserve the last room for the night!"

I hurriedly wiped my mouth and hands and followed her to the phone. I took care of the reservations and felt relief once the transaction was complete. I wanted to hug the two servers for helping me, but deemed my impulse too obtrusive and reigned myself back from acting too emotionally. I decided instead to show my appreciation through a generous tip.

After profusely thanking the two servers with a dedicated smile and a few thousand bows for each, I went back to my seat and enjoyed the rest of my meal in peace knowing I had a place to sleep for the night. I couldn't linger though because of my limited time to visit the Astoria Column. I tried not to rush and uncharacteristically declined dessert. That was a tough call. I added a large gratuity to the bill, visited the restroom, and walked towards the door within a few minutes. I called out another big "thank you" to the kind women who helped me as I exited Farrell's Burger Basket. They both encouraged me to come by again so I could enjoy a dessert on the next visit.

I re-entered "my baby" transport and deemed my first mission in Oregon a huge success. I cracked up at myself. I hadn't considered the high degree of difficulty for finding lodging. Here's to flying by the seat of my pants! I've committed to travelling wherever my nose takes me and that cavalier attitude extends to finding a place to sleep for seven more nights. If I mull over the situation, I might hesitate so I won't think about it and handle the matter as needed. It's a stupid plan for a seasoned traveler, but I'm not a seasoned traveler. Stupidity excused, right? Though I am a thorough a planner. In this case, the thrill of not knowing where I'm going outweighs my compulsion to plan every step of the way. This is new for me. The anticipation is exhilarating.

I took a deep breath as I started up my baby, put on my seatbelt, and headed towards the Astoria Column. The two servers also gave me directions to the site. They are awesome! I should have gotten their names to write in my journal, but I've never been good with names. I don't know how often this happens for others, but I easily forget within seconds of introductions. I try to work on my short-term memory loss issue, but I look a bit moronic pounding my head as I repeat names during introductions. It's not a sociable action.

"Anyhoochiemamas! Oh, yah. I should record this." I pulled over to ready the music and camcorder for travelling again since I hid everything from view. I had to reach on the floor for my binder. I uncovered the camcorder and placed it on my lap. I re-entered traffic and did a U-turn so I could re-approach Astoria and videotape the drive into the city … "Well, here we are. Looks like we're approaching … Astoria. And I already ran into my first little setback."

I restarted Eagles and the intro for "Take It Easy" finished in perfect timing for me to sing with Glenn. I sang through the chorus and stopped to relay my recent activities. "Okay. I had my first meal. I'm kinda backtracking, looking around, exploring the place." I approached the diner. "And … there's my first meal. I went to Farrell's Burger Basket. There's some nice people in there. Say 'hi' to them. They helped me out. That was really nice." I thanked God for their kindness and panned across the cityscape. "This is Astoria." I focused on the Astoria-Megler Bridge. "There's the bridge crossing over to Washington. So, we're looking back north." Back to the matter at hand. "I tried to get a room in Astoria. No vacancies. The bed and breakfasts are filled. Everything is full. I had no place to sleep." I laughed at the prospect.

"Luckily, the server gave me a reference and I've gotta go back into Washington for the place I'm gonna sleep tonight. But that's … okay." What choice do I have? Beggars can't be choosers. "Now, I was told to head down this road and I'd see signs for the Astoria Column. Oh!

Look at that! There's a sign for the Astoria Column right there. That's where I'm heading."

I followed the signs and kept recording while Eagles filled the audio void. "Witchy Woman" played while I passed a few churches. I drove through mixed-use areas reminding me of the Wallingford neighborhood in Seattle. I noticed a good number of "four-square" style homes and a few bungalows here and there. The ambience is pleasant. I scanned left and right as I drove through more and more residential streets. The commonality of the experience is that I kept climbing upward. I'm anticipating that this tourist attraction is located on higher ground overlooking the city.

I didn't see any more signs for the column. I came upon a T-intersection. "Where the heck am I going? Huh? I have no idea where I'm going! Woohoo!" My sixth sense told me to turn right. "So, people are … you are all going to see me get lost. That's just wonderful." This is a smallish city. I can't get lost. I continued following my instincts and finally came upon a sign. "Oh! Astoria Column! Look at that. Not so bad." It pointed left so I turned up another hill. On the street was painted a large image of the column. "Ohhh! That's the symbol for the Astoria Column. It's on the road." I drove up a meandering street weaving left and right through trees. I played with the camera and tilted the view with each turn, making formula-one racecar engine sounds at a swift 20 mph. "We're having lots of fun now! Hoohoo!"

On one imaginary, steep-banking turn, I noticed the column peaking above the horizon. "There's the column, right there!" I stopped goofing off and sped up so I could finally get to the site. I continued recording.

The view opened northward, high above the mouth of the river. The south remained thick with trees. I drove west and greenery finally gave way to reveal the column. Situated in a hallowed position above everything in the city, the final approach further enhanced a reverence towards the landmark. Even the driveway leading to the site is set at a lower elevation than the base of the column, providing a sense of dignified formality.

I coasted to a stop behind other vehicles parallel parked in the driveway. I sat still and steadied my recording on the monument. My first impression is that it was designed to look like a Roman column and a spiral frieze adorns the entire column length. Within the frieze, the carved strips spiral towards the sky, artwork embellishes the entire surface. The base of the column rests on a concrete box where visitors enter. An observation deck is situated near the top of the column. I don't know anything about it so I'll research the history of this area later. For now, I'll be a tourist and enjoy.

I stepped outside. The wind is noticeable. It's steady. I videotaped the surrounding area and zoomed in on the awesome truss structure of the Astoria-Megler Bridge. After videotaping the bridge span, I made my way towards the entrance of the monument. I noticed the simple but beautifully maintained landscape.

I stopped at the base of the stairs roughly six feet lower than the entrance to the column. It's only one flight, but reminds me of a large altar. I was inclined to bow before ascending, but refrained from doing so and made my way up. I crossed the grass courtyard and entered the open doorway welcoming visitors.

The first thought that washed over me as I stepped inside was a contemplative one wishing for an enlightening experience as I ascend the column, but that image scattered into nothingness as I followed other tourists up the spiral staircase and a large butt loomed within an arm's length of my face. My hope for enlightenment became a silent plea that this elderly gentleman in front of me did not have gas that might explode and encase me. I did not want to experience the particulate matter of a man with digestive issues or anyone else for that matter.

I tried to look away, but I just couldn't. I had nowhere to look and suddenly became conscious of my own butt. I snuck a peak behind me and found no one. I happened to be the last tourist for now. My bowels are fine, but this is still an awkward situation.

I climbed slowly, one step at a time, keeping one eye on the butt ahead of me and the other on my own butt. The column's cavity echoed the voices of children, women, and men speaking simultaneously, nothing close to enlightening for me. I must have counted over

Erwin Lazaro

one-hundred-fifty steps before I breathed a sigh of relief and exited upon the observation deck.

This would have been a wonderful place for me to deliberate my existence if it weren't for so many tourists in close quarters. The irony is that we are above the city, estimating over a hundred feet above the ground, and open to the cloudless Oregon sky. In fact, I'm looking eye-to-eye with the sun right now. It's brilliant. Too bad I can't find peace here. Instead, I turned on my camcorder and recorded more footage of my travels for review later.

When I first learned about the column and being as late as it is in the afternoon, I thought that I could potentially be here with minimal disturbance. I thought that most tourists would be eating dinner by now and making their way to other places at this hour. I thought wrong. I'm such a selfish prick. Denied.

I'm not wasting my time here though. I'm making the best of it and trying to keep things light. A little darkness managed to seep in, but the sun is inspiring. It's inspiring me to look upon the brighter side of life. No shadows can exist from where I'm standing. I'm looking directly into the sun with my eyes closed, absorbing energy. Even the penetrating winds at this elevation are telling me to enjoy these moments.

I stood in place, my camcorder still recording. I abandoned my search and somehow found serenity as a reward. The voices softened to ambient noise, mixing with the winds, the helicopters, and the planes. Is it that simple? It can't be that simple.

I opened my eyes, absorbed a deep cleansing sensation, and discharged fragments of my caged emotions. A helicopter closed in and I focused on the pilot. He veered away and I followed until the image became too shaky and unstable. I zoomed back out and panned across the environment.

I felt calm for an ephemeral moment. I want more of that. How can I get it? Where can I find it? I crave it.

The noises came back at full volume.

It's time for me to leave. I stopped recording, descended the column, and quietly left the site. I looked in the rearview mirror. This visit was worthwhile. For that one precious moment, visiting Astoria was worthwhile.

The rest of the evening I wandered northward, enjoying Eagles hits with the camcorder recording, singing along to every track. I wanted to stay in Seaside, Oregon for the night, but here I am crossing back into Washington. The sun is setting and I'm heading towards a lighthouse at Cape Disappointment on Washington's southwest peninsula. My office bro, Brian, had told me about it from one of his trips so I figured I'd try to visit it myself. The horizon is rapidly overtaking the sun though. I'm not sure if I can make it there with any daylight left.

By the time I arrived at the parking lot it was 7:57 pm. Only three vehicles remained in an otherwise empty lot. A sign specified the park being open from 8 am to dusk. I parked, contemplated, then decided to leave. I couldn't leave my valuables unattended as darkness creeped in. I don't remember how far I drove, but this was an unproductive one-hour excursion.

I shrugged my shoulders and deemed myself satisfied for trying. It just didn't work out this time. I drove away from Cape Disappointment. Now, all that's left for my first full day on the road is to get into bed so I can rest up for the next day.

I drove back up highway 100, but didn't get far before I pulled over. It sure seems as if the water is going crazy. I was drawn towards the intensity of the waves. I had to stop. The power of nature is fierce and I had to admire that ferocity. It's scary. And I realized that this is my first opportunity to stand in the presence of these grand waters. Well, I'm about a stone's throw away. I rested my head on the wheel, admiring the scale of its power. The water's voice is ominous, easily felt within the confines of my baby. Continuous roars overlapping one another.

The horizon is about to blanket the sun and remnants of the day lingered. I stepped out of my baby and witnessed the transition of the twilight sky. With the sun disappearing, human and wildlife activity virtually nonexistent, and the temperature rapidly cooling, the atmosphere was still except for the waves warning everyone to beware. I anticipate that every evening is like this. Mother Nature puts on a show and all else halts to give their undivided attention.

I was parked on the highway shoulder. A few drivers not currently paying homage passed from either direction. I leaned against my baby and faced the ocean. My heart is racing. This is the sensation of feeling alive! The roar of the waves crashing is being compounded by my imagination. I'm projecting myself standing at the edge of the shore. This exhilaration stems from my fear of the waters swallowing me whole. Though that fear has never deterred me. I'm almost welcoming it.

After all, I was the fool who learned how to water ski in Tulalip Bay amongst fishing vessels and their nets. I didn't find out until much later that normal people water ski on placid lake surfaces. I'd often go airborne and face plant into the water because of those volatile waves in the bay. The wake of fishing boats passing by compounded the turbulence of the bay waters. A countless number of times I failed. I wore a life vest, but my head, and particularly my face took quite the beating. I drank so much sea water. It was a cleansing of sorts. I can't complain though. A great friend and his family spoiled guests like me and I had a blast every time. Great homemade breakfasts at their cabin followed by the attempts to conquer the bay. I amused myself.

That's just it. I'm not afraid of facing my fears, but at the same time, I'm terrified. I'm more terrified about failing than being terrified by fear itself. I was always scared out of my mind going out on that boat, but fear didn't stop me. I don't know how to swim, but that didn't stop me either.

I proved to myself and to my peers that I could do it and I did. I'm not stupid though. I'd punch the person in the face that'd dare me to do something stupid. No, I'd laugh, call them an idiot, and then feign a hefty punch to their face for mocking me in the first place. Idiot. I'm not stupid. I'm just dumb.

Pride is dumb. I never conquered that bay, but I tried and tried again. I did okay. It's not the water skiing itself I'm referring to either. It's the fear. I still feel that same fear standing here. This fear is intoxicating, but I'm not going to do anything stupid. I'm not stupid. I'm just dumb.

I folded my arms and admired the endless waves taunting anything to approach. Purring in anticipation. The shore-wide cirrus of water retracting anything oblivious to the circumstances.

Whereas I felt calm near the top of the Astoria Column, electricity is coursing through my body near the shores of Baker Bay. The night time here is a different animal. I'm wearing a t-shirt and shorts. This rapid transition of the horizon swallowing the last rays of sunlight dropped the ambient temperature and I began shivering.

I am pleased that I witnessed the sun set beyond the horizon. No green flash though. That's fine. I'm not with anyone and it'd be a waste if I did see the green flash while I am alone. I guess that's a relief.

I scurried into my baby and started her up. My automatic lights engaged with the darkness and I quickly raised the thermostat to get the heater blowing. Just like that, the day had passed. Limited visibility is making me aim for one target. I turned off the music and rolled down the windows. The waves are broadcasting their own music, powerful and mesmerizing.

I drove with the windows down until I couldn't hear the crashing waves any longer. I froze, but it was well worth getting goosebumps. The blasting heat from the vents barely compensated for the biting winds flowing throughout the cabin. After shutting the windows, I turned down the blower, put on music once again, and looked forward to a hopefully, comfortable bed.

Time plays tricks. I swear. Driving in unfamiliar territory completely skews my perception of time. I am so worn out. I only have a general idea of where to look for my destination. I just want to get in bed. I refuse to look at the time and continued scanning ahead.

When I finally saw the signs for the Westport Motel, relief washed over me. I was getting a bit worried thinking I had missed it. Funny that the lyrics of "Hotel California" were floating through my brain waves.

My grip on the wheel loosened as I parked. I apologized to my baby for holding on too tightly. I caressed the wheel, told her I love her, and thanked her for bringing me here safely. My baby needs rest too. "Good night. Rest well. Thank you."

I checked in and thankfully all is well. I brought in everything except for my mountain bike. It's time for my last video entry for this first day on the road. I yawned and pressed the red button. "Okay. We're at the end of my first evening and I'm at the Westport Mor … Mort …

Errr, uh, yuh … Westport Motel." The camcorder recorded the plain white setting, kitchenette, wall-mounted television, and gaudy bedding. I added a personal touch by dumping my belongings throughout the room.

"I'm exhausted." I turned to the digital clock on the nightstand, but couldn't make out the numbers through the screen. The image is cryptic. "That's weird. The numbers are distorted on the screen. What the heck?" I had to use my eyes to read the clock. "Oh, it's supposed to read 10:57 pm." I zoomed back out. "Anyway, this is the end of an evening. My first evening, on my own. Good night everybody."

Short and sweet. I set the camcorder down and called it a night. Time to replenish my energy for whatever lies ahead. While brushing my teeth, I hurt myself, careless in my groggy state. I was aloof to any discomfort and changed my clothes. When I flicked the switch to turn the lights off, I felt scared. Pulling up the covers, I buried myself within this unknown place. Comfort took over and I didn't have energy left to care. I forgot everything as I closed my eyes. I didn't feel anything either. Before losing consciousness, I balanced my state of awareness between apathy and fatigue. I also thought about the Bates Motel, but that's as far as I got.

X

Questions Or Answers

I WOKE UP and I'm grateful to be alive. I see daylight around the curtains. That's a relief. My last thought before sleeping was The Bates Motel and my first thought upon waking is The Bates Motel. I'm just not comfortable travelling alone.

I didn't linger in bed. I felt the pep in my step and arose with nervous energy. I'm anxious and nagging tension remains deep within. I want to be on the road as soon as possible. I'm still in Washington and that sucks. I'm wasting time here and I'm easily annoyed, but I'm trying to keep a positive attitude. Trying ... It's my fault for not planning.

It didn't take me long to pack up and reload everything into my baby. I decided to have breakfast in Astoria. I'm hoping to have enough belly fuel to last until dinner, if possible. Time is wasting away. It's thirty minutes plus to breakfast.

No grand farewell for the Westport Motel. I quietly drove away and I quietly entered Astoria. I found The Berry Patch and devoured a marvelous breakfast: two large buttermilk pancakes, four savory sausage links, two eggs over medium, two glasses of freshly squeezed orange juice.

I always place the delectable, fried eggs over my pancakes. I always pour a generous amount of maple syrup over everything, puncture the eggs, and let the oozing yolk and syrup mix together to create golden, liquid swirls. I'm stuffed now, but it's heaven on a plate. Well, it would be if I weren't dining alone. Meals are not just about the food. Meals serve an important social function. Sharing a good meal with good company always accentuates details of the experience. I remember more vividly. I recall more vibrant hues and greater clarity while sharing food.

Of course, I am blessed to live with an angel on earth who always cares about every detail. Our meals at home are always lively. Mom laughs so much at my silly humor. She's the perfect audience. I look at her with pure love and adoration and I learned to be a good listener because of my mom. Unfortunately, I haven't reciprocated one hundred percent of the time like Mom does for her family, but I'm trying to do better and be a better son. I fail her constantly. Mom is my ultimate role model for understanding people. Nothing gets passed her. She does it so naturally.

My heart deflated as I drove out of Astoria. My family standing on the doorstep as I drove away from home, just yesterday, came to mind. I know they're worried. I left without warning. They have no idea where I'm going; neither do I, for that matter. My family is waiting for my return whenever that will be. Without doubt, they want me to hurry back and come home safely. I almost want to turn around, but if I do, nothing will change. That's what keeps me looking forward.

I shook my head, took a deep breath, and tried to reset myself. I'm blessed for starting the day with a great breakfast, thanks to the people at The Berry Patch, the chickens that laid the eggs, the cows for their milk, and the pigs for the sausage links. The details sound morbid, but I am truly grateful for the food and remember intently where my food comes from, just as I remember where I have been and what I've done to be here today. I must build on that.

"Ah … so far behind this morning. Can't cry over spilt milk, though. I feel warm and fuzzy inside thanks to The Berry Patch. Had to release the demons and *that* made my meal complete! My spirit is lifted too so I can't complain; I press onward." I patted my belly with one hand and pointed the other towards the windshield, my right knee taking control of the wheel. "Duh, duh, duh, duh, duhhhh; Duh, duh, duh, duh, duhhhh; Duh, duh, duh, DUH, duhhhh; Duh, duh, duh, Duhhhh! Yes! Onward, I say! So, corny." I paused. I should have packed *Die Walküre*, though it's probably a good idea that I didn't. If I had, I might be encouraged to fly off a cliff or something. "Oh boy, I'm not only talking to myself, I'm reacting too!" I gave myself a toothy grin. "Let's take care of that craziness by picking the next CD."

I grabbed the wheel at a curve and fumbled for my CD binder. I had listened to a local station driving into Astoria. The weather forecast sounded promising, but the sky is partly cloudy. My vision drifted and the scene triggered a reaction, "Dang it! I haven't recorded a greeting this morning, but music comes first."

I instinctively knew who to choose and help me sing my blues away. Music tugs at my heartstrings and this man knows how to toy with my emotions. The music and lyrics speak volumes about experience or I imagine, both stem from grueling introspection. In my opinion, Bobby Caldwell is a wise guy playing in a bar and empathizing with any patrons willing to listen. This man knows about love even if love never stays. I could have written the lyrics for his music if I had those experiences for myself. That's my way of declaring a kinship with this soulful and jazz-driven performer, though I consider him one of my primary therapists. I have no idea if I'm even close to understanding Bobby Caldwell, the man, but that's what I gain from the music he sermonizes. "Sermonizes? Huh, that's a good one." I popped in one of my Bobby Caldwell CDs and grabbed the camcorder.

"Good morning, everyone! Just enjoyed a spectacular meal at The Berry Patch in Astoria. Great people. Great food. Looking forward to the day. It's supposed to be a sunny one." I looked up at the sky. "I hope these clouds clear out. Hmm, going to bypass the lighthouse, no time. I'll make another trip out of it. That'll be fun. As much as I love Washington, I keep lingering here so it's time to move on!" That's the spirit and I roared a thunderous burp as an exclamation point. "Excuse ME!" My knee took the wheel again and I covered my mouth.

"Bobby Caldwell's keeping me company, so we can sing together along the Oregon coast." My spirit soared with the music. "Let's see how far I can get today and *also* get lodging. I intend to go as far south as I can. Don't want a repeat of yesterday!"

Of course, it didn't take long before I found the first diversion of the day. Del Rey Beach must lure and capture every traveler onto its shore. How can any first-time visitor bypass this experience? It's just not possible. I haven't had an opportunity to drive directly onto a beach before now! Of course, I couldn't help but question whether it's alright to *actually* drive on the beach. So, I slowly progressed inward and found a line of vehicles neatly parked near the entrance. I tentatively passed them, drove towards the water, and wondered how many Oregon beaches I could share this experience with my baby, feeling this beautiful sand beneath her four-wheel drive.

I stopped within a playful distance to the water, the waves teased my baby. I was the only one parked so close to the encroaching waves, but I figured I'm not going to stay for long. I'm going for it. This is my time. Of course, if I'm approached about violating beach rules, I'll gladly comply, but until that time, I'm living for this moment.

In fact, I took a few moments to simply appreciate my position on this beach. Staring out towards the ocean beckoning, I'm feeling the urge to drive directly into the water. Driving parallel to the waves seems so appealing. I didn't take long to decide.

I smiled a mischievous smile, stopped recording, and placed my baby into drive. I think she's excited too! "Here we go!" As we started to move, I couldn't help but think, "I hope I don't get into trouble. I hope I don't get into trouble! Wait, I said that out-loud, didn't I?" I felt a crazy grin plastered on my face. I slowly gained speed and quickly closed the gap to the waves. My heart raced as the wheels plowed into the foam. I tried to dance with the movement, following the water's advancing and receding.

I don't know how far I travelled, but after I was satisfied with one run, I turned on the beach and plowed through the waves towards the place I had started, retracing my tracks. I stopped dancing and let the child in me bulldoze my way through, splashing water back onto the ocean, a little boy playing with a big toy at the beach. I did a few more runs, back and forth, before coming to my senses. A wave of guilt washed over me and I glanced towards the beachside wondering if people were yelling at me to knock it off. I breathed a sigh of relief upon observing a quiet setting, as far as I could tell.

That was a lot of fun, but I calmed down, and found a quiet place near the water, away from people. I didn't want anyone to be encouraged and approach me, just in case. The clock read: 10:30 am. I parallel parked, turned the front wheels toward the ocean, grabbed my camcorder, and stepped outside. It's time to videotape on the beach and listen to the ocean. It has much to say, after all.

I started recording, sweeping across the beach and over crashing waves. I did just as I intended. I remained silent. I'm in awe. The morning fog is just breaking away. The waves are intense and incredibly volatile. Progressive layers of roaring elements are crashing over one another, gradually collecting sand, retrieving the grains to take them where they belong.

Washington beaches are nothing compared to this. That's my feeble opinion determined from my severely limited experience. I should thoroughly explore Washington shores and compare beaches one of these days. Of course, comparing natural features really is kind of lame. It's like comparing toes on the same foot. It's just a matter of the preference between the big toe and the pinkie. Every part of nature is beautiful when appreciated for what it is.

I continued recording as I judged what lay before me, despite my preceding thought. My weak mind had a first impression and I said it out loud, "This is a violent act of nature." And then, I immediately countered myself. "Violence has nothing to do with this. The alluring dynamics of the waves crashing upon the shore, the tremendous volume of the waves crashing upon themselves; it's truly captivating. Not as if the waves have any intention or will to crash upon the shore nor the sand being frightened by the ocean bully. No concerns, no thoughts, no heart to screw things up, no mind to clutter the action with intent, just energy colliding." I finally shut my trap.

But, not for long, "I could stay here the entire day."

I averted my eyes from the screen, continued recording silently, and absorbed this experience. I perceived this expansive scene, using as much of my periphery vision to capture a live panoramic view. An immense choir undulated before me, tempting me to join in their deafening roar. I deeply inhaled the dense ocean air as crashing water spewed upward and became airborne. I felt the constant vibrations emanating from the earth, a trembling that I could not resist. I tasted these moments and enjoyed a sensual experience that only poetry can portray.

I could stay here forever. But, because I can't, I must seize forever; if only to savor for a few minutes and then, let it all go. I could use my camera, but a photo represents one moment. One reproduced, visual moment is not enough. Though, a photo can evoke similar emotions, it's not the same. How can one moment fully express this which transform with time? I'm anticipating that watching my video footage will have a diminished effect, as well. Even though I'll replay this experience, I can't immerse myself by viewing timeframes on a screen.

The answer is simple, of course. This experience cannot be reproduced. That's what makes this time invaluable. That is, unless all my senses can simultaneously relive this, the recollection will always be flawed. I'll go further by understanding that each moment is unique. Only time travel would make it plausible to re-enact unique moments and the entire point would be moot because a lack of awareness would negate the purpose for reliving the experience. Isn't this entirely about awareness?

Memories represent the closest means for duplicating this amazing experience. Which leads to a more important question. Why be fixated on reliving experiences, anyway? When something is invaluable, emotions swell. A profound appreciation for the present inspires a need to preserve associated emotions. Specifically, a reproduction of feeling is desired. Yet, memories transform over time. Photos and videos serve as tools to preserve memories and help to, at least, recapture feelings identified with these important situations. I imagine myself to be one who feels this way when my dreams are finally realized. I'll capture everything and save all that I can. But, again, why?

Is it a waste then to do what I'm doing right now, by recording with this camcorder on which I spent a thousand dollars to use? I don't know. I just have a feeling that I will relive this time. I have no idea when or for what reason, but I have a hunch these videos will be important for my future. The details will be important to me, as important as they are for me now.

Also, my interest in capturing visual moments is similar to my fascination for quotes. I'm interested in more than the typically recognizable saying. I create my own. I consider my personal quotes as footnotes, phrases that condense expansive ideas into a few words. Words fascinate me, especially when associated with music. I love the connotation of words, layers that bring depth to words. Words are not one-dimensional. In fact, understanding words annotatively is shallow. Sure, a picture is worth a thousand words, but don't devalue words. Just as a painting is comprised of a myriad of strokes, words are placed together to create moving imagery a painting cannot render. I can keep going on and on debating with myself, but it would be a waste of my time here.

My mind is wandering so freely, only because I'm free from distraction, not being cluttered or overwhelmed by needless stimuli. Free from distraction … but opening the flood gates to emotions I'm repressing deep within. I'd imagine if I were standing here in a state of happiness, I'd be capturing as much as I can for the sake of posterity, but I'm obviously not here to nurture happy feelings. Frankly, I want to scream at the top of my lungs. The beckoning roar has transformed into screaming and I want to scream back until the ocean recedes completely, deferring to my callous will.

Letting my guard down has invited waves of insecurity, doubt, frustration, and anger. Just last evening, standing on the side of the road as darkness fell, I was awestruck by those precious moments. That's the feeling I was hoping to build upon right now. Apparently, not. As violence was my first impression this morning, conflict is an indication of my true state of being.

I'm glaring out towards the ocean. I feel my brows intensely furrowed. My expansive vision has become a focused beam of rage. I'm still recording and now I'm making a concerted effort to pacify myself before I say something I might regret. Thankfully, I'm not impulsive like that, but I'm also not the person I can rely on. I'm afraid of what I might do in this state of mind.

I pushed the red button and stopped recording, dropping my arm to my side. My shoulders tightened. I continued glaring outward without purpose. Screaming would be of great benefit to me right now, but my pride is making me hesitate in fear someone might hear me and become concerned. I don't want to attract attention. I can't explain my circumstances.

Muscles flexed throughout my body in response to the glaring expression that is really turned inward, so I turned my attention to the fog retreating. I wish the fog could take this self-loathing away and cleanse me, but if life were that simple, lots of people would be standing with me now. I'd bet that most people would return for more cleansing. I'd also bet that a great number would repeat the process repeatedly. People love convenience and this potentially magical process would just be abused like so many conveniences already available in this world. So, of course, it can't be easy. Also, wiping a conscience clean would be disastrous for people. People would no longer be accountable for their own actions. That convenience would simply desensitize moral values.

"Forget it." I released my tension and dropped my shoulders, feeling defeated. The ocean has won and I'm glad it did. "That's right. Don't let a moron like me get my way, the spoiled brat that I am. I'll figure it out, but thanks for entertaining me." I dropped my vision to my feet, smiled a bit, and turned to leave this therapy session.

I started up my baby and smiled fondly towards the ocean. "I'll be back a little further down the coast and we'll continue where we left off." I slowly accelerated and turned back towards the path from which I came, retracing the tracks I made so as not to further degrade the quality of the beach, my attempt at paying respect for my time here.

I didn't feel like singing as I re-entered Highway 101. I let Bobby take the solos as I travelled southward. On the approach to Seaside, the traffic intensified and slowed to a crawl. I spent so much time moving a short distance that the CD ended and since I didn't want to sing, I chose music to quietly appreciate. I automatically thought of the smooth bossa nova sounds of Stan Getz and João Gilberto. Their Brazilian infused jazzy combo takes me away. I popped in the audio medicine to counteract the traffic pissing me off. Getz and Gilberto made the lost time tolerable.

When I finally made it to the heart of Seaside, I turned onto Broadway Street, driving towards the water. I passed the PIG 'N

PANCAKE on the south side of the street and drove around the loop introducing the beach, allowing me a quick glimpse of the sands completely inundated with people. This is the most unattractive scene I've witnessed on my journey, thus far. I detest this scene; "too many people" is an understatement to describe this. I'm not in the mood for crowds.

I didn't hesitate and immediately drove out of Seaside, hoping that Cannon Beach would be a better fit for my emotional state. I don't know much about either city, so I hope Cannon Beach is more appealing to me. Maybe, when I'm feeling more sociable, I'll develop a favorable opinion of Seaside, until that time, this is not a place I currently wish to be. "See ya, Seaside."

I observed the odometer and estimated that less than ten miles passed between Seaside and Cannon Beach. When I entered the City of Cannon Beach, I lit up. The streets are crowded here too. Waves of people are moving in and out of buildings and crossing streets, but I'm not appalled. Somehow, I'm feeling an affinity for this place. If I had to determine why that is the case, I'd say it's the planning and architecture of the business district here and above all, the character of this area in which I'm driving through. "Very interesting ..." I mumbled to myself.

"Let's think about this ... My first impression of both cities is distinct." Heading southbound and exiting Highway 101, I entered Seaside. It's a straight shot to the beach, nothing is left to the imagination. Cannon Beach, on the other hand, has an inviting quality through a meandering approach into the city. It's a statement that encourages people to stay for a while; no rush to leave. The approach already speaks volumes about the planning for both municipalities. Entering from the north, people cross endearing waterways to enjoy the primary commercial areas of both Seaside and Cannon Beach. The difference being the actual approach between the two is significantly contrasting; one is as straight as an arrow, the other appears to follow the lay of the land, giving a more natural feel upon the discovery of what lies ahead. "Yah, I think that sums it up."

I'm such a nut-ball when it comes to the environment. I'm always looking around and analyzing. It's not a matter of like or dislike, either.

Erwin Lazaro

I love appreciating. Even during my struggles, my mind never turns off or gets fixated on my feelings. It's a wonderful distraction for that reason. As angry as I get with myself, I can turn on a dime, and devote my attention to a butterfly or a building or ice cream. Maybe it's a failsafe mechanism within me. That's a good thing. I'm thankful for it. Though, the description defines me as a scatterbrain, I don't feel like that is the case, simply because the things that take my attention are positively driven, typically spontaneous, like this debate I'm having with myself about Seaside and Cannon Beach. I'd define this speculation as an objective analysis.

Anyway, I've used so much time analyzing and considering why I am the way I am, that here I am, having driven almost entirely through the business area of Cannon Beach without recording any of it. But, in this case, it's not a bad thing since I don't want to stop here, either. I'm getting happy feelings by driving through, but I'm not going to walk through this throng of people. I'll revisit both, Seaside and Cannon Beach, when I'm not so grumpy.

I smiled on my way out of Cannon Beach. I genuinely felt good about my visit and I'm looking forward to exploring more someday. Hopefully, I won't be alone next time. Though, if I do return on my own, I'm anticipating I had successfully found some semblance of peace. Otherwise, I wouldn't make the effort. I wouldn't repeat this type of journey. I just know that I wouldn't. I would come here to enjoy. In fact, I'm counting on it. One day.

I made my way back onto Highway 101 and backtracked a bit, heading northward. I lowered the windows and took in the comforting ocean air. The next diversion wasn't very far and I turned off the highway within a few minutes. I had seen a beach access sign while approaching Cannon Beach, but I was too impatient to stop earlier. I know that every time I see an opportunity to witness the ocean, I'm always going to be enticed. That's certainly going to make my entire trek along the Oregon coast an interesting one. The temptation is too great and I'm willing to go back with the intention of moving forward.

My second diversion for the day is Indian Beach. I just love this approach. Without taking my eyes away from enjoying the view, I reached over and started recording in one fell swoop. Keeping my camcorder on is convenient since I don't worry about batteries running low. I might seriously consider getting a microwave for my baby somewhere along the way. I could eat my way down the coast. Wait ... That sounds awful. Okay, bad idea.

"I love this approach. I'm driving through a densely, wooded area. I have no visual of the ocean, but I know I'm driving towards Indian Beach." I'm listening to the cool sounds of Stan Getz and João Gilberto. They're making me feel good. Add the sultry voice of Astrud and wow ... the famous voice of "The Girl from Ipanema". If I recall correctly, Astrud wasn't a professional singer when she recorded the single. Also, I can't remember if these are the tracks with Antônio Carlos Jobim. "Who picked this music? It's really good." Cool. Cool. "Whoever it is, has really good taste in music. That's all I have to say. Outstanding. Cool. Cool." I keep thinking and saying "cool." The irritation is rising. I need another ... cooler adjective.

The land fell away from the road and the path started curving between trees. This is transportation engineering navigating the terrain. This is what I mean by an interesting approach. My curiosity is piqued. "I better keep to the fifteen mile-per-hour speed limit."

I continued video-taping while driving towards the ocean. Not more than a minute later, as I rounded a curve without sight beyond the trees, a truck stayed tight to the turn and sped directly at me. "Dude!!!" I barely had time to react and instantly veered to my right while managing to avoid disaster. The truck passed inches from my baby. I couldn't even swear at the asshole. Man, or woman, a complete idiot, never slowed down and sped away.

My heart stopped. My sight was fixed on the valley below to my right. That was an instant when time stood still. I had swerved off the pavement and instinctively knew I had little room before my baby and I ended up in the ravine. My right hand was occupied by the camcorder. With a reflexive jerk of the wheel, my left hand moved right to avoid a collision and instantly moved left to also avoid falling into the adjacent ravine. "FUCKER!!!" I thought in my head. I couldn't say it out loud, but my heart was screaming it.

Once my voice returned, I gasped. "That was almost the side of my vehicle!" I maintained velocity and continued towards the beach while my heart rate normalized. If either of us had been moving any faster, I would have been toast. "What the heck, man?"

I fell silent to overcome the shock, but the forest gave way to reveal the ocean. I inhaled deeply and became overwhelmed by the revelation. The view is beautiful … beyond the parking lot filled with vehicles and people cluttering my way, that is. I raised my chin as if that would improve my perspective of the ocean.

I pushed back into my seat, repulsed by the social sight. I know I can't ask everyone to be gone. I have no right. Nor is it appropriate under any circumstances. I'm just being a spoiled brat. I don't think I want to step outside here, either.

Vehicles pulled out in front of me. I paused. Pedestrians crossed in front of me to get to their vehicles. I smiled and paused. Bicyclists passed me from behind and moved directly in front of me. I scratched my head as they slowed upon passing.

I patiently maintained my composure, keeping my sights on the reward ahead. I don't want to be around people, but I can't pass up this opportunity. So, I made my own stall in a full parking lot to take in this scenery. I don't want to mingle, but this amenity is here for me too. I'll just keep to myself and stand somewhere relatively quiet with my camcorder.

Once I found a decent place to stand, my senses were immediately drawn towards a view to behold. The rock formations in front of me are a sight I haven't witnessed until now. Simply fascinating. Add the fierce waves crashing into the rocks and it's a continuous battle between two natural states of matter. I'd imagine a child automatically believing the rocks winning this clash, but the persistent ocean is crumbling those rocks with each thrust in this war of attrition. This is truly an incredible sight. Those waves crashing into the rocks are spraying the world with tremendous force. "Wow …"

After a few more waves of rhythmic collisions, I turned my attention to the crazy people going in and out of the water. So many surfers on this beach. Crazy people. Gleeful screaming blending with the ocean roaring. I'm standing high above the action so the volume is modest. I don't know whether to smile or shiver for them. I think screaming in their direction so that these people regain their senses sounds about right, but they won't be able to hear me. I'm not even going to try.

Crazy sums it up well, I'd say. That water is probably in the mid-fifty-degree Fahrenheit range. The deadly rip currents known to exist off the Oregon coast, and witnessing the rough conditions first hand, is enough to make me grab onto this log fence for support. "They're crazy." I'm thoroughly mesmerized by this scene as I stand silent, taking it all in with my free hand holding the fence. I love this.

I'm sure these people standing on this observation platform have similar feelings. That's why those of us standing high above the beach remain where we are, infatuated with this experience. Those crazy people below are just crazy people. My philosophical nature supports their proactive approach, but those dangerous waters cannot be taken lightly.

My swimming skills consist of hanging onto one side of a swimming pool and splashing my way to the other side of the pool where I can grasp the pool gutter. I know that once I get to the other side, I'll be okay. I also love diving off the highboard and touching the pool floor twelve feet below the water's surface. I'm not afraid within a controlled environment, but here, anything goes. Those people down there better be strong swimmers. I understand that their surfboards act as floatation devices, but still. Don't mess with Mother Nature.

The camcorder's been recording since I found a comfortable place to stand. I pleasantly realized I hadn't said much, so I changed that. "This is captivating. I keep wanting to stay forever. Why is that? I want to observe things in nature or more accurately, things in their natural state. The rock formations are molded by the waves. The waves are influenced by the moon's gravitational pull. Volcanic and seismic activity formed these rocks and this land above the ocean's surface. The ocean is jealous. The ocean is possessive and trying to reclaim that which was lost, finding a way to encompass the land and cover it once again." I rolled my eyes thinking how I twist reality into an overdramatic, romantic metaphor.

Erwin Lazaro

"It's so chilly, just standing here. That water is so cold and people are out there. Presumably, they love being in these waters to endure the conditions." I've always grown up around water, but never learned how to swim. I'm going to be continually reminded by this fact travelling down the coast. "It amazes me that people freely go into the ocean without the fear that something unfortunate might happen. Though, it's more than likely that these people harbor a certain degree of fear and they have a certain confidence level that allows them to find a thrill here. It's also partly my misinterpretation as an observer. Maybe, they're like me, just as I purposefully stepped into that boat every time I went water skiing, trying to conquer my fear of the unknown. These people want to prove to themselves they can do it and be thrilled by the experience at the same time. Or simply, these people love the challenge and they truly have confidence in their skills."

I understand these contemplative viewpoints, but I can't empathize with any surfer since I can't swim, so my confidence level is very low. Even though I crashed into the Tulalip Bay countless times and continually swallowed salt water, I faced my fears head on, with full confidence in my friends and my life vest. I should probably add a little crazy and dumb in that equation too. Even from this distance, I look at the waves here and I feel true fear within me. I am willing to learn how to swim, but my life has just led me elsewhere. I can learn if I gain a desire to learn, but up to this point in my life, my time in the water is almost nonexistent, except for my daily shower. No swimming skills needed in the bathroom.

I looked more closely at the people on the beach. A good number are children. Those are the next generation of surfers. They'll grow up with experience in these waters and hopefully, always be safe when they venture out on their surfboards.

"I'm not a person who finds a place to sit and watches people as a hobby. I am a person who observes people when I'm amongst other people. I can further generalize and affirm that I am an observant person. I'm enthralled by life. I pay attention to where I am and time flowing around me, noticing a dandelion floating by, moving shadows, a person sneezing, and the toy poodle in a woman's handbag. I love to speak, but I enjoy listening even more, especially listening to the sounds of nature and children's voices." I bit my lip and looked up at the hazy, blue sky. Listen to me. I sound like an ad for a single person looking for love. Am I desperate or am I just being me? I don't know anymore.

The laughing children caught my attention. "I'm enjoying the children playing on the beach. It looks like they don't have a care in the world. It looks like they don't have thoughts for anything else but these wonderful times, simply having fun. I wish I could be like that again."

As a child on the beach without a care in the world or a man having peace observing these children? Which one am I seeking to be? I'm torn watching this scene. Am I wishing to be a child again? No, that's not it because I am a child. No matter how old I get I am always a child. It's important not to forget that fact. I feel like a child throwing tantrums because things are not going my way. Then, is it a man who has peace? No, that's not it either. I'd interpret that as being a man who has conceded. Peace doesn't necessarily mean answers have been revealed. Peace doesn't mean that dysfunction or strife has been resolved. All peace represents is a compromise between opposing forces. That's not what I'm after. If it's neither, then what am I seeking? Why am I here?

This is so frustrating. I'm so frustrated, again. I was enjoying myself. Now, I'm just plain irritated. I'm also noticing the growing number of people where I am. It's getting uncomfortable. I quickly scanned the area with my eyes while I kept the camcorder focused on the beach. I noticed the people behind me are looking at me. This guy standing close to my side is looking at me talk to my camcorder. He's probably thinking I'm "one of those artsy-fartsy weirdo guys".

I was cradled by serenity and feeling incredibly content within a personal bubble that has shrunk since these people have moved within my vicinity. Seagulls passed overhead. "I do love the picturesque scene of seagulls flying near the ocean." I should dissipate these negative feelings. I'll observe the children playing on the beach to sooth my ill will. Where are they?

Observing young children is the most wonderful part of people watching for me. A young child is as close to their natural state of mind as they will ever be. Minds get cluttered with age. Adults complicate

Erwin Lazaro

everything. Adults need to learn from children. I don't mind mischief because it's honest and their fun makes me laugh. I don't mind a child lying because I can read their expression and understand the truth of the matter. I can work with apples if I know they are apples. Somehow, when people grow up, honesty becomes one of the most complicated feelings to convey, especially to oneself. Adults are idiots for the most part, especially when adults forget they are children. The irony is that that denial is the most childish act of all. "I am not a child." Seriously? "Yes, you are a child and the sooner you understand what that means you'll finally be honest with yourself." Idiot.

I'm trying to clean out the garbage from inside. Even though I'm angry and frustrated, I acknowledge that my efforts are productive. I'm being honest with myself and seek to unravel my obscure personal truth. I'm trying to comprehend. I'm desperate for it and the anxiety I'm experiencing is driving me crazy. I am facing myself head on and I won't back down. My actions are helping me. It's true.

"Listen to them. Listen to all of it; the wind, the ocean, the birds, the people, all of it. At Del Rey, I was so close. I'm further here, but these sounds … so rich. The sound is so rich, rich and full of energy."

I was almost lost in thought and then I felt self-conscious. I finally realized the guy next to me had turned and faced me. I immediately stopped recording and turned to face the stranger.

He offered a wide smile, an older man, "I didn't want to disturb you so I waited until you were finished."

Idle conversation. I thought, "Too late." I felt my right eye twitching as my irritation level grew.

I had almost completely drowned out the words being uttered by this man until he said, "Looks like you're searching for something. No, you look like someone who's in need of a conversation. A specific kind." He nodded towards my camcorder. "I'm going to come right out and say that I noticed you immediately. I could be completely wrong, but I'm a bit of a gambler. You see, someone approached me just like I'm approaching you." The man scratched his head. "That was years ago, but those few minutes sure made a big difference in my life."

I pursed my lips together to prevent saying something I'm going to regret.

After a short pause, he continued. "I was enraged at the time. I had my hands on this fence. Holding real tight just like this. I felt like I could crush this wood with my bare hands. It was terrible." He demonstrated. "I guess my face or my whole body showed that I was visibly upset." He laughed while remembering. "A complete stranger came up to me and looked at my hands. He wanted to know what the fence had done to deserve that kind of treatment from me. I must have given him quite an awful glare because he backed up and started a conversation in the same way I'm beginning this conversation with you, young man." He winked at me.

I sighed inside with my lips pursed tightly.

"Looks like I'm here for a reason today. You're not trying to crush the wood, but from the look in your eye, the intentions are similar." He turned to face the ocean. "I come here every once in a while. Like many, I'm drawn to the ocean. Like you. Just hear me out for a few minutes and I'll be on my way."

He gave me a sidelong glance before continuing, just to make sure I am paying attention. "This might actually be for me as much as it is intended for you. I might have been waiting for a moment like this."

My irritation started rising again. I want to tell him to get on with it. The word "rambling" came to mind.

He gave me another sidelong glance. "I sense your irritation. I'm glad you have the good manners to …"

I turned to face the ocean.

He continued speaking. "I was at a crossroads in my life. Well, to make a long story short, I was making a big deal out of nothing. I beat myself up over the smallest stuff. I took my anger out on the people around me. I kept on asking myself 'Why?' I eventually discovered that I was asking myself the wrong question. Instead of 'Why?', I needed to ask 'How?'. I also learned to ask myself 'What?', 'Where?', and 'When?'. 'Why?' is the easiest one to ask, but it's also the most difficult to answer. The answer to 'Why?' always lies in the past and the only person who can answer 'Why?' is *you*. No one can help you with 'Why?', but you can get a lot of help to answer the other questions. You'll always be alone with 'Why?' My point is reconsider your position, step back, and ask yourself those other questions instead of beating yourself up."

I decided to face this presumptuous man and ask him a rhetorical question, "Why are you even bothering to share this with a complete stranger like me?" He already premised his oratory by answering why he approached me and I just told him I'm not listening. I felt bad, but my emotional response prevented me from understanding anything further.

"It appears you're not ready. That's okay. I should have guessed that you'd react the same way I did. It comes full circle, I understand." He paused, hoping I might come around, but I refused. "Well, I'll be on my way. I'm sorry for troubling you. You take care now." He turned and walked out of my life.

My anger shattered, the cloak of irritation disintegrated. Underneath my breath, I replied, "You don't know anything about me. What do you know?" I was speaking to the ocean and it's relentless pressing upon the shore.

The ocean earnestly replied. I heard it loud and clear. "Answers lead to more questions; therein lies the answers, the questions." My heart stopped beating and I am alone. No one is here to rescue me and I just turned away a man who tried. What do I do from here?

XI

Lily

I DON'T KNOW how long I stood in the same position, but time stood still once again. No sound, no motion, no feelings, but I am aware. This must be a state of shock. Something similar just happened when I was almost struck by that oncoming idiot and able to react accordingly. It's as if I'm outside of myself, observant, questioning whether this is really me or whether I'm having an out-of-body experience. If I am having an out-of-body experience, it's breathtaking. Observation of one's self is forced; the reunion of soul and body reveals the truth, good and bad.

The ocean answered my muted scream. No, it was a revelation in the form of words. Those words came to me: "Answers lead to more questions; therein lies the answers, the questions."

Was I listening to that stranger because I did ask myself a question and it was in the form advised to me: "What do I do from here?"

That phrase revealed, and that question, they were both automatic responses. That man said something about seeking the answer to the wrong question. I'm going to delve deeper into that later. It's unusual, but I'm not angry. Either, I was reset by the impact of the encounter with that stranger or I am aware of progress as a result of that encounter. Either way, I'm not angry. I'm nervously excited with hope. Hope is leading me to act based on my desire to seek. I've been wandering aimlessly, living without purpose. I'm extremely hungry to act with purpose. I recognize that.

Sound resumed in the form of the waves crashing upon the rocks below and children laughing. My vision cleared and I looked upon the frothy movement and the people undulating with the frigid ocean water. I had my hands upon the fence for support. And, someone's obnoxious perfume filled my nostrils. That is probably what brought me back to reality, the smelling salts that struck me as a counteracting disturbance to arouse my consciousness. I tasted an alluring hope for the first time in a long time and I am eager for more.

Turning around, I discovered a slew of activity. I looked for that man who came to my aid, but couldn't find him amongst these people. I smiled and navigated between running children, baby strollers, and leashed dogs. I wasn't irritated by any means. "This is quite interesting" is the thought that came to me upon re-entering my baby. I paused and scanned the area once again. No sign of that man. "Where ever you are mister, I'm sorry and thank you."

I relaxed a bit and that's when my belly told me it's time to refuel. I thought I could last throughout the day, but audible grumbling from my core is openly communicating a need for nourishment. I guess that having an out-of-body experience consumes a lot of energy and it was well worth it. I instantly decided upon revisiting Cannon Beach. I didn't anticipate going again during this trip, but I am infatuated with my first drive through and now I have an important purpose. It's time to feed the belly. Of course, it's a bonus that Cannon Beach is only a few minutes from Indian Beach. More reason to return now. I'm looking forward to a good meal.

When I returned to the heart of Cannon Beach, I picked up the camcorder and described my experience in a more jovial manner. If I had recorded earlier, reviewing the tape would have been a downer. I'm always amazed by influences that help me choose wisely. I'm even more grateful in paying attention and recognizing the signs to make those choices, though I'm certain I've missed exponentially more than I've noticed. Noticing is always a work in progress.

During this drive through, I intently searched for places to have lunch. "Okay, I'm in Cannon Beach and my mission is food. I'm *super* hungry and stuck in traffic. I'm looking for a place to eat." My stomach started growling when a waft of deliciousness filled my baby with alluring flavors I could readily taste. "Oh, I smell something right now that is *incredible*!" I didn't realize how hungry I really am until I drove through that particulate wave. A quaint sign for "Lazy Susan Café" came to view and became the first choice on my list. "Maybe, I'll have lunch with Lazy Susan."

A hopeful spirit allowed some humor to surface and the atmosphere in Cannon Beach encouraged me to enjoy being here. "I like Cannon Beach. Darling ..." I channeled my inner Billy Crystal. "Uh, that's a bad ... That's a bad Billy Crystal impression, but hey, I try. Cool. Okay." I drove all the way through before deciding where to feed the belly. As I passed the PIG 'N PANCAKE in Cannon Beach, it became an easy decision to dine at the Lazy Susan Café. "It's time to ... I'm going to find a spot. Talk to you guys later."

Parking towards the south end of the business district, I looked forward to a good meal with Lazy Susan and wondered if I would find a café filled with tables that had revolving trays. "Ten-minute parking, okay?" I smiled, hid the camcorder, and secured my other valuables. On a whim, I had grabbed the camera and began walking northward. I may stumble upon an inspiration to remember. Along South Hemlock Street, my senses absorbed the environment until arriving at the café. Good feelings emotionally charged me while entering the building. Lazy Susan has an appealing sense of comfort, openly welcoming guests. The café is lively and the turnover appears to be high.

The hostess greeted me with a big smile and promptly escorted me to a table. I'm quickly appreciating this single-diner option, especially when I'm starving as I am right now. A starving belly overcomes the awkwardness. Hunger is a good mechanism for quelling uncomfortable situations. The non-essential emotions go out the window. Feed the belly.

I peered at each table. No revolving trays.

I was seated with my back to a wall. It's a great perspective of the café. I'm able to look at the entire space without obstruction. More importantly, I'm able to take notice of the artwork being displayed here and window shop while dining. That's how these tourist areas are designed, of course. It's a great way to advertise and hopefully appeal to a captured audience. At least, for the patrons who pay attention.

Erwin Lazaro

Every table is seating a party of two or more. People are engaging one another so it's easy to overlook the background. Overall, that's good. I'd probably do the same, but I'm going to make a true effort to always pay attention to my environment, whether I'm making sure all is well or because I'm appreciating details. I'm currently dining alone so my options are limited. What else can I do? I can only study the menu for so long before I decide. After that, I choose to entertain myself. Otherwise, I'd revert to that awkward position of wondering what to do. I don't want that to happen.

Sitting in silence, an energetic community sped around me. My head and body barely moved, but my eyes followed the action. I sat alone and ordered a hot seafood salad with a cup of hot water. Amongst the hustle and the melding ambient noise, I decided to turn around and look behind my seat. I was stunned because I hadn't noticed the artwork on the wall upon sitting down.

The one place I needed to give the most attention was right behind me. This is another sign for my presence here. I am an arrogant person by nature so I believe I'm not here by accident. I should probably think of a more amiable adjective, but it's true. I have an ardent opinion of believing in myself. To truly believe in my efforts, I must be obstinate, but I also purposefully temper my arrogance with an equally obstinate position of humility. It's a tedious dichotomy that constantly tests my sensibility, but I must do so to continually improve. Even in this sad state I'm currently in, I fight with everything I have. I haven't given up and I'm proving that to myself by acting on my beliefs. The harbingers I identify are also reinforcing my faith. They work together. I'm encouraged to keep doing what I'm doing.

The cup of hot water was placed down behind me. I responded without turning. "Thank you!"

I read the caption under the unframed painting displayed behind my seat. It's a rendition of Haystack Rock. It says that Haystack Rock is the third largest of its kind in the world. I think that's hard to believe, but what do I know? It's located nearby so I should visit if I can, but I don't think I have time. Anyway, that's not what captured my attention.

A poem accompanies the scene. It's titled "Walk the Beach" and it's written by a Cannon Beach resident.

The ocean perpetually inspires people. Art and poetry are obvious expressions to share that inspiration. I read the poem several times through because the sentiment moved me. I could have another one of those out-of-body experiences. In fact, I paused, but nothing happened. I smiled knowing that it won't happen because I want it to happen. Three's a charm, but it's more like three's a crowd.

I turned back to face a heavenly salad being placed before me and angels sang until the plate came to rest on the placemat. I looked down and realized it was my stomach singing joyfully in anticipation. I thanked the server, quietly gave thanks for this meal, and immersed myself. My face lowered and became firmly affixed to the plate with my table manners on the floor. I'm certain I displayed unsightly behavior from another patron's perspective, but I didn't care. I'm not devouring the food. I just don't want my mouth very far from the plate. Everything fell silent as I lost track of time and awareness, savoring every bite. I'm not sure if I made noises and I didn't look for reactions. It was me and the salad. Nothing else mattered.

After that delightful meal, I sat upright in my chair, completely satisfied. Thank goodness it was a salad, because if I had ordered a porterhouse and a beer down the street, I would have been full of regrets. I complimented the servers for their hard work and praised the salad being soundly digested with the help of the hot water.

Turning around once more, I reread the poem. A Cannon Beach resident wrote it. Peter D is written next to "Walk the Beach". I'm sure to find many reproductions within the souvenir shops here. I'd love to take a copy with me so I can recite it for the camcorder while standing in front of the ocean. I could even be so cheesy as to recite it while videotaping the scene at Haystack Rock. I am a romantic spirit so I'll determine whether the effort is worth the time when an opportunity presents itself.

Lazy Susan deserved a good tip and I gratefully placed my contribution on the table. I gave a hearty farewell on the way out while rubbing my tamed belly. Stepping into this glorious sunshine negates bad moods, but I'm teetering on the edge. My resistance is so low that I can retreat from the slightest tremor of discouragement. I wish I wasn't so weak, but I'm smiling now and I'm grateful for it. A satisfied belly should keep me in good spirits for a while. I can only hope.

I stood in front of the café window with the intention of seeking two things. The first is "Walk the Beach". The second is ice cream, magnificent ice cream. I've wavered from my typical craving lately, but the sunshine is helping me channel good vibrations. My meals are not complete without a healthy serving of ice cream. I'm thinking two generous scoops on a waffle cone. I know ice cream is nearby. Follow my confectionery radar and I will discover my treasure.

The sun's rays feel incredible. Can I bottle this feeling and take a dose when needed? I shrugged as I realized I sought the easy way out again. Too much convenience never works with people. Complacency always takes over and the value plummets. So many cruel jokes placed upon mankind. I've witnessed time and again how stupidity is ingrained within human nature. As much as I fight to strengthen my resolve, the instant I let up, temptation creeps in. The temptation to make poor choices or complacent choices is the default.

I stopped in my tracks and looked up at the sky. Is that the crux of my dilemma? Am I simply complacent because I lack purpose? Yes, I lack purpose and that is a spirit killer, but no, it's more than that. Maybe, that's why I'm seeking solitude. Without any disturbances, I'll be able to focus on the root of my suffering. That's a good clue, I think.

My eyes fell upon the sea of people swerving around me and my statuesque pose on the sidewalk. This is not a good place for me to stand was my first conclusion. The second that came to mind was that I'm not going to be able to dig further within this flow of activity.

I shook my head at the sky as if to say it's the sky's fault for making me feel happy right now and then I refocused on my two objectives. I turned into the first souvenir shop and easily found the poem in multiple forms. For convenience sake, I picked up poem bookmarks and decided to buy a few so I could potentially gift some later.

As I approached the register, several figurines were on display to entice customers, but my heart nearly shattered when I noticed a little ceramic frog looking at me. The frog. Lily … I stumbled and regained my composure before anyone noticed. I hope nobody noticed. I thought I was over that, but every time I think I won't fall apart, I do. This is so embarrassing. This is not the time nor the place to fall apart. I exhaled deeply and paid for the bookmarks, pretending as if nothing out of the ordinary happened.

Rapid reset in front of a stranger; I'm fine. I am fine …

One down … I perked up. Ice cream is next. The fastest way to get back on the road again is to ask the attendant for directions to the nearest ice cream shop. With the exchange of money for the receipt, a finger pointed across the street. I smiled widely and bowed generously in appreciation for the help.

Blazing out of the shop and jay-walking across the street, I made a beeline for ice cream. The shop door was propped open to reveal a long line overflowing outside. I smiled outwardly while gritting my teeth on the inside. Well, waiting in a long line is a good way of depleting positive energy, but ice cream is the goal here and the anticipation is keeping me in check.

I dared not look at my watch and inched forward ever so slowly. Easily deciding on two flavors, my face squeaked across the display case. I have this thing about not caring how people perceive my actions, but I do notice how others react. I'd like to think it was my doing that to one side of me, a child was doing the same thing. On the other side, two adults were kissing the glass. I cringed because I wouldn't go that far. I'll wash my face later, but I draw the line at inviting unknown germs directly into my body.

Usually a well-mannered person, I put on a good show, but when ice cream is involved, I purposefully restrain myself. The time had finally come and with my tongue wagging, I snatched the ice cream cone from the server's hand and basically threw money at the person. I whisked through the crowd and out the door. Dawdling was no longer an option as the day moved swiftly with barely any physical progress on my journey, but I won't discount my time in Cannon Beach because of the salad, the poem, and some insight from my "bicameral mind" for speculation at a more appropriate time and location. Who was it that coined that phrase? I think it was Julian Jaynes from his 1976 book *The Origin of Consciousness in the Breakdown of the Bicameral Mind.* Good year, by the way ... I sometimes refer to Tina as my "bicentennial baby sis."

I licked my way back to my baby, strapped myself in, and gave a fond farewell to a positively energetic, little city. As I merged onto highway 101, I reached for the camcorder with my free hand and drove with the ice cream cone in the other.

"I'm back on the road again. I spent an incredible afternoon in Cannon Beach. I'm in love with that place. I met more nice people. Oregonians are friendly people. I don't know why I'm surprised by that. I'm just gabbing away. Anyway, I ate at that café I mentioned earlier. I ordered a hot seafood salad with scallops, bay shrimp ... and bacon! ... from the aquatic swine." I cracked up. "All of that was served hot over romaine lettuce. A chardonnay vinaigrette brought the flavors together and I said 'yes' to parmesan cheese grated over my plate. Delicious meal."

"I have a surprise in my hand. Whoa! Whoa! Whoa!" I WAS driving with my hand. Well, it was more the side of my left hand, grasping as much of the wheel as I could with my pinkie, because I am clutching something very precious with the rest of my fingers and thumb. "I'm driving with my knee right now, but I gotta get this on the video! My favorite food in the whole wide world: Ice cream!!" I gleefully wiggled the ice cream-filled waffle cone in front of the lens. "I'd say; the highlight of every trip. Ice cream! Yes, Ice cream!" It's melting so fast. I had to lick up the sides as I continued to knee-drive while recording.

"Okay. Anyway ..." I took a lick. "Great ice cream place, but going back to the Lazy Susan Café" I took another lick. "It's a beautiful space. I took a picture inside and the people were truly nice. I really loved the local art being displayed within the café, all for sale, by the way." Lick. "I was told where I could find more of the artists' work nearby." Lick.

"I did buy something that I was compelled to take with me. Right behind the chair where I was seated, on the wall, the perfect poem was placed just for me, specifically for my soul searching. It's about these incredible beaches. A local resident wrote the poem. After lunch, I went to a store where I could find more printed versions of the poem and bought some bookmarks." I'm glad I did because it means a lot to me.

"When I return, I'll take a longer stroll through the shops. The shops were incredible. I'll spend more time browsing the local wares, which is what I enjoyed tremendously. I didn't have leisure time to ponder through because I was parked illegally. I had parked in a ten-minute zone for about … two-and-a-half hours. It's okay. I'm a Washingtonian. If I had gotten a ticket, I wouldn't have to pay it, right!?"

I got distracted by the view of the ocean and took notice of a road that seemed to disappear downward, over a steep incline. "Wow! There's a road *down*! *Really* down! That's what four-wheel-drive vehicles are for." I contemplated the possibility for a split second, but I passed it so fast that I let go of the notion instantly.

"Okay. Anyway, I'll bring out that poem later. I discovered this incredible poem that happens to fit my situation and my mental … hmm, upheavals … questions. It's funny too because It may seem as if this product placement is a coincidence, but really, I found it for good reason, leading to a higher consciousness or understanding of what lies ahead. I'll read it later."

I was going to leave it at that, until I could find a place to read the poem, but I continued. "The poet describes the feelings I held at Del Rey, about what the ocean means, and the sensation of being overwhelmed by the incredible beauty of the experience … and … and … What? And, yah." My thoughts derailed.

"Okay, I'm at a loss for words. My stomach is full. What's on my mind right now is that I make it to Tillamook, which is about thirty-six miles away, without having to take a *shit*. Okay?" My exasperation started growing with my concern for soiling myself. "I haven't done *that* and I know this is gonna be on tape now … but I gotta do *that* soon, since I ate a humungous, fibrous lunch and I just finished two huge scoops of ice cream." I managed to keep up with the melting treat, speaking between licks, bites, chewing, maintaining the speed limit, video-taping, and driving "safely". I'm the multi-tasking champion! I just praised myself. I did.

"German Chocolate Cake and Butterfinger in a waffle cone … I'm sure my overstuffed belly is going to take a toll on me. I showed you earlier." I raised a brow as I realized something. "I don't know who I'm speaking to, but I'm referring to *you*. Yooz. All yooz all. So … I gotta not think about taking a *shit*. I laugh when I say that."

The red light turned off with a quick thumb press and the camcorder was almost thrown onto the passenger seat. Even though the air conditioning is blasting, the temperature rose in the vehicle. My face began to flush. Speaking became too difficult because of my predicament. The reaction to stop the recording was prompted by escalating discomfort. "I don't think I can make it to Tillamook." My left knee quivered and the air in my lungs ejected through pursed lips. "I'm not going to make it to Tillamook."

Thank goodness, the highway is lined with convenience stores and gas stations because the next one is my target. Within a few minutes, I slowed and turned off the road. The situation became dire as the goal was positively identified. "Oh man, oh man, oh man." My bowels reacted to visual confirmation.

I made a parking spot next to the men's restroom and moved as swiftly as possible. Geisha-like steps ensured that nothing escaped as I rushed in. My careful, yet harried pace transformed into a knee-high march upon determining the coast to be clear. Unfortunately, I slammed the stall door behind me. I cringed and hoped no one was alarmed enough to check out the ruckus while I frantically lined the toilet seat with shreds of toilet paper that refused to cut cleanly from the dispenser. I turned on The Flash mode with my lower half and sat down in a blur of super speed. A wave of relief … a niiiiiiice waaaaaaave offffffff … relief … washed over me. Not much compares to the satisfaction gained from the … release. It's almost as good as the meal itself, almost, but not quite. Normalcy returned upon exiting with emptied bowels and clean hands. I felt like a new man.

"That was a close call." I can't fight my nature. I eat. I poop. It's as simple as that. It would be great if my body slowly digested food, but it just doesn't work that way. The machine runs efficiently. It's my nature to empty the tank when it's full. I am thankful though; very reliable, if anything.

A deep, cleansing breath was required and a renewed purpose is in front of me, but before driving away, I took the opportunity to fill up my baby. She needs care too.

After we both reset, I looked at a map for nearby beaches. I'm going to Tillamook, but I want to visit a beach beforehand, so I can recite that poem. Manzanita Beach is clearly marked on the map. That's good and bad. I'll check it out and find a quiet place for the poem. If I happen to stumble on a different beach access any sooner, I'll probably opt for that. Living by the seat of my pants gives me a refreshing sense of freedom and it seems to be suiting me, for now. That's difficult to admit for a planner at heart.

As it turned out, Manzanita Beach was close. I was nearly at the beach access when I made the emergency diversion to the restroom. A couple of minutes on highway 101 and I slowed to enter the Manzanita Beach parking lot. To my surprise, the area was relatively quiet. The pleasant discovery of a natural scene propelled me to move quickly, find a secluded spot, and read the poem.

It's taking a lot of effort to avoid being hypnotized by the ocean. My impulse is to record mindlessly. Absorbing nature's energy is free therapy and though, I haven't found resolution yet, I know I'm following footsteps, or bread crumbs, that are leading me someplace meaningful. It's just so difficult not knowing or understanding what I should do.

Wait a minute … What if I'm sorting through my feelings in the wrong way? Just like that man told me, am I going about this incorrectly? Am I off base for seeking answers to why I'm about to explode? Am I off base for trying to identify the causes of my frustration? "What?" is making me question "Why?" Somehow, that feels … right. Now is not the time to be fixated. I should force myself to think differently.

Okay. How about I forget about "Why?" … It's strange, but now I'm feeling … scared … and worried. I closed my eyes and focused on my fear and then I focused on breathing. The image of the frog, the image of Lily, came to mind. I … I don't think this is a good … a good place for this. Okay. How about I calm myself and read the poem? That's a good idea.

Lily … a private place is necessary to "open up" about Lily. Maybe,

I'll be foolish enough to record myself later, so I never forget. I pulled a bookmark out of my pocket and read "Walk the Beach" aloud. The camcorder was focused on the ocean as I conveyed more about my experience in Cannon Beach and concluded by reciting the poem. I made a wise choice discovering the Oregon coastline on my own terms. Mother Nature offers free therapy and I'm certainly taking advantage.

Staying longer at Manzanita Beach was not wise as the sky raced past the sun. Always aware that time knows no mercy I took another look at the map and planned for the evening. I confidently decided on Newport roughly one hundred miles from my current location. It's crazy for me to randomly choose these cities, purely relying on hope for a sanctum from the darkness, but that's what I'm doing. The uncertainty is unsettling and is exactly what I need. Unpredictability is serving as a distraction from the burdens I normally carry and counteracting the complacency ailing me. Everything I'm doing right now feels … worthwhile. Good signs, I believe.

Zooming away from Manzanita, the CD binder remained closed and singing acapella fueled the drive towards Tillamook. My favorite album over the last two years is *Return to Pooh Corner* by Kenny Loggins. Nostalgia and comfort are two blankets that envelope me when I play the music from *Return to Pooh Corner*. It's an album of children's songs that entrances my heart. Kenny Loggins' music from this album especially suppresses my insecurities and helps me overcome the fears I've been facing alone.

Separating from my ex-fiancée opened a large void in my life. The album was released in 1994, but after our separation during the spring of 1996, I relied on music to help quell the sorrow. Even though our union was not meant to be, the pain from letting go of valuable time remained and I had to find a way to overcome it. Music always rescues me and I found solace through *Return to Pooh Corner*.

I love every track with great passion, but four are etched within my heart: "Rainbow Connection", "All The Pretty Little Ponies", "The Last Unicorn", and "Return to Pooh Corner". Nostalgia and comfort blanket me, but if I looked into my own eyes, I'd see melancholy within their depths. I hope to change that one day, but as I am, too much reside too deeply.

I brought the CD, but I didn't pull it out. This time around, by singing acapella, I'm able to release emotions through my voice. Listening to my own voice helps me be accountable for my actions and reaffirms my feelings.

I'm not sure what type of person I'd be without music; an angry person, I believe. I don't want to consider it and shivered as my thoughts spiraled downward. Usually, music is enough to rebalance my emotions, but I had to seek an additional therapeutic method. I'm so grateful for this opportunity. Music and this road trip must be the way for finding what I've lost or maybe, yet to discover. It has to be.

I looked at the sky to adjust my sensitivity. I am a mess, aren't I? So much introspection and no clue as to what I'm doing, except driving. I'm driving to a hallowed place for ice cream where the best cows bestow the best dairy for the finest ice cream in the land. It's a good distraction to tell myself fanciful tales. Maybe, that's important too.

"What exquisite flavors shall I find in the land of Tillamook? How many confectioneries shall I visit to satiate my desire and indulge in the ages old craft of ice cream making?" I spoke in my best attempt at a regal British accent. Smiling released the building tension and more ice cream lays ahead, two satisfying reasons to subdue the self-loathing. I think I'll try something fruity this time. "Mighty scoops: three and four await me! Possibly, scoops three, four, and FIVE?" Spoiling dinner is no problem. I'm on vacation.

With my chin up, I sang the songs of Loggins and performed with my heart. Upon purchasing the CD a few months after release, I easily learned the music with great passion. And, as with all new music that attracts me, I memorized and trained with my mind so that on days like these, I can give it my all. Even though I am an audience of one, I give the best I can offer. "Train with your mind, perform with your heart." is what I say.

One-hundred-ninety horsepower led me into the land of Tillamook to reveal but one mighty castle securing the treasures I sought, and feast I did. Three massive orbs of fruitful delight adorned a golden waffle horn. Together we found a cloistered refuge where the proper attention was given towards my adoration for this blessing. For these precious moments, I'd dedicate any measure of time. Thus, my full attention and devoted passion enjoyed every portion until the very last, when nothing remained, except for the yearning of the next opportunity for such a treat. Riding away on my valiant steed, my belly roared its satisfaction, savoring the memories, new treasures for my heart.

With the horizon approaching the sun on this second day of introspection, I used the remaining daylight to burn calories gained from a total of five decadent scoops of ice cream with dinner yet to come. Towards Newport, I ventured into more parks and changed into hiking shoes to explore trails. Breathing the ocean air and walking through forests is incredibly refreshing. After numerous hours seated in my baby, I don't feel as much fatigue because of ample opportunities to physically experience nature. And, as the horizon overtook the sun, serenity approached as the last people under this peerless sky disappeared. The intensity of stillness penetrated my position and heightened my senses. I felt the environment. I stationed myself on a moss-covered log and sat passively. Serenity teased me and I became too scared to close my eyes, gazing in every direction, trying to identify every sound. Within this forest, the sun's light was entirely replaced with overlapping shadows. Remaining still became difficult, trying not to let fear get the better of me. Yet again, I succumbed to my lack of faith and scurried out of the last state park for the day as dusk settled in.

Pressing to hurry, I managed to keep pace with the posted speed limit. "Whoa! I can't read *that* sign. What is *that* posted? Umm ..." the numbers were at least three feet in height. I was amazed by the enormous size. A second later, I passed three familiar cyclists. "Wow! I passed these three about twelve hours earlier. That's so strange because I've only been on the road for about ... eight!"

Newport surprised me. A lonely sign, affixed to posts set in the grass, made me realize I was already within the city limits. It was time to settle for the evening. Immediately scanning the area for accommodations was the easy part, but I found that stop after stop, bright lights posted 'no vacancies' at each location. Nervousness crept in as my choices dwindled. My heart sank with the last confirmed full motel that I could find in the area.

Driving along the Oregon coast in August is teaching me a severe lesson. Relying on hope alone is not working out very well. Retracing my path through Newport, I stopped at one of the full motels to seek help. Hope was not lost and I was directed towards a community of townhomes that are sometimes available for rent. It didn't sound promising, but I had little choice.

I crossed my fingers as I entered the rental office and with great relief, I gave thanks after exiting. I had the same feeling as I had earlier in the day when I exited the restroom. I almost kissed the key to the last townhome available because it became mine for the evening.

As I unloaded my baby, I counted at least six state parks that I had visited today. Fatigue started to set in as I entered the unit with my belongings. I placed the "Do Not Disturb" sign on the front door and began videotaping.

"This is what I had to pay for because there were no other vacancies. It's August. I'm in a townhome all by my lonesome. Look at this. I'll give myself a tour." The next few minutes were spent videotaping the two-story, full kitchen, one-and-a-half bath unit, with a deck at each level overlooking the ocean. I was impressed, especially for a reasonable price.

It wasn't until being in the kitchen that reminded me, I hadn't eaten dinner yet. It's 7:40 pm on a Sunday evening so I concluded the tour in a snap and rushed out the door. I really want to relax within the privacy of the townhome so I didn't meander through the city and sightsee. The waterfront at Newport seemed an attractive option and I perked up with clam strips and chips with a beer. Digestion encouraged my fatigue, but I had an important goal this evening. I'm going to sit in front of the camcorder so I can recap the day, plan for the rest of the trip, and most importantly, focus on Lily … I am the fool.

Time is without a doubt an illusion because, by the time I made it back to the townhome, it was already approaching 11 pm. The beer kept me relaxed and I set up the camcorder in front of a rattan loveseat for two. Purposefully preserving the darkness surrounding the recording area, I used the camcorder to illuminate my personal revelations. I pressed the red button and sat cross-legged with a pillow on my lap.

I started by recalling some experiences of the day, followed by singing more acapella of *Return to Pooh Corner* songs, this time with lyrics in hand so I could sing the rest of the songs I didn't know by heart.

The singing is an opening act so I can warm up to the serious stuff and while I sang, I thought of that man at Indian Beach who stepped forward this morning and challenged me. He emboldened me to challenge myself this evening. This is a gutsy move, but I must act on signs I believe are being presented for my benefit. My arrogant nature won't accept another explanation, just as my former pastor encouraged. I am asking. I am seeking. In response, I am receiving. I won't ignore the signs. From the One without limitations, I am receptive.

After finishing the last song from the album, I set the CD insert down and mentally prepared myself. Here I go …

"Okay. Wow … How do I begin this? Let's see. I've travelled for two days and my emotions are scattered. For the most part, I'm trying to be light-hearted about everything, but it's been a struggle. The smallest thing sets me off. That's not good."

Looking towards the camcorder and its blinding light within a dark room makes this feel like an interrogation, but I continued. "I have no idea where the lens is. The light is blinding. Go to the light! Go to the light! Anyway … I've kept most of my troubles within my head and speaking out loud will help me process my feelings differently and hopefully, more effectively. When I have the camcorder on there's almost a sense of avoidance because I'm afraid to confront what is bothering me. My mind can dismiss my feelings, but speaking out loud about my troubles makes me accountable for what I'm saying."

What am I doing? This is not an informative lecture. Stop avoiding the problems, idiot. "Oh boy, okay. Okay … avoidance. Yes, avoidance is a big part of my problems. I'm afraid. Yes, I'm afraid. The next feeling is guilt. Guilt is suffocating me or I'm drowning in guilt. That guilt comes from me not wanting to disappoint anyone. I'm trying to overcome feeling guilty for disappointing people for any reason. This trip is making me feel guilty and yet, here I am. I feel something important lies beyond what I know right now or maybe, it's the other way around? Have I had it backwards the entire time? I don't know."

"I'm not trying to discard my past, but as I already mentioned, I've been avoiding … avoiding things like … Lily. Oh man … do I really need to do this?" I stared into the surrounding darkness. "I didn't want to think about Lily when I was in that souvenir shop and now I'm going to talk about it? I think I've talked about the frog, three or four times. Each time I've talked about Lily, I've lost it. I just have a lot of wires when it comes to the emotional stuff. Those wires electrify and I can't handle the load."

More distraction: not good, dude. "Ugh. It's not that big of a deal. I'm sure anyone who listens to this is going to laugh at me. Recording this is a mistake, after all." I motioned towards the camera, but hesitated.

I settled back into the rattan. "I should explain who Lily is in the first place. Lily or Herbert… Whatever the frog's name is… aquatic frog or toad… I don't even know. For the sake of this video, I'll choose Lily and make her a frog." It'd be too confusing if I keep waffling. "Lily *was* a tiny aquatic frog that once belonged to my ex-fiancée's younger sister." I felt the heat rising around my face and my eyes started getting misty. "I'm not going to cry. I'm not going to lose it. I'm going to do this. I've barely started. Come on, man!"

"The younger sister had Lily since she attended the University of Oregon and on a visit to Seattle, she asked my ex to care for Lily because she wasn't able to properly care for the frog any longer. Of course, my ex agreed. That was during my ex-fiancée's stay at a UW dorm. Eventually, the two sisters moved in together and Lily moved with the sisters, from apartment to apartment. That was about a six-year period." I thought about that detail and deemed it to be correct.

"I spent a lot of time with both sisters and Lily was always there. Through the yelling, through the tantrums, through the times I had to sit quietly while my ex battled on our behalf. Did I feel cowardly? Yes. Did I feel strong? Yes. Is that a contradiction? No. I made a promise not to interfere with their familial disputes even though I was taunted, ridiculed, and disrespected as if I wasn't a person who existed in their presence. My will is strong and it took everything I had not to react, but

I remained stoic because of my dedication … almost all the time … not including the one time and one time only, when I put my fist through their apartment wall. It was scary. I was scared and glad that I didn't punch a stud instead of the drywall. I would have had a broken hand, I think."

"Through everything, Lily did what aquatic frogs do and snapped at the fish that swam too closely; must have lived through, at least, four sets of fish. That frog lived for about eight years. The bowl was the one place, whenever I entered their apartment, I always greeted. I always paid my respects to Lily. I'd go to the bowl, tap on it, get the frog's attention, swirl my finger into the water, and tease the frog for a bit. Lily swam up and always tried to get my fingertip. While I was at the bowl, I'd always ask my ex if the frog and fish had been fed. She'd reply with a 'no, could you feed them for me?' I'd always reply with, 'Okay.'"

I felt the tears welling and had to pause, "I'm not going to get emotional about this again. I'm passed it, really …" I thought about Lily's peaceful life in a peaceful home compared to the chaos the ensued regularly in the apartment beyond the glass bowl. The sisters didn't share a home when I was involved. They only shared a space to eat and sleep. That's my opinion, anyway. No one will change that. I kept my promise. I maintained my integrity, but I refuse to suffer any longer.

"Thank goodness, their mother wasn't always around. I lived with the sisters for about three years and when their mother visited, I was welcomed home to the love and peace of my parents and my sister. I didn't stay away though. Upon planned visits and outings with the three women, I had to intensify my defenses. I was as gracious as I could manage. As much as I tried to understand their volatile behavior, I could never accept that as being normal. Whenever the arguments erupted, typically within the apartment, I'd always go to the bowl because I knew Lily would be there and greet me in the same way, every time. Lily was always the same, always stable, always playful. Lily easily became my refuge within the chaos. So, throughout a six-year relationship, the frog was my rock to keep me from getting swept up by the negative energy that always threatened to collapse my defenses."

"Eventually, my ex and I separated amicably and we continued to go out with mutual friends. On a night that we had plans for dinner, I visited and immediately went to the bowl as I always had. I crouched to peer into the water for my traditional greeting, but I couldn't find Lily. My first thought was, 'Does she know where Lily is?' I didn't want to tell her without investigating, just in case the frog had jumped out of the bowl, and her cat, Ashes, had found the frog and ate it. Those were my first thoughts. I picked up the bowl and held it in my hands. I remained crouched in the corner of the living room, with the bowl up to my face, looking through the glass, trying to find the frog. I turned the bowl in several directions to gain different perspectives because Lily might have been camouflaged among the rocks and plants as I had witnessed in the past. By inspection, I couldn't find the frog. I always had before."

"We had to rush out and I decided to ask about Lily at a later time. Of course, once we left, the situation slipped my mind until two days afterwards. I had been invited over while my ex prepared for a trip to the Philippines for her best friend's wedding. She had prepared a list, and on that list, she mentioned the need to clean the fish bowl. That's when I remembered. 'By the way, I have a question for you. Where's Lily? Where's the frog?' At that point, she stopped what she was doing and focused on me. She cocked her head to one side and asked in a distressed tone, 'Didn't I tell you?'"

"That's when I started crying because the answer became clear from her expression. I couldn't stop crying. My ex came over to where I stood and gave me a supportive embrace. She held me until I stopped. She held me for thirty minutes."

"That was about a month-and-a-half ago. Since Lily passed away, my life has turned upside down. I became unstable. The intensity from that loss made me explode inside. I didn't realize how much significance I had placed on Lily and I underappreciated the fact that Lily held everything together for me. I had never experienced so much anger, rage, frustration, angst, passion, and so many other emotions as I had through the relationship with my ex. Lily became my place of solitude and stability. I had projected so much onto that tiny creature. I had found a way to maintain my own sanity through Lily and when

I learned Lily was no more, I just lost it. I lost all of it." I felt quiet tears on my cheeks.

"I'm not crying ... maybe, a little watery-eyed." I wiped away the tears. "Lily ... the aquatic frog. I had never cried like that before, in such a devastated manner, never. In a way, it was good, because it helped cleanse me, at a time when I couldn't carry those bottled-up feelings any longer, when my symbol of hope during those difficult times disappeared. And, even though I claim to let things out, I know there's still much pent up inside. I think it's common for people do that, whatever can be withstood, which leads me to ..."

The timing was impeccable as the camcorder shut down signifying the end of a tape. Wow ... and I was just thinking how I don't want to go any further with this. "I don't want to talk about this anymore." I stated my intention out loud to make it firm and sat back into the rattan, contemplating in reticent gloom.

The frog represented a symbol of peace when I was with those three women, throughout the six-year relationship with my ex. Together, my ex and I were well matched. We learned much from one another and we also taught each other well. It sounds like one side of the same coin, but it's not. We were both good students and good teachers. She taught me about passion. I taught her about peace. We learned some very important lessons the hard way. Along with those lessons came emotions I personally couldn't process and chose to keep them inside hoping they would never resurface.

Prior to that six-year period, I lived in a bubble. I lived with angels. I had never experienced anger. I had never experienced rage. I had never experienced frustration. I had never experienced angst. I had never experienced passion. Once the floodgates of anger, rage, frustration, angst, passion ... emotions that ripped me apart from the inside, opened ... I forever changed. It sounds horrible, but I was forced to evolve and shed a protective skin. I would have tweaked it a bit here and there, but ... I softly laughed at myself.

Not that I'd want anybody to experience the volatility that I had, especially with the peace from where I came, but those adverse times made me a stronger person. Unfortunately, it's human nature to learn the greatest lessons through adversity and I am certainly working through some now. I'm not done learning from that time. I'm trying to become a stronger person. I really am.

A smart person would get help. A stubborn person would not. I'm obviously the latter and here I am. This is my fight and I am going to overcome this on my own terms. Thoughts of my mom spilled into my head … the love and strength as she faces her own struggles, raging every day. They filled my heart. The tears flowed … "Stop! Stop it!" I can't. I can't right now.

Still … Be still. I closed my eyes in the darkness. Stillness… Breathing …

When I discovered that Lily passed away, the defense I had built to protect myself completely shattered. Lily was my foundation and over the last two years, I've built up more unfamiliar emotions since the separation. Wait … turn that upside down. Lily was at the small opening of a giant bag filled to the brim, holding everything together for me, but now that Lily is gone … It's no wonder I'm a mess. I'm releasing those pent-up feelings that have accumulated for eight years.

I like how I'm psychoanalyzing myself, sitting in the darkness on this rattan and processing these emotions, battling myself. I'm either dumb or dumb for tackling things this way. Sounds about right, I'm double dumb for doing this to myself.

So many other people are facing much larger problems. People are fighting for their lives … people are starving … people are being abused … people are dying … the tears started again. "Stop … Stop! Stop it!"

I'm not worth any of this, am I? Am I worth anything? I'm so selfish for having these feelings. "Mom, I'm so sorry for doing this to you …" I couldn't stop the tears, after all, and I bawled in the middle of the night, alone.

When I had no more tears to shed and my face hurt so much from crying, I stood and shuffled over to the bathroom where I flipped the light switch. The brightness repulsed me. I squinted until my eyes adjusted. It's approaching midnight and I haven't finished recording yet. Washing my face helped and I stared into the mirror, looking at the mess I am. I smiled and tried to rebalance. Aside from the blood-red eyes, I'd guess I'm fine. I just need to lighten up so I can wrap up the video log and finally get to bed.

The darkness is my friend, a place of solitude and comfort where everything is equal. When shadows pervade from a night light or ambient lights around a curtain or the dawn of a new day, distinguishable forms signify their inequalities. Sometimes it's safer in the dark. I am no better or worse than anything around me, but I know it's not real. It's temporary, a sanctuary where I can disappear for a little while, before I must face reality where light treads. I flicked the switch upon exiting the bathroom and I disappeared. I disappeared within the townhome and felt my way back to the rattan.

Each moment is monotonous in this quiet obscurity, with nothing to compare. I sat until the darkness within me became equal to the darkness of the room. When my mind finally calmed, I stole a few more moments before reaching for the camcorder. I fumbled for the button, but shrugged as I felt my way to the kitchen for a background light before returning to my place in front of the camcorder. I was tired of the interrogation routine.

"This is getting tedious" is what popped into my head upon abandoning my temporary sanctuary, again. Gathering my thoughts also required some mental review, trying to remember how I intended to conclude this recording. It took me a few minutes, but the points in mind returned to me. And, with a deep breath, I reached over to press the record button ... but I didn't press it.

I sat back and looked towards the camcorder, feeling numb. It's so hard to pretend. That's what I'm feeling right now. That's just not me. What's the point of recording these videos if I'm not being honest? Well, I was honest about Lily, but I'm done with being honest for tonight. Instead of revealing anything enlightening, I'm sinking further. This video is going to end on a sour note and I don't want to do that.

I reached over and pressed the red button. "Alright, I had to take a little break, but I'm back ..." Instead of going further into emotional turmoil, with the night about to turn into a new day, I wrapped up the session by mentioning how fun the day was and how much I'm enjoying this trip so far, which is the truth, overall. Plus, ending on a happy note will help me rest tonight or at least, give me a good reason to be at peace before I start again in a few hours. "Good night."

I stopped the recording and exhaled. I thought that speaking openly about Lily would help me release more tension, but it seems I'm just spilling more from that overflowing bag of ... I sat back into the rattan, one more time, and returned to Lily. Maybe, Lily is orchestrating from a different place, knowing very well, after all this time, exactly why I was always at the bowl. This is going to sound silly, but "I miss you, Lily ..."

Erwin Lazaro

XII

Ravings Of A Madman

THE BOWL IS completely empty. Where's Lily? Where are the fish? "Oh, there they are." I walked over to the bowl and swirled my finger just beneath the surface of the water. "You scared me for a second."

Inhaling sharply, I startled awake, finding myself in an unfamiliar setting. It took a bit for me to realize I was dreaming. My body was twisted with my face firmly nestled into the sheets. I straightened out to lie on my back and stared at the ceiling. "Oh yah ... I'm in Newport." I rubbed my face with one hand and dropped it back to my side.

Numb. I'm not feel anything. I'm lying in bed staring at the ceiling and feeling numb. I tried recalling more of the dream, but couldn't remember anything else. I'm losing my touch or maybe, there wasn't any more to it. I must have awoken when I realized it wasn't real.

Anger swelled from within. I don't want to start the day this way. What day is it today? Monday ... It's Monday. I tried a session of true confessions for the camcorder last night ... after a long day. I thought it would help, but it sure doesn't feel like it. I'm such an idiot. Why am I feeling angry? I'm the only one here. No one's doing anything to me. What time is it? Never mind. I don't want to know.

Emotions began filling me ... spilling from me. Without looking at a mirror I can tell my face is flush. Sweat is forming on my forehead. This is like Friday and the reason why I left for this road trip. Nothing has changed. Frustration grew, so I closed my eyes to concentrate.

Stillness. Concentrate on being still ... be still. Concentration turned into focus. Focus on being calm. My brows relaxed. My body relaxed. My breathing relaxed. Extending my breathing helped stop the emotional overflow.

This is so … This is … Why am I feeling this way? There I go again asking "Why?" Think about this differently. What is at the root of my problems? Reviewing last night, I breathed slowly and focused … Avoidance. Fear. Guilt. That's what I identified last night, feelings that surfaced instantly when I spoke openly.

I ran my hands through my hair and closed my eyes. My sister came to mind. "Oh boy, here I go … but this time, I'm going further." Tears started welling before I could even develop any thoughts.

Sadness … I feel sadness. "I finished with disappointment, didn't I?"

"My wonderful sister, Kristine …" I stared at the ceiling with tears running down my cheeks. "Tina … first and foremost, I do not deserve to be your brother. Maybe, it is because Dad put so much pressure on me to succeed for you and take care of you. I have always been afraid of not living up to those standards. As much as I have worked hard to meet those expectations, I am nowhere near capable of helping you, especially as I am now."

"When Patrick died, I started to seriously focus on my future. He became a catalyst for me in understanding how short life can be and that scared me. Dad kept telling me it's my responsibility to take care of you. When Patrick died, I was thirteen years old. You were four years old and I was only concerned about myself." I covered my face, ashamed of my revelation.

"When you were born into this world and blessed our family, you automatically made me a better person. Before you were born, I was a demon that tormented our family. Outside of Mom and Dad, many had no expectations for me. That was made apparent later in my life when relatives, and others that knew me as a child, told me straight up that they were surprised at the person I became. I felt sharp pangs from those remarks, but they were true. I couldn't deny their feelings. I knew they were being brutally honest, understanding the truth behind the humor they used as a cushion to soften the blow. I did cause harm."

Through feelings of pain, images of Randy filled my heart. "When Randy took his own life, I considered the unbearable pressure that forced him to act and make that irreversible choice. I connected a level of his pain with my own feelings. Don't get me wrong. Taking my own life is not an option. It's the self-doubt. I connect the pressure and the self-doubt. On the outside, the smiles are intended to keep everyone at bay. On the inside, the fear is overwhelming." I extended my arms to reach towards Heaven. "And Randy, I failed you too."

Crossing my arms upon my chest, I prayed before continuing. "I credit my sister, Mom, and Dad for keeping me tied to this world. If I didn't have the three of them, I wouldn't be … I wouldn't be as arrogant about my life." Forming fists and firmly pressing down with my right hand, I beat my chest several times with my left, over my heart, to attest to my conviction.

"It doesn't mean I don't waver. I can't help but dwell on so many of my failures. Failures I can never recover from. I think about Randy constantly. I failed him and I will forever regret my selfishness and lack of understanding for his feelings. Randy is another reason that ties me to this world. Patrick too. I made a promise to Randy and Patrick that I am living for them." Anger convoluted the building sorrow. Anger directed at myself. Anger intensified my tears. "That's an arrogant promise, isn't it?" Rage took over. "It's really for me, isn't it?" I started striking myself. "I'm just taking advantage of their tragedies as motivation for my own life. Aren't I?" The tears and gasping grew too loud and I covered my mouth to stifle the emotions.

I strained to see the ceiling through tears. I dared not wipe them away as testimony for my punishment. This entire time, I've thought so selfishly and here I am at a crossroads. I'm frozen, but I'm … I'm screaming and trying to wrestle free from … from … The frustration is so thick.

These are ravings of a madman.

Other people will probably think I'm crazy for having these feelings … for beating myself, for punishing myself. That's also why I don't want to burden anyone with my problems. Even to me, my problems seem so insignificant … insignificant seems so callous. My family is not insignificant. Randy is not insignificant. Patrick is not insignificant. They are not problems either.

"I am insignificant. I'm not worth the trouble and yet I'm so blessed … and I'm a spoiled brat. I don't know what I've done to have so much. Throughout my life, angels have blessed me. I'm so selfish for destroying myself because of *feelings*?"

I'm not facing famine. I don't live in a war-torn country. I'm not a refugee. I'm not being persecuted. I'm not a criminal. I'm not homeless. I'm not battling an incurable disease. I'm not mentally ill … or am I? I shook my head. I'm not mentally ill.

"I have everything … I have everything, except … purpose."

Clarity came for a moment before disappearing again.

"Purpose. People who face life-threatening situations have an immediate purpose. They are fighting to survive. People who are dying want to live. People who have a strong desire, work towards satisfying that desire. People who are hungry seek food. People who lack want more. They all have one thing in common. They all have purpose."

What is my purpose?

I've been told what to do throughout my entire life and there's nothing wrong with that. That's how children learn, but at what point was I supposed to think for myself? I was so dependent on being told how to act, what to do, what needs to be done. I didn't learn how to think for myself. I'm being ripped apart from the inside out, screaming to find a voice of my own. But, I can't figure out what that is. It's still indistinguishable to me.

Thinking about purpose brought me back to my family. The only clear purpose for living revolves around my family. It always has, but the question is, should it always be? Family is my rock. My family is my foundation. That will always be, but what goes on top of that foundation? How do I build upon my values? Values … I am always afraid. Is fear preventing me from moving forward? Building values and moving forward …

I finally wiped the tears using my wrists and stood up. Walking over to the deck, I drew the curtains open and peered out towards the daylight through squinting, tear-filled eyes. The sun's vital energy radiated everywhere. It was already high overhead. I welcomed the warmth through the sliding glass door.

A gaggle of geese is feeding on the lawn below. I stood with hands clasped and observed their movement. The sight is a welcome distraction. Getting out of bed was a sound step for reshuffling feelings. However, inciting this explosion is important to me. I've been avoiding this for so long. Acknowledging emotions that have festered over the years is agonizing, but necessary. I'm determined to overcome this situation I'm facing. This is the time I've set to do it. If I don't do it now, I'll just waste more time within the status quo.

Remaining frozen terrorizes me. Lately, I keep thinking about being frozen. If I don't push myself, complacency takes over. Complacency is the worst. Complacency is a fatal enemy that will leave time snickering as I fade away. I have much to do with this precious life. I have received so many blessings and every wasted moment is an insult. How can I look at myself in the mirror knowing I haven't done all that I can do with my life?

Within a long list of blessings are the angels. Some angels are of my blood. "Who could be so blessed as to live with three angels? I am. That's who. Mom has raised Tina and I with complete adoration and devotion. Dad gives us everything we want. And Tina, you are the perfect counterbalance to the chaos I brought upon our family when I was young. Your peaceful manner and glowing smile has made everything brighter and happier for everyone. My little sister ... you have always been the sweetest angel." I paused to stifle more tears. "Dad is absolutely right. You deserve the best of everything. I'm a worthless brother who can only think of himself, when it comes down to it."

"Tina, do you remember when you were nine years old, I had graduated from high school and spent most of my time away from home? When I became a freshman at the UW?" Before I moved forward with those questions to my non-present sister, I fondly reminisced through the first nine years of Kristine's life, my little Tina-pa.

"For your first nine years, we were inseparable. You were the chubbiest, smiley-est, happiest, cutest, everything-good-est, little girl in the world. You followed me everywhere. You and I spent so many wonderfully, joyous times together. Your glowing smile never faded as you crawled on all-fours in diapers. You were always adorable chasing me around our home in your yellow, circular baby walker, bumping into everything along the way, grinning from ear-to-ear. You were the prettiest four-years-old girl with the most pronounced dimples. You wore everything pink. We used to play a game of kick the ball down the hallway where I'd close the doors. You had to get the ball passed me on my knees and hit the closet door at the end of the hall to score. I'd feign often and you'd win. We laughed uncontrollably as you swiped at the ping pong ball and usually hit nothing but air. The two of us played all sorts of games, sporting our matching permed hair with big curls. We even got those hair perms together." The thought of us sitting in salon chairs brought a big smile to my face.

"We also tried to spend as much time as we could with our cousins. I gave them nicknames too: Chonini and Meming. Chonini is Jason and Meming is Jamie, of course. Whenever Jason and Jamie had an opportunity, they would spend entire weekends with us. Mom always took incredible care of our foursome. You and Jamie slept together. Jason slept on my floor. During the day, I'd drive the four of us to the park and we'd play football. Jason raged when he was on the losing team, which was most of the time. We also hung out at the video arcade for hours. We'd visit grandma and grandpa's store, D'Philippine's Best, and then we'd go to the dime arcade nearby. The Lazaro cousins spent as much time together as possible. You and I were always sad when Jason and Jamie had to go home." Those wonderful memories swept through me and brought a well of love and happiness with them.

"Without Jason and Jamie, we'd just spend time together doing everything and nothing, though I always sang. I sang all day long. I'd draw and sing. We'd do homework together and I'd sing. The radio would play and I'd sing. We'd play games and I'd sing. You'd play with your toys and I'd sing. You and Mom would be in the kitchen together and I'd sing with my bedroom door open because I knew my family was my audience. Our hearts were always smiling."

A realization dawned on me. "Now that I think about it ... Is that why you refuse to sing? I messed that up for you too, didn't I? All those years I never asked you to join me. Even though we're nine years apart, I should have encouraged you to sing with me and maybe, you'd share

Erwin Lazaro

a beautiful voice yet to be enjoyed … another reason I've failed you and one I didn't think about until now. The list grows longer."

I peered intently into the reflection of my own eyes through the sliding glass door. "We had spent so much time together … so many wonderful memories … and now my realization of holding you back, that includes singing … you were a doting nine-year-old and then I abandoned you."

I pressed my forehead against the glass. "I graduated from high school and immediately left you behind. After some time, you wrote me a letter. I have cherished that letter throughout the years. You wrote about how much you missed me and that you wished we could spend more time together. You even slept on my bedroom floor waiting for me to come home."

I lightly tapped my head against the glass. "I know … I know. I'm just festering in my own self-pity. It's quite pathetic, isn't it?" Alas, the foolishness of counseling myself. Images of Randy materialized through the glass while contemplating his last moments, what they were, I can't begin to imagine. I looked to the ocean beyond the beach. I spoke to Randy's image superimposed over the ocean view. "Did you try to convince yourself to stop the madness or did you encourage it? Did you seek any self-worth or did you relinquish everything?"

Just standing here thinking about the possibility makes my core shudder in desperation. "That's why I'm speaking about it out loud. Thinking is too destructive. Speaking gives me a chance to listen to myself and process what I'm saying. I learned how to do this after your death, Randy. I needed to speak out loud to process your suicide."

The images of Randy faded. The ocean became clear and my family emerged, reflections of the people I love most. "I lived in my own form of Eden and never wanted more … The consequence was that I didn't know how to live beyond my home. Reality set in with each passing day. Adolescence turned into a life beyond Eden. I didn't realize I was only doing what I had to do. I stepped into an expansive world and didn't look back. My curiosity piqued and I neglected the world that raised me."

Alongside visions of Mom and Dad, accentuated by the sun's

glorious light, Tina's dimples were a welcome image to remind me of how easy it is to get distracted. "Within my Eden, I had nurtured only one dream. In doing so, I developed that dream within my heart, the dream to reproduce an Eden of my own. The only dream I have is to become the best husband possible and through that union, become the best father possible."

"High school graduation came and went. Time left me no choice, but to act. That's when I left my Eden behind with naivete leading the way. I returned to the garden ten years later after learning much, broken in a way that my Eden could only repair. I needed to be coddled by complacency. In doing so, I lost my way and placed my dream on hold until I mended. Here I am two years after returning and feeling more lost than I ever have."

"I'm still so far from my dream coming true. I've been on so many dates lately, but haven't felt any lasting connection to nurture. What I do know for certain is that I have two golden rules that I will not break. One: I will never meet a woman through church. I am within a sacred place to give thanks and will never seek for myself. I am not in church on my behalf. Two: I will not scope out women at a wedding. I am at a celebration for two people who have invited me to honor their union. I don't attend weddings on my behalf. *I am absolutely adamant about those two rules.* Other than that, friends have recommended dates for me. I've taken the initiative to speak to women that have led to dates. After two years of actively seeking, I have not found anyone who has captured my heart."

Pain surged from within. Sadness and loneliness exploded outward. "How did I get on the subject of women?" I looked high into the sky. "That's a book's worth of contemplation. I don't have the time or the energy to go further about romantic love. I'd never leave this glass door." I laughed out loud. "At least, I still have a sense of humor. While I was driving, I stopped myself from talking out loud *to* myself, feeling weird about the situation and now I'm spending an entire morning doing just that. It goes to show I'm not always thinking about what may be best, but I'm willing to follow my feelings and try."

I shook my head vigorously several times and almost lost my balance.

"That gave me a bit of a headache, but I strayed way too far. Where was I? Eden … dimples … distractions … Ah, yah. I set myself up good for that, didn't I? I fell into it so easily. Well, let's see. Is my mess centered around women? I'm thirty. I'm single. All those years ago, I predicted twenty-five years old and married. Didn't happen. I tried … and within range, but ultimately … I made a wise choice in not forcing the matter. I tried. I really tried, but dad's wisdom saved me. Dad says, 'When you get married, you don't just marry one person, you marry their entire family.' That clinched it for me and I haven't forgotten. It's a lot to ask, but I hope and pray I will one day find *the* woman of my *one* dream, raised within a loving and nurturing family, similar to my own … and together, our two families will merge into one. I will love her family as my own. Support them. Respect them. Protect them."

"Ahhhhhhh! I did it again! Distractions … but this is a good one. It's a good dream to have. I can't wait for it to come true. It's just a matter of time … and luck? Good luck, I hope." The air from my lungs released at an incredibly slow rate before I inhaled to concentrate on my previous train of thought.

"Stay focused, man!" Where was I going with my thinking … "Distractions … dimples …" It wasn't coming to me. "Shit! Fuck! Shit! *Fuck*! *Shit*!" I covered my face with my hands, pushed upward until my palms rested on my forehead, and leaned forward with my knuckles on the glass. "Where did I begin?"

"I'm always an idiot. I think of women and get all messed up. What's new?" Standing upright, I laid my hands to my side and dropped my shoulders in defeat. "… but, I'm a fighter." Straightening my posture, I stared intently towards the ocean. "I feel like I'm on the verge of something. It's a nagging feeling. I have it on the tip of my tongue, but I can't seem to figure out how to say it yet … to recognize it yet … whatever *it* is."

Hoping silence would lead the way to inspiration, I kept my mouth shut, but nothing came. I looked down upon the geese still lounging, occasionally feeding. The simplicity of their actions is captivating. The camcorder came to mind and I rushed over to grab it, the air engulfing me as I slid the glass door open, a refreshing breeze carrying the ocean's essence.

Pressing the red button alerted the geese, reacting to the beep that marked the beginning of the recording. I'm surprised they heard that, but no one else seems to be around and I startled them. Remaining as motionless as possible, I zoomed in on a few of the geese wandering off and I became lost in pondering.

I followed the geese around the lawn, videotaping their mundane behavior. After several minutes of recording, I slowly stepped backwards, through the opening, and stopped the camcorder. My self-counseling session was over for this morning.

Finally acknowledging the remainder of the day, my stomach and the sun urged me to get on with life. Some progress was made through the tears and emotional outbursts. Every effort to explore is leading me closer. I can feel it with some clarity.

Being alone seems counterproductive, but my instincts are telling me I'm doing the right thing. "Well, this is interesting. Exactly, how is this trip working out for me so far?" But, before I answered myself, I went to the bathroom to wash away the tears and blow my nose. Bloodshot eyes last night, bloodshot eyes this morning. I scolded myself in the mirror.

While brushing my teeth, changing my clothes, and repacking my belongings, though not all at the same time, my mind actively defined and justified my actions. Firstly, being alone minimizes the distractions, almost in a meditative way. No one knows me better than me, especially with my determination to get answers. This route is only for certain personality types. I'm a tenacious problem solver and I have a willing, open mind that must always consider options beyond my own meager abilities. My knowledge and wisdom is miniscule so I'm actively learning with each effort. I also have a strong desire to resolve this on my own.

The potential issue is if I fail on this trip, what then? I stopped what I was doing. "Well, that's a glass-half-empty approach." … Or, it's realistic to consider failure. Some neurosis is effective, as long as I don't succumb to spiraling negative emotions as I've been prone to do lately.

Erwin Lazaro

I am getting headaches from this soul-searching rollercoaster, especially from crying. "I don't think I've cried this much since second grade. Such a bummer adding to those tears of old."

Secondly, I'm my own cheerleader because no one else is going to cheer me on. I don't expect anyone to cheer me on, either. Everyone faces problems. I can't rely on others to persistently motivate me. I learned from my dad. Dad has carried the weight of his entire family on his shoulders. Dad's entire family depended on him to make a better life by moving to a foreign land thirty years ago and build from nothing. Dad certainly has taken good care of his loved ones. The fire in his eyes is forged from adversity I've only heard in stories, but he has managed. Dad hasn't relied on anyone else except for himself. I took a few cues from his lesson book and personalized it with both Mom and Dad as my role models.

Thirdly, these efforts are my soul searching. This is a better-late-than-never rite of passage. Australians have something called a walkabout, I believe. "No, wait a minute … or, did I get that from a movie? Oh, wow … Crocodile Dundee! Geez, I think the movie came out when I graduated from high school in 1986. If I can remember, I'll go to Blockbuster Video and check the label. What was the actor's name? Hmm … I think the guy's name is Hogan. Paul Hogan." He has some great lines in that film. "Something about itchy feet … being elsewhere … something about … you can't quite touch it … and … go find it because you know it's there … or something like that." Maybe, I should go for a rental. "Walkabout … yah, except I'm not walking, I'm driving. Drive-about." I crack myself up.

"I'd say those are three good reasons I'm a few hundred miles from home trying to touch something. Wait, that doesn't sound very convincing. I gotta find it and then touch it. Uh, that sounds worse." The funniest thing about speaking off-the-cuff? The words that come out can be confusing, entertaining, or just plain misleading. "Glad I didn't record that on the camcorder. It would have been embarrassing to witness." It dawned on me. "Ah, another good reason to do this alone … so, I don't needlessly embarrass myself in front of others. This is my private battle. No need to share my sob story."

My stomach let out the loudest grumble. "Holy crimmonies! Dang, the echo in this room is crazy." I rubbed my belly in an attempt to soothe the hunger. "I've overstayed my welcome here. Reload my baby and I'm off to explore some more." This was a good place to vent. "Definitely. Thanks, Newport."

XIII

What Other People Say

THE REARVIEW MIRROR framed a valuable memory, a trembling image while driving away. Behind the closed door of that townhome, I found enough courage to confront fears I had previously refused to acknowledge until now. Arising from my efforts here in Newport, a feeling of satisfaction is encouraging me to keep seeking. If I could recall this feeling on demand, I would. I turned my attention forward. The hardest part about progress is that failing is inevitable. Life is a dance, movement in every direction, conveying any emotion, at any given moment. Any given moment is unpredictable, even when everything seems to be going according to plan. That is the key point for living, isn't it? I can plan all I want, but life cannot be planned, no matter how many preparations are made. All that can be done is to set goals and do what's required to meet those goals. More often than not, I am forced to adjust plans and even more often, I am forced to adjust goals. Any given day is filled with inconveniences.

The easy way out is to wish for everything to be convenient, filled with happy feelings for an entire lifetime. But anyone seeking that path is delusional and misunderstanding the value of living. Nothing is wrong with seeking happiness, but defining that happiness is also as unpredictable as life. The definition of happiness changes with the wind. I understand what makes me happy now may be completely different from what will make me happy in the future. Life is cruel. Or, more accurately, from the perspective of those who wish for convenience, the unpredictability of life is cruel.

Preadolescent innocence once protected me from emotional turmoil and then I grew up and became complicated. When I wanted to do something as a young child, I did it, good or bad. If it was bad, I learned from that experience … eventually. The value of learning was not typically a priority for me. Being a repeat offender was more common than not. My poor mom. The point I'm trying to make is that fear was not a factor for the intrepid child I was. If I thought it, I did it.

Right now, I'm one of those complicated idiots that wants everything to be convenient, mostly because I'm tired of struggling. I am a spoiled brat, so I have no right to complain and yet I do. Feeling entitled is also another human failing. I know this and yet I succumb to that selfishness on a daily basis. Both convenience and self-entitlement lead to apathy and complacency, forms of rot that consume the soul. I silently chant these warnings, a personal mantra to bolster my defenses and yet I still fail much too often.

I'm intensely fearful. I can't remember for how long. That desire for convenience stems from deep-seated anxiety developing over time. The easy way out is a convenient way to avoid my fears. Apathy and complacency are paths of least resistance. In other words, it's easy to give up. Did I really give up?

I believe I did give up and then, somehow, I woke up and realized what I was doing was wrong. It was a helpless feeling. I had never given up before, but I was beaten down and at the time, I didn't realize how much I had lost. If I had revealed my suffering to my mom and dad, they would have been devastated, especially my mom. I didn't want to add to her suffering. I tried to deal with it by myself and obviously failed … or not. It took me a while to act. Two years for me to act. I'm acting now. It's only too late if I spend the rest of my life wallowing, but I couldn't stand my self-loathing any longer. I took baby steps and the first step was the hardest.

The first step was when I learned how a good defense rises from a good offense to stop destructive emotions from dominating me. Tired of wallowing, I became angry. I couldn't look myself in the mirror. I only saw shame. That shame disgusted me. Enough for me to do something about it. I finally acted. That was the first step. It didn't matter how I acted. Anger sounds destructive, but in this case, anger reinvigorated my spirit for living. I found the spirit to fight my intolerable condition. I'm continuing that battle. I obviously don't have a firm grasp on managing destructive emotions and during this trip I'm encouraging the havoc. It's dangerous, but I'm willing to take the risk. I've tried to suppress the suffering, but that strategy just froze me. That wasn't a solution. It was a band aid.

At first, self-pity consoled me. Then, self-loathing bound me. And through it all, self-doubt always crept in to deter my path towards personal enlightenment. In hindsight, I probably should have sought help and not try to do this on my own, but this is the course I chose. I can't rewind and do this again. I don't want to do this again. I'm diverging here, but I really think finding solutions ultimately depends on the person. I'm confident in my problem-solving skills. I can do this. It's just a matter of ... *how?* Yes, "*how?*" drives forward or more specifically "*How do I ...?*". "*Why?*" recedes in time to seek causes. I know the causes, for the most part. My failures are more stepping stones towards my future and I need to keep forging ahead.

A strong sense of pain wracked my entire body. I grabbed my shirt and dug into my chest. "There's more ... more I need to confront. I'm not done yet, but this is not a good time. I just started driving for goodness sake." I'm going to find a more appropriate place, a private place, just in case I have another emotional breakdown. I'm not stupid enough to let my emotional instability affect other people, especially on the road. I could make a rash choice I may regret for the rest of my life. That can't happen.

I need to find a place that will allow me to explode without harming anyone else. Even in the townhome, I had to restrain myself. I had to stifle my sorrow. I had neighbors and having the police knock on my door in the middle of night was not an option. I'm not doing this to make things worse, I'm doing this to get better. I need to let everything out. My gut tells me I need to empty everything. A violent expulsion will occur if or when I don't hold back. I must ride the wave until I get to the end. Only then will closure be at hand.

The scary thing is that I want to find someplace to let everything out, but what happens if I lose control ... lose all hope ... and I'm alone.

What would I do then? That possibility scares me. If no one is around to stop me from doing something stupid … No, I won't do that. I can't do that. "I'm such a frickin' arrogant prick … but this arrogant prick … believes."

These self-deprecating demons are byproducts of my arrogance. I set myself on fire. Arrogance is protecting me from apathy and complacency, but walking that tightrope is exhausting. Exhaustion is a daily endurance trial, but it's not because I'm caught up in every detail. This mental fatigue is connected to my lack of purpose. I'm spinning my mental wheels and going nowhere. My status quo is exhausting.

So far, this road trip is making the wheels churn effectively. The progress is exhilarating. I want more. This "drive-about" is also giving me a tangible way to transform my destructive actions into constructive reform. Being outdoors is cleansing me too. It's clearing out my system, giving me a fresh start, but I still have much to air out as this morning reinforced.

I'm going through seemingly life-encompassing ideas, but something doesn't really mesh or make sense. The unpredictability of life and adjusting goals started this particular train of thought and within my introspection, exhaustion came into play. I determined that the cause is my lack of purpose. Am I convincing myself that I'm exhausted because of life? Because I'm continually adjusting goals? If I define goals further, the lack of purpose I described last night refers to long term goals whereas the unpredictability of life that forces goals to change are generally short term; although, not exclusively.

A **BLARING** honk erupted from behind me. I don't know how long I was stationary at the driveway exit, but it was long enough to piss someone off. I raised my hand to the rearview mirror and apologetically waved to the driver waiting for me to do something. Gritting my teeth, embarrassment took over and I drove into the heart of Newport to find lunch.

"Really … the thoughts that run through my head." If I contemplate without pause, I'd probably overcome my problems just by thinking too much. So much mumbo jumbo would fill my brain that the poison would be squeezed out naturally. I laughed at the thought.

My brain bulb lit up. Laughter is a mechanism that instantly gets me out of these periodic funks. I simply move on. Now that I think about it, I'll see any random person genuinely smile or laugh and that energy makes me feel better as if I'm siphoning from them. Somehow, I find humor in the things I do and I'm able to laugh about it. I think that's a good thing. Maybe, even a measure of my sanity. It's a temporary fix though. That's also a band aid, but it still makes me feel good, if only for a short time.

A low murmur resonated into a horrific grumbling. Rubbing my stomach brought attention to my current task. Feed the belly. I hadn't eaten since dinner last night and it's already the afternoon. I've drained my energy through these mental exercises. I'm truly surprised I'm not grumpy … or am I? "I'm just wimpy. Yah, I should be able to go for days without water. Yah, weeks without food. Yah, yat's duh thicket. Godda wub Jon Wubitz and duh 80s." Somehow, I channeled Bugs Bunny towards the end and pretended to gnaw on a carrot.

I didn't really know where to search for lunch outside of the waterfront area, so I headed that way. It's another beautiful day. Enjoying a meal with a good view is always a bonus. That's enough motivation for me to search no further.

As anticipated for a Monday afternoon, that odd time between lunch and dinner, the waterfront is relatively quiet, except for fellow tourists wandering about. Parking was not an issue. No view, but I strolled into Mo's and was led directly to a table without waiting.

Everything looked yummy on the menu. I couldn't resist the fried combos. Ordering was a snap and I had nothing else to do but observe my surroundings. Empty tables and servers trying to keep busy comprised most of the scenery within the open space floor plan of the restaurant. A few customers trickled in, but they took orders to go. Within a few minutes, the hostess led a young family my way and seated them directly in front of me.

The parents don't look much older than I am. Maybe, we're about the same age? Their son looks about four years old. They have a newborn daughter, dressed in pink from head-to-toe. She reminds me so much of my little sister under that pink, frilly bonnet.

I can see she is wide awake and as content as can be; gentle and smiley. The image takes me back to my baby sis at the same age as this little one. I don't ever recall my sister crying. That can't be right, but that's what I fondly remember. The vision melts my heart. I looked away as my eyes watered just a bit. I had to stop my emotions from going further.

Rubbing my temple helped as I feigned an eye irritation and diverted my gaze to the tabletop, but my attention was drawn back to the family of four. Awkwardness crept in because this family *is* my view. The restaurant is sparsely populated. They were seated next to me most likely because this is the servers designated area. I can't help but feel I am an audience to their actions. If they look my way, I'm really going to be embarrassed.

I'm not a pervert. I admire them. I admire this scene.

Observing without appearing to care, I casually scanned the restaurant while periodically resting my mind upon their activities. I didn't linger too long for fear they might notice. Hopefully, my consideration is light enough that I won't draw their attention.

What makes this period of time more awkward is that I'm waiting for my order, so I really have nothing to do. I'm just a single guy sitting at an empty table facing a family and the other tables are empty. It's oddly laughable, but I wouldn't blame the dad if he suddenly faced me and issued a warning glare.

As it turned out, dad had his hands full with his son who was not sitting still. Mom's eyes were locked with her daughter's adoring twinkle. Two pairs representing the yin and yang of their family. The doting mom and the scolding dad, both parents were too preoccupied to be disturbed by a random stranger. Hardly any words were exchanged while I was in their presence. All four simply communicated through their actions. When the boy tried to scurry pass his mom, without losing focus on her baby, mom scooped him up until dad retrieved him. Their expressions spoke volumes. If I could hear their inaudible language it would be an overwhelming cacophony only tolerated within a family structure as this one before me.

When my prepared plate was set on the table along with a cup of hot water, I thanked the server and gave thanks for the meal. It's against my nature to scarf everything down, but I did. I had already pried too much into the privacy of the young family and ate with my eyes fixed on my food. That was probably the fastest I consumed a large meal out of consideration for my obtrusion. I prayed I would not regret devouring every morsel. I hope my bowels aren't going to scream at me for causing such suffering. No amount of hot water is going to relieve me. I also quietly apologized for not appreciating the meal properly.

The server brought out food for the family as I finished up. Even through my beast-like consumption, I noticed their smooth orchestration of care. I witnessed harmony. Their behavior didn't change while incorporating food into the mix. I wanted to applaud the entire production, encouraging them to synchronize for a lifetime. I would have unforgettably embarrassed myself with grease all over my face, if I had acted. My unseemly appearance paired with good manners prevented me from playing the fool.

When my plate was cleared, I leaned back and felt bloated. Starving just a few minutes prior, my stomach now feels as hard as a rock. The server left the ticket for me and I could barely reach forward to grab it. As I snatched the paper from the table, I somehow connected with the boy who was grinning at me. I returned a closed-mouth smile that turned into a toothy grin. Through that exchange, I tried to convey to the boy with my own inaudible language. I told him, "Cherish this time. Don't forget. Love your family and be grateful your four hearts are beating as one. Protect that with everything you have and then make it your own ..."

I couldn't believe it. *Was I telling him or was he telling me?*

Dazed by the thought, I don't remember what happened next. I'm almost certain the server took my payment and I was on my feet, but I just stood in place. I looked at the boy, but he was back to his silly antics. It's typical of me to want affirmation that I'm not going to get.

Walking briskly passed this loving family, I overheard two words that made me take notice. I heard, "Devil's Punchbowl." I instinctively knew they were talking about a tourist attraction, but I was afraid to ask them directly. Instead, on the way out, I asked the hostess about it and she told me it's a local water feature that is popular to visit. She warned me that it's probably too late to enjoy today. The tide is probably too high to access the punchbowl.

Feeling somewhat disappointed for missing out on a water attraction, I went for a stroll before returning to my baby. Burning some calories and digesting this food became a priority. Access to restrooms was at the top of my list, too.

Mo's is located on the landward side of the boulevard. The inlet is on the other side, so I wobbled across and started walking southward to get a glimpse of the water. It's a shame. These buildings are obstructing a scenic amenity, but that's how it goes. Local businesses rely on direct access to docks. It's their livelihood. I'm just a spoiled tourist that wants convenience. Lots of ways for me to witness a beautiful view and I'm making the effort to go see for myself. I'm not the only one. Other people are walking the boulevard and I'm certain some are tourists with the same intentions.

Upon the path, a group of elderly couples blocked the sidewalk while browsing over a map. As I approached, they were considering options for a late lunch. I loved the smiles on their faces. Smiles are infectious. The energy that radiates from smiles inspires me to join. I had a beaming smile when I asked, "If you don't mind, might I offer a suggestion? I couldn't help but overhear your conversation about having lunch."

It turned out that they were also explorers from Washington. This is their first visit to Newport and they had just come from the area surrounding the Devil's Punchbowl. I expressed my enthusiasm for the attraction, but they told me they weren't able to venture inside. The tide had already risen fairly high. They did enjoy the view overlooking the punchbowl though. Apparently, a lookout sits directly above the feature. They did witness a few people inside, but didn't want to risk getting trapped if the tide rose too high for them.

They saw my excitement grow and one spoke up, warning me it's too late to try. One of the gentlemen advised, "You should wait for another opportunity ..." but I had already started back-peddling, about to turn and sprint to my baby. Then, I realized I hadn't offered my suggestion for lunch yet. I pointed from where I came and said, "You can't go wrong at Mo's! Their menu is spectacular. Their chowder is a must!" I waved, turned, and ran.

The timing was perfect for me to release the demons. The running churned my stomach and probably disturbed my digestion. I bolted into Mo's and asked the hostess if I could use the restroom. I had exited just minutes before and she pointed with a smile.

After finishing my business, I paused outside, took a deep breath and felt a rush of adrenaline; anticipating a chance to discover something I'd only find at the Devil's Punchbowl. The name is already foreboding and I want to find out for myself.

The afternoon wore on. I bolted to my baby only to do a 360 and go back into the restaurant, huffing and puffing. This time the hostess was perplexed at my repeated sudden entrance. I told her that I am crazy, but I'm going to the Devil's Punchbowl to see if I can get in before the tide rises too high. By the look on her face, she thinks I'm crazy too. "I was about to drive away, but I don't know where to go. Would you please give me directions?"

She proceeded to tell me. It was simple enough. Clasping my hands and bowing profusely, I thanked her for being patient with me. She gave me a final warning, but I ignored her as I backed out the door with a beaming expression. "Thanks for your help!"

Time knows no mercy. Intuition is guiding me. I'm determined to see for myself because this might be the place I'm seeking. The adrenaline mixed with nerves. I tried not to speed, but I couldn't help it. I drove safely, but I pushed the limits and pushed forward. I couldn't let this slide. I'm tired of waiting. I'm tired of looking ahead. This is my time. This is my chance to seek and discover. Of course, it's another challenge and I'm facing it head on. I don't want to regret any longer.

Carefully thumbing my binder, my sight darted between the road and the discs to find Al Jarreau. His music is incredibly uplifting and always emote a sense of hope. He is a warrior of music for me, the one on the front lines that faces everything head-on with a smile. His scatting is unrivaled and serves as munitions to keep everyone at bay. "No other … I say no contemporary artist even comes close to Al Jarreau's ability to scat." Ella Fitzgerald immediately comes to mind from an era long past. Just thinking about Ella Fitzgerald performing with Al Jarreau is beyond this earth. "I wonder if they ever performed together. I would have loved to experience that. Fitzgerald's big band stylings mingling with Jarreau's vocal acrobatics …" That would be mesmerizing, but I think she passed away a couple of years ago. Louis Armstrong, Cab Calloway, Sarah Vaughan, Al Jolson … Bing Crosby scatted some too, all past legends and many others. Only a few now and none that come to mind as Al Jarreau does for me. Jarreau's music entwines the glorious past stylings of iconic scatters with contemporary Jazz, R&B, and Soul. A strong spirituality shines through Jarreau's music. Al Jarreau is serving as a guardian of sorts, paving the way for me towards the Devil's Punchbowl.

XIV

The Mind Is A Powerful Enemy

A FRANTIC RACE and Al Jarreau calmly leads the way. Though the sun is high, the horizon appears to be creeping eastward at an accelerated rate. "Staying calm ... driving safely ... I read too much fantasy, but Al, wherever you are ... can you please use your magic to slow down time while I speed ahead, so I don't miss this chance?"

I was told that the punchbowl is roughly eight miles north of Newport within the community of Otter Rock. Once I see the signs and exit from highway 101, I'll be very close to the parking lot for the trail that leads down to the beach and tide pools, "Heading north ... of course!"

The traffic was light and the turn off from the highway was visible in no time. I blindly reached for the camcorder in case I missed signs for the punchbowl. I videotaped the approach. Happy ... "Just enjoyed a great meal at Mo's. I'm heading towards the Devil's Punchbowl to see if I can make it inside." The tall-standing trees to the west ended to reveal a cliff and the ocean beyond. "Whoa! Is that the punchbowl? I have no idea, but it looks like I'm quickly approaching." I slowed down. The road transitioned into a parking area. The east side of the driveway is lined with public buildings for visitors. I couldn't help exclaiming, "Ice cream!" A big sign is displayed on one of the gabled roofs. "All right, I'm going to park."

That didn't take long. "Thanks, Al." The lot is relatively empty. I took the camcorder and an extra battery, just in case. The view is magnificent, of course, but it looks like I'm going to walk further to the punchbowl. I don't see very many people. That's a good sign ... I think.

The path led to a breathtaking view. A few visitors are standing where I want to be. I moved a little further and started videotaping this captivating scene. A wooden fence lined the safe area for good reason because it's a long way down.

The Devil's Punchbowl is aptly named. The cavity looks as if the devil carved it out himself. A natural formation in the shape of a circle? At least, that's what it looks like from where I'm standing. I *think* this is a natural occurrence. The rocks could have collapsed at some point and exposed the huge cavity within. "Could the ocean have actually carved out caves within this land mass? … Form a volume in the shape of a circle? That's very strange."

It's intriguing. I had to ask. "Excuse me?" I approached the group talking about the view. "Do any of you know the history of the Devil's Punchbowl?"

The visitors were kind enough to chat. They took turns sharing their knowledge. They had read some information regarding the Devil's Punchbowl and Gull Rock. One of them pointed to a large mass projecting out of the water, about one-half mile beyond the punchbowl, exclaiming, "Surfers like that area!" That reaffirms my idea that surfers are crazy people with big kahunas, especially the women.

I asked whether the punchbowl was manmade or formed from natural erosion. Another person from their group mentioned that clams dug out a sea cave through the sandstone rock dated from the Age of Astoria Formation, about eighteen million years ago. The ceiling eventually collapsed.

I was clearly shocked and they told me, "There is a way to go inside the punchbowl, but it's too late now. The tide is too high." They were just at the shore and turned around. The tide had risen to a point where they would have to wade through the water in order to enter. The group wasn't prepared for that.

"I'm going to try to get inside since I don't know when I'll be visiting next." The visitors looked at me as if I am crazy.

One of the women stared me up and down, "You don't look like you're prepared either. I think it would be a mistake to try."

Smiling on the outside, I was genuinely irritated. "Well, thanks for

Erwin Lazaro

the info. I appreciate the chat. I'm going to check for myself." I waved and turned to head down the trail, but my eye caught the whitewater filtering through the westward opening into the punchbowl. The rhythmic roar easily distinguishable from the cavity, echoed upward. That looks to be a cave entrance before the ceiling collapsed. Water crashed in with each wave, but the broken rubble is clearly visible at the base, so I have time to walk around if I can access it.

My imagination rendered the water gushing through with the rising tide, fiercely swirling about and flooding the punchbowl. This is a deadly natural occurrence. The whitewater erratically churning and crashing on all rock faces. That's no joke. Those visitors said the water is supposed to roil and foam. "Roil?" I must have looked perplexed by that word. One of them clarified with, "You know, agitate real good." Okay, *that*, I understood.

Looking more intently, I see the shadow of another cave entrance facing northward. Water wasn't coming through at this time. That's probably the way into the punchbowl. It makes sense that I could enter from the north side by walking along the rock face. That must be it. That's where I'm heading.

My inclination is to stay longer and video tape the water gradually rising. That would be cool … incredible … to watch the basin fill as the tide comes in, but I didn't rush all this way to be a spectator. I'm done reflecting behind the fence. I ran down the trail.

As I ran, thoughts of everyone who spoke about the punchbowl ran through my head, as well. No exceptions regarding their warnings. Everyone clearly cautioned me that it's too late. I understand they mean well, but this is paramount for me. Passing up this opportunity is ludicrous unless swimming is the only option. Drowning is not on my agenda. Al got me here quickly so I don't want to waste that valiant effort. Plus, none of them know for certain. Everyone's speculating. The last group basically conveyed they didn't want to get wet. That's not enough to stop me. "Where there is a will, there is a way."

A sign came into view. It looks like this is the trailhead to the beach. I started videotaping at the sign. It read: DANGER TRAIL NOT PASSABLE. I walked passed the warning anyway. "I'm going to try to get into the Devil's Punchbowl. I was told not to go down there by several people. The water level is getting higher and higher. Of course, I'm not dressed to go into the water, but I'm going to see if I can get over there. I have to hurry."

Videotaping in silence, I walked a path cut through the wild brush. One wide curve and the sand became visible beyond the greenery. I paused the recording and ran through the brush until my feet landed on the beach. Surveying the area with a sweeping glance, a few people were spotted on the north side. Otherwise, the beach was almost entirely bare, except for a family heading in my direction. I walked towards them. It looks like they also turned back from the punchbowl.

Acknowledging them with a nod and a sidelong glance, the dad gave me the same warning everyone else had. I retorted with, "I'll be fine." I admit I was not friendly. I'm just tired of the repeated warning … I sighed … but it's no excuse for lashing out at a person who is concerned for my welfare. That was downright rude of me.

Back-peddling, the dad reacted, "Don't expect anyone to come save you if you put yourself in danger." He didn't wait for my reply and rejoined his family.

Boiling in my tracks, I deserved that, but I still felt anger shooting through me. I turned to face the dad, but he was well out of earshot and looked to be conversing with his wife … probably about the idiot who might do something stupid. Hand and camcorder on my hips, I turned back around. My eyes fell upon two sand angels, most likely created by the two children with that family I had just passed. I didn't have time to dawdle, but my eyes lingered on the angels before I pressed forward.

"Whoa …" Bringing the camcorder up to record, megalithic protrusions delineate the area where I am heading. These rocks make up the cliff edge where I was standing earlier. Mounds of jagged boulders line the beach towards the natural wall. This is part of the same structure the punchbowl was carved from. I continued southward. No one else is in sight.

The sandy area along my way diminished as the beach and the ocean converged to a point in the distance. Some large, rounded boulders spotted the area ahead. My heart raced with anticipation. That point of convergence is where I will have to decide.

Approaching the doorstep of my destination, the path is shrouded in shadow. A massive rock looms over the area I must pass. Large rubble lies within the convergence zone. The exposed surfaces are covered in algae. My pace quickened and I walked into obscurity.

Within the shadow of uncertainty, I paused to acknowledge this heavenly ocean view. Pristine by sight and raucous by sound, the contrasting senses modeled my feelings. My heart is drawn towards progress and my mind is reeling from truths I'd rather not face ... just a little further.

My attention turned to the rough-hewn rock face. It's showing incredible decay from the ocean's pummeling. The ceaseless action even formed a few crevices. One is large enough to be a small grotto, a space for candlelight and offerings to the ocean. Another crevice curves around rocks that were forcibly split; toes for this monstrous megalith. The space is large enough for me to enter. I walked between the toes to see what I could find ... just sand.

Stalling ... I'm trembling. The megalith stands guard and blocks my view. Here is where the water begins. In front of me are algae-covered rocks above the water's surface. I must traverse them to see what lies beyond. "I don't think I'm going to make it ..."

With my right hand preoccupied by the camcorder, my left hand supported my weight over the rocks. "Okay ... well, let's see ... how slippery is this?" I carefully stepped onto the first rock protrusion covered with algae. "I don't want to fall into the water."

Securing the first rock, I surveyed the path ahead. A series of similar protrusions lined the way. The rocks here really do look like toes. One by one, I crossed over toes. As funny as that seemed, I focused on one step at a time. Still within shadow, every step forward revealed an incredible view ahead of rock formations bathing in sunlight.

I turned westward in awe of the ocean. "Wow, look at those waves." Somewhat close to me, the waves crashed against obstructions unseen. I'm certain that rocks are preventing those forceful waves from hitting me right now, but not for long. "I wonder how much time I have." I continued moving. "No one get mad at me for doing this."

"The last toe with nowhere else to go except into the water before me ..." Looking down, the depth seems manageable. I estimate knee high. I also estimate about fifty feet of water to wade through before reaching exposed rocks I can walk upon. The water is calm here. I have to jump in. This is the time. This is my time. I jumped.

Crouching down, I planted my left hand on the rock beneath me as my feet went airborne. My right hand extended as high as I could reach to protect the camcorder. Exhilaration swept my body as I entered the water, excited that I am on my way and electrified because, "The water is *freezing! It's so cold!*"

I looked down. The water is deeper than I had anticipated. The items in my pockets are submerged: my wallet, keys, receipt from Mo's ... extra battery. Most of my shorts are submerged. That makes this about thirty inches deep. "If I knew how much time I had ... Whoa!"

"*Whoa! Whoa!*" First step and I almost dunked myself. What the heck, the algae are hazardous! Duh ... somehow, I managed to rebalance with the help of the wall. My right hand still held high. Now, most of my body is soaking wet. "It's cold! *It is so cold! Huh, ho ...*" I shivered vigorously. "I don't know how I'm gonna get back. I'm soaking and I'm cold."

For fifty purposeful steps, I carefully moved along the rocks. A track of sand made a nice ramp up to the solid platforms ahead. After taking a few steps on the sand, I inspected the camcorder. "I did get my camcorder wet." The lens appears to be fine though. "It doesn't look so bad." Peering over my shoulder, I convinced myself that I'll make it back safely. With the water in shadow, I reacted with a shiver. The blurred distinction between rock and water are making the tide level appear higher. I hope my perception is just fooling me.

In front of me though ... Wow. I could easily spend hours absorbing this environment. The north face opening into the punchbowl became visible. I see light from the other side. With my goal in sight, I trembled and continued walking in the shadow of the rock wall. The sand ramp ended at the large rock platform I observed from the megalith's protruding toes.

Forced to resume my careful pace upon the rocks, the blanket of algae slowed my advance to a crawl. Trying to appreciate this naturally evolving scene is difficult when every step requires attention. I can't take anything for granted here. I'm alone and if I get hurt, no telling if help would come, just as that dad warned. Ignoring the danger could cost me dearly.

Roughly one hundred feet south of my position, the rock face turns westward and forms the enclosure for the punchbowl. Where the two walls meet, I noticed a much smaller fissure that penetrates through. It looks wide enough to sneak in, but I dare not enter that way. The large entrance is my goal.

At the threshold, all the way through, and on both sides, a sandy floor welcomes visitors. Each deliberate step led me to the sand. Relieved on safely reaching stable footing, I stood before the opening, dripping wet. The sound emanating from within is intense. This truly is a cave mouth screaming to all who would be in my position: "STAY OUT OR GET IN!"

I walked into the Devil's Punchbowl.

Sound savagely echoed throughout. I could now distinguish that the two openings into the Devil's Punchbowl are almost connected. The northwest portion of the enclosure is basically a stout pillar, rounded by the ocean's current. Water will flow freely between the two once the level rises high enough. Currently, froth crashing through the west side is steadily rising. Relentless waves are creeping in to fulfill the daily cycle.

The sandy area allowed me to visually examine this enclave. I'm at the base of the punchbowl and my imagination rendering the water gushing through with the rising tide, fiercely swirling about is even more terrifying. The whitewater erratically churning and crashing on all rock faces from within is more threatening. My nerves rattled with the thought of being caught inside here if both exits are filled with water.

Images of devastating turbulence filled my mind. I am finally within. An awesome concentration of energy is swirling here. The intense sound is first to consume. And though not visible, wind is funneling throughout and upward. Ocean spray is mixing in the air. I can feel and smell it. The sun's energy is penetrating, now that I'm able to walk in the sunlight. The heat feels concentrated down here in the Devil's Punchbowl.

I raised my arms with my palms facing upward. This enclave is a mecca. I can feel in my heart that I'm supposed to be here.

My emotions swelled. This mixing bowl spurned my feelings. Imminent danger combined with my fragile nature blended together into an overwhelming surge of energy. Kinetic flow made me tingle all over. Hands raised high I turned in place and gave thanks for this moment. Silently, I cried for this moment. Tears streamed down my cheeks.

I couldn't help being overpowered. I was helpless before and now … now, I don't know how to describe this situation. I lowered my arms and moved further in. Only the area in front of the openings has sand. The rest of the base is a seaweed and algae-coated, rocky obstacle. I'm not sure what possessed me to move, but I climbed those rocks. I slipped the entire way. I bled, but it didn't matter. I moved away from the water until I couldn't move any further.

Once again in shadow, I placed my left hand upon the rock face, the camcorder in my right hand also against the rock face. "I'm here …" I whispered. Not sure who that greeting was for, but I announced my arrival. Turning around, my knees buckled. I sat in place and closed my eyes. "I did it, Mom. I'm doing it. Everyone told me I shouldn't … I couldn't, but I did."

Weakness filled me, emerging from my heart. I listened to the rising tide. I envisioned the sand almost entirely under water, but I didn't react. I was powerless to open my eyes. The pressure from making it here anchored me in place. A sorrowful flood poured out. "I know you didn't want me to go on this trip … Dad and Kristine, either. I know you all mean well, but at what cost to me?"

Already submerged by my own tears, this was the final push I needed. Constantly at odds with myself, I always knew why, but I never had the courage to face it. I had to go to this extreme and force this self-confrontation.

"I can't ask for anything more and yet I want *more*. I have everything I need and yet I need *more*. You never ask for anything. You never want anything. I'm trying to be like you, but I can't. I'm trying so hard, but I can't overcome my desires. I want to give back all that you've given to me, but I only think of myself. I want you to be happy, but I'm helpless to do anything for you. You have suffered through the years and you continue to fight for your life so that your family can have everything we need. I'm not strong enough to do that for you." I buried my head beneath my arms. "I'm your worthless son."

Sobbing uncontrollably, I pulled my head down over my knees. "I know that if you saw me now, you'd be in overwhelming pain, even more pain than I am experiencing." Especially in the last year, I had progressively fallen into a sulking rut. "You've been aware the entire time. Every day, you never fail to ask me how I'm doing or express your concern for me." Every time you ask me, I become more consumed with my failure to ease your concern. I only add to your burden and that, in turn, adds to my pain. Maybe talking to you directly is the better course, but I'm too afraid to make you suffer more. "You worry so much." I know if I discuss this openly you will be consumed by it. I'm the stupid one for not trusting you enough to help me. I know you'll do anything to help me. "You live for Kristine. You live for me."

"You are the person in this world that means more than life itself and I continue to add to your suffering. Ultimately, that's the reason I am on this journey. Ultimately, *you* are the reason I am on this journey."

XV

Martyr And Her Cross

M Y ANGUISH TRANSFIGURED to a semblance of clarity. It petrified me. My mind throbbed. I couldn't feel anything else, but then, the throbbing shattered. A void remained. All barriers encompassing me were broken too; the humor, the anger, the frustration, the sadness ... all gone. Entirely exposed, all that is left is me.

Even so, regardless of my circumstances, no matter my failures, no matter what I do, I could be in the worst place within the worst conditions. I may be threatened right now. No matter ... One thing is certain. I will always be connected by the inseverable thread that leads me to you, Mom. You are my confidence. My future is certain. I'm going there.

It's the path from here to there that I haven't been able to accept because of you.

"Mom ... I don't know how you do it. I don't know how you endure. Yet, you wake up every morning with love, kindness, and effortless smiles to greet your family. You work tirelessly through your suffering. You are a martyr carrying a heavy cross."

The moment you left your own parents, siblings, and friends, you were alone. For thirty-years you have been alone without anyone to confide in, always being self-reliant for consolation. I understand this every time you cry in solitude. You reemerge with a smile, not wanting anyone to see your pain, but I'm aware. Your family is aware.

Sometimes, I approach you, but you smile and tell me not to worry. You tell me you'll be fine, but I can't help but worry. In fact, I worry more. I get that from you. "You know, I'm just like you, Mom." I try to help, but you'd rather carry the entire burden than let others carry any portion for you. I recognize your sacrifice, but you won't really accept my help. Your gentle nature absorbs the negativity around you. You accept all instead of distributing the load. You'd rather protect your family than let us suffer even the slightest amount. How can I leave you behind knowing our family is your only comfort from this world?

In addition to your daily trials, you've relied on memories to connect with your parents and siblings. Communication with them is sorely limited. Your own family lives more than six-thousand five-hundred miles away in the Philippines. They need you and you miss them dearly. They relied on you as the eldest of eight children, the Até of the Mijares family. You left them for Dad and for me; for our future, thirty years ago. We visited a few times, but it's never enough. I couldn't imagine being away from you or have no communication with you, indefinitely. Three of your siblings passed away. Your auntie; my Grand-aunt Felicisima passed away. Your dad; my Grandpa Manuel passed away. Loved ones have passed away. You've mourned from a distance.

Which leads me to the worst part of ... of living in this world ... it's unbearable for me, but you're the one who rises with incredible resilience. I weigh your circumstances and agonize, but you're the one who laughs and makes the most out of every moment. Your heart beats with firm resolve. My heart is constantly aching. Not for me, of course, but for you, Mom.

1989: The most devastating year of our lives. That most devastating year has turned into the most fearful nine years. Today is August 10, 1998. Our family is trying to live with a semblance of normalcy. In fact, normal is a blessing. Balance is a blessing. I am in the Devil's Punchbowl upsetting that balance for my own selfish needs. I'm adding to your suffering and if you knew what I am doing now, I don't want to imagine how you would feel about my reckless actions.

Our family is always praying for one another, for our good health and well-being, for our safety, for our prosperity. Although, I don't want to be consumed by the gravity of your situation, I'm always praying for healing power to restore you, Mom ... somehow. A miracle is needed.

I almost wish I could blame someone or something for what

happened to you; for what's happening to you. No one and nothing is identified to receive my wrath. Maybe it is so because Dad and I would be vengeful. As it is, we are altogether helpless. All we can do is love you … support you in every way our feeble efforts can be of value. Between the four of us, we are trying to live as best as we can, thankful for every day we have together.

I can't help but go back to that vacation, between December 1988 and January 1989, when we enjoyed the Christmas season in the Philippines. In retrospect, trouble began just before that trip. A bad omen warned us, but we couldn't associate our future with the crime that violated our home the evening we took care of our passport photos, preparing for that trip.

Pulling into our driveway, the front door was broken and wide open. Our beloved puppy was inside. I was enraged, but you stopped me from running in. Headlights remained on. I stomped outside with limited visibility at night. Screaming at the top of my lungs, I threatened the criminals while you pleaded for neighbors to call the police.

After the police secured our home, we were grateful that our puppy was unharmed. The robbers stole electronics and jewelry. They had broken our backyard fence to escape. We live on a street connected by a walking bridge over a freeway. At least one of them escaped over the bridge. The following day I found items in our backyard and one of our remote controls on the bridge. Our home was defiled. We were violated.

In my mind, that was the beginning of unceasing hardships befalling our family, the beginning of unending personal tragedies for you, Mom. Your family and friends wonder why an angel faces so many misfortunes when all you aspire to do is care for your loved ones.

You are the embodiment of love. I have never witnessed you become angry. You have never raised your voice. Your emotions are pure and evident. You are among the strongest warriors this world will ever know. The weakest of mankind uses violence, rage, anger, or anything that would crush others for selfish gain. You, on the other hand, always genuinely radiate an aura of love, compassion, and everything a human spirit should be. You harbor no ill will even though you have endured so much. Your will must consist of the strongest energy because your spirit never falters.

None of your afflictions make any sense. I believe in karma. Your reality defies karma. For the kindness you willingly share, as our family and friends would attest, you should be receiving a fortune of good will in return. I could ask my friends whom you feed lumpia shanghai and their fond recollections of you would solidify my testimony.

Maybe, I'm correct about your thirty years of self-deprivation. Maybe, you're hiding the dark truth of your feelings … but I can't believe that. I refuse to believe you conceal any ill will. Maybe, you have been experiencing what I'm going through right now … for thirty years. Could it be that everything you're feeling, I'm also feeling? Is it because we're innately connected that I'm spiritually empathizing with you and how you have been feeling throughout the years? I can sympathize with your solitude, though I'm not sure if I truly empathize, since my life is filled with the boundless love of my family with every blessed breath. Some are blessed to know each other so well that words only get in the way. That is how we are. Maybe, our connection is the reason I'm bound so deeply and fiercely speculating.

If reasoning is involved, I can't fathom your circumstances. Unfortunately, the truth is the human body cannot endure endless suffering. Spiritual, mental, and physical health are intertwined. If one is ailing, all could succumb or one will compensate for what is lacking. Mentally, you isolate yourself and carry great burdens. Physically, you are reacting just to survive. Thus, you are a spiritual warrior. Your spirit is strengthened to endure.

For you, Mom, it doesn't make any sense. The last nine years have been an endurance trial for living. I don't get it. I also don't care about another person's karma, because I cannot affirm nor can I judge them. It is not my place. I can judge myself, though. I certainly affirm that I am not worthy of the tremendous blessings I have received throughout my life and yet, I receive innumerable blessings. I say this because I feel it. I am given so much and genuinely appreciate as many recognizable blessings as possible. I give thanks for blessings: great and small; past, present, and future; accountable and unaccountable. That is my daily hymn. I know you do the same. It is because of you that my every breath is a prayer, always brimming with zeal and sincere intention. I know you are the same. Yet, you suffer so much. For the blessing you are, it doesn't make any sense that you suffer endlessly.

I wish I had the foresight to stop our family from going to the Philippines in that December of 1988. Maybe, your suffering would have been averted. I clamped down on my head. This is speculation. Nothing is going to come of this. "**IT'S NOT FAIR!**" I roared with anger. "It's not." I whimpered.

The vacation itself was priceless. We stayed with Grandma Luz and family for three of four weeks, enjoying Luzon where three of us were born. We had a wonderful time in the Philippines and didn't want to leave. Vibrant imagery flashes of family and precious experiences. That was only the third visit, and unfortunately, that became the last visit to our birthplace.

Our lives turned upside down upon returning from that vacation. Your health immediately declined, your energy depleted. Normally, you're always up early and starting the day ahead of the rest of our family, but you couldn't function normally. Dad was frantically concerned and took you to your physician.

I wasn't aware until after several visits. You didn't want to alarm Kristine and me. You were given various tests, including one for bone marrow because your red blood cell count was dropping. Your physician suspected leukemia. The tests were inconclusive. Nearly one month had passed before you were referred to a specialist. Your physician drew a conclusion that required confirmation.

Your medical records were transferred to a nephrologist, who identified your emergent need for treatment. Your kidneys were failing and a urinary catheter was placed to finally relieve your deteriorating condition. The next step was to quantify your kidney function. Further testing revealed the devastating results that *ninety-seven percent* of your kidney function had been destroyed. The shock left us ... unable to comprehend.

That marked the first day of dialysis which has become a part of your routine ever since. I drove you to the dialysis center three times a week. You were forced to sit still in a chair for four hours at the mercy of others. Even that didn't go well for you. Some employees were negligent, unresponsive, and rude. I had threatened several times to go in and confront them, but you always held me back. I understood the potential ramifications that you might suffer further if I interfered. You endured the selfish acts of others.

After some time, Dad liquidated our family assets and secured a dialysis machine for your use at home. The machine and materials required to properly support you are an overwhelming financial burden. Dad didn't hesitate to act and is providing everything he can for you. Dad is always doing a remarkable job providing for our family. He is even cleaning the house, washing dishes, and doing chores that you would normally do; all after his own hard day's work.

Our lives adapted to your hemodialysis. Your overall health stabilized and we were grateful for your returning energy. One year passed after your tragic diagnosis and your nephrologist recommended your placement on a kidney donor list. We offered our kidneys to you. Dad tested, but he wasn't compatible. You and Dad refused Kristine's participation and my participation. Your dual refusal was reinforced by consulting with the specialist. Because Dad was incompatible, you both told Kristine and me that our chances of matching you were fifty percent at best – not enough to qualify as suitable donors. The best potential match would be a sibling. You have reached out, but haven't received any offers. You have graciously respected their privacy and we don't have any right to demand.

Two years passed after your diagnosis. In 1991, you received a phone call regarding a potential donor. We were excited for you. Hope rose, though at the expense of another person's life. The donor found was a match of four out of six HLA antigens, enough to consider compatibility. Cautiously, you and Dad agreed to the surgical procedure.

A new wave of tears consumed me. Another tragedy beset you. Surgery is already terrifying and during the attempted transplant, your body completely rejected the donated kidney. You were almost lost on the table. *"You almost died, Mom."*

I wished I could say that was the last of it, the last of the danger that threatened to take you away from us, but it's not. We are a family just trying to live happily, trying to nurture love through these adversities, but calamity hasn't let us be. Misfortune didn't conclude with your near death. In 1994, you were diagnosed with breast cancer. You're living with breast cancer. Neither side of our family has any history of breast cancer. I screamed again, "*HOW IS ANY OF THIS FAIR!?*" My tears and saliva mixed together, flowing upon the rocks beneath me.

Every step of the way, with every horrific development, you're the one consoling our family. We are speechless and you are reassuring us that everything will be okay. You're the cheerleader, the patient optimist, willing hope to emerge and save you from this tragic reality, but the burdens grow with every passing day. No relief is in sight. Your name was placed on the transplant list again. You're willing to take that life-threatening risk *again*.

In the meantime, you are doing what must be done and you are not just surviving. You are living as best as you can without letting your conditions compromise your love for your family. You are living as if you are a healthy woman with fully functioning kidneys. You are living as if you don't have breast cancer.

You never complain. You have no energy. The hemodialysis process is extensive and you must be meticulous for fear of contamination. You had to inject yourself every time, alternating areas to let the scars heal, until you had a permanent catheter implanted which makes hygiene even more critical. You must prepare before and clean after every session. You must maintain your schedule without fail. You must sit in place for hours at a time while the machine cleanses your system. You are your own medical professional to function normally.

Even so … You're always in a good mood. You continue smiling with a contagious radiance. You continue laughing uncontrollably at the silliest things with gleeful delight. You continue nurturing with passion. You continue praying with unwavering diligence. You continue loving with everything you have. You continue persevering through incessant afflictions.

That is your spirit shining through. That is your warrior status. You give everything you have without asking anything in return. All we can do is pray for your immediate recovery and clean bill of health because we are otherwise powerless. You alone must live through the pain and suffering. Life is *definitely* not fair. It's unpredictable.

XVI

My Greatest Supporter

WEAKNESS ENTANGLED ME within this explosion of despair. I am powerless to move, forced to dredge further into the depths of this pain. The brewing danger surrounding me is not impeding my frantic impulse. This vulnerable nature is making me scour the depths of my own suffering. My broken spirit longs for the world that was once my vivid spirituality. My search keeps leading home when I returned two years ago, when I could no longer function on my own; the culmination of my torment rooted in my return as a failure.

Two years ago, my family received me with open arms. Dad was comforted by our family reunion. Kristine was happy for her big brother's homecoming. And Mom, you were comforted by our reunion and happy for my homecoming, but most of all, you were concerned about my circumstances. You knew that being home meant my dream didn't come true.

Mom … you and Dad expressed your mutual concern about my wedding proposal. I reinforced my feelings and you both relinquished, believing in me, saying, "You know what you're doing, son. You have our blessings." I was scared neither of you would approve, but your perpetual faith in me is firm. You both implicitly trust me and always wish for my lifelong happiness. For those reasons, I wanted everything to go well. I wholeheartedly worked on my intentions becoming reality, but the opposing forces remained unyielding.

To my ex-fiancée's credit, she warned me many times. She kept telling me that we will face endless conflict. She reminded me that I will always have to concede and she will always have to fight our battles. She also trusted me. She was also willing to have faith in me.

I was the one who continually insisted we make it work. I had faith in our bond. I was willing to concede for us to be together. I wanted to be worthy of her trust. I wanted to support her for upholding our relationship … but when our wedding was being considered, when I would commit for a lifetime, I realized, this was not my dream. Ultimately, I didn't believe she wanted this for our future either.

Our bond may have been strong, but our future was not attractive. We spent six years trying to develop a life we could share. I was the one forcing our union. My ex-fiancée compassionately believed in me and I'm the one who let her down. I gave our love hope and in the end, I abandoned it when she asked me one last time. "This is not going to work. We should end this now. Agreed?" That last time, I finally agreed and haven't looked back.

She might have wanted me to keep fighting for us, but I couldn't do that any longer, not without my heart's conviction. I gave everything to an invaluable relationship that wasn't meant to last a lifetime. I believe we both learned important lessons to carry forward. I tried to force my dream upon tumultuous circumstances, but our worlds will never harmonize.

Dad's wisdom put everything into perspective. The pursuit of my lifelong dream doesn't mesh with a simple truth. I can't force my dream to come true, the dream must come to me.

Sometimes, I look at my own hands. I look over my arms. It's strange, but sometimes I feel a separation between my body and soul. I wonder, *"Is this really me?"* I'm completely aware but somehow, I have difficulty believing, sensing that I am living a dream. Within a few moments I'm reunited, feeling whole and then I think, "Having an out-of-body experience is breathtaking, observation of one's self is forced; the reunion of soul and body reveals the truth, good and bad." It's that truth that allows me to look into a mirror and cherish the good, the bad, and everything in between; the person I am as a whole. I have to love me.

But, I stopped loving me over these last two years of healing and

Erwin Lazaro

my world degraded into a static existence. Looking in the mirror has been difficult and I haven't been able to look myself in the eye. I started making compromises with myself. I started making decisions that didn't sit well. I started thinking "It's okay," and *it's not okay.*

I used to stare deeply into my own eyes. I'd challenge myself. If I could look into myself without flinching, I'd confirm I am the person I want to be. Integrity is everything. Dad taught me that. The true tests to prove my worth are derived from mistakes; new wisdom or more folly. I'd hold myself accountable, acting as necessary, but failure is inevitable and for good reason. Failure is the most successful path for learning. Nevertheless, I'd beat myself up vowing not to repeat the same mistakes. Even through my vigilance, failure after failure, I'd renew my vow to do better, but my will faltered. My determination receded for two years … until recently and now, I'm finally confronting my failures and my fears.

Lily's passing shocked me into an emotionally charged reaction. That cleansing wave purified me and ironically, the beginning of my rejuvenation occurred within the arms of my ex-fiancée. She truly deserves a person who will love her unconditionally. The fact that we always had to maneuver around conditions reinforces my decision to never look back.

I have a dream that must be fulfilled unconditionally. I dream of ideals. I've envisioned my dream coming true from the day of my birth. I dream of unconditional love because of you, Mom. Every experience shapes my dream and you are the spirit who has and will always mold my ideals. You are the reason I don't give up, Mom. You are the reason I aspire and dream.

I was broken two years ago and I have purposefully broken myself today. This place where I am now, this crossroad in my life, this swirling vortex of energy that is aggressively stirring, this mobilizing spirit … is building to a magnitude where I'm being forced to choose and it's not a clear path. It's not a comfortable path, either.

It's such a horrible feeling… the doubts. I've caused distress at home. I came home to heal and inadvertently put my will aside in the process. Being home has restored me to a certain extent, but as I healed,

I realized two influences are opposing one another. It's this opposition that has frozen me, but recently, one influence is pressing to lead.

One influence is forcing me to choose, but I'm scared. I'm scared for many reasons, but I'm mostly scared because someone is going to suffer, either way. If I accept this status quo, then nothing will change. I know that without risk, there is no progress.

The dream I was living had slowly disintegrated, but the dream is not lost. Hope is always counteracting. Lily triggered a reformation. My will is intact and finally gaining the resolve to push back. I was despondent, but I'm a fighter. My heart protects the precious memories that are encouraging me to rise.

My heart also protects a spiritual guide that has always advised me. I am blessed to share that counsel with so many throughout my life, beginning as a child; helping and protecting others. This spiritual guide gives me an intuitive ability, the reason I was assertively approached to become a priest at one time.

Somehow, I stopped listening to my advisor. Somehow, I forgot I had many advisors and in doing so, I forgot the greatest advise of all. I turned on myself and internalized everything. I didn't want to burden others with my problems. Pride took over and I hardened. Somehow, I overlooked the most important lesson about counsel. Guidance is for the counselor as it is intended for those counseled.

I'm here because I implicitly remember what I forgot. I am at my limit and now, I'm releasing, letting go. I was good at doing that as an eight-year-old. I forgot about my second grade. I was beaten and shamed, but it didn't matter after the tears stopped. My body hurt. My mind didn't understand. I was resilient because of my heart. It's all because of you, Mom.

You are my heart.

Before I returned home, I had forgotten my resilience. I never wanted to admit it, but I was scarred by people who took advantage of my heart. I had gambled for the kindness that never came and my heart devolved into a hardened shell. Intellectually, I remember, but emotionally, I had forgotten. I forgot what it was like to let go. I learned shame as an adult and forgot that I am a child. No matter how old I become I am always a child. It's important not to forget that fact, but I did. I returned home and the child in me reemerged, urging me to release the shame, along with the negativity I had stored away. My hardened heart softened because of you, Mom.

I'm here to release the negativity and transform the damage into the positive spirit that has always guided and nurtured me, the spiritual guide that has never left me, willing to lead if I am willing to accept. The child within is my spiritual guide.

The shell softened and my dream reshaped by spending time with you, Mom. Time with you naturally reformulated the vision for my future, but the imagery wasn't entirely clear. The ideal for a fairytale romance I once sought was not only tempered by my experiences, but also by the unpredictability of life. I emphatically understand I can't gain my desire by force and the unpredictability is you, Mom.

The child in me reemerged due to going home and remembering. I reclaimed myself. It has taken two years but now, the child within wants to roam free. Angst looms because I'm about to commit and I can't help but look over my shoulder to fix my attention on you, Mom.

I'm such a momma's boy and I'm incredibly proud of it.

Mom ... you are a living dream. I am eternally grateful that I was born into our family. If anyone had an ultimate goal for reincarnation, I wholeheartedly claim it is to be your child; to be raised and nurtured by you; to be loved by you.

Boldly, I claim I have achieved the ultimate goal. No other will surpass you. My dreams are vibrant and if I am recalling past lives to serve as reminders of my path to you, I humbly appreciate every experience to evolve into a soul that will carry everything I have learned and pay it forward ... to anyone I meet ... to the future, especially to my future family.

In other words, Mom ... you are everything I aspire to be. The least I can do to repay you for everything you have done for me, for our family, is to honor you with my dedication. I have always dedicated my energy to shine as brightly as possible so that when others are in need, I can offer my help. I will be a beacon for others. Never do I seek to offer though, I offer only to those who seek because those who seek already have a willingness to learn and that willingness is the key to understanding what I have learned from you … what I learn from you … with each blessed moment I have with you.

Mom … you radiate an immense energy of love, of hope, of faith … an enriching spirituality that attracts. Those of us who are nurtured by your tremendous, yet gentle love, always want to be next to you.

Your attractive aura projects through your eyes, your smile, your expressions, your actions, your way … it's seemingly impossible to define or identify entirely. Your way is unspoken, astonishingly fragile. Anything can destroy it. Yet, your way is mighty and boundless. You teach without teaching. You speak without speaking. You give without giving.

I clutched my hair between my fingers and pulled. I haven't the words to express your abilities, nor can I accurately characterize who you are, but I do know that you are a brilliant spirit I must protect and yet, share at the same time.

Protecting your contentment, while sharing your way, is my bewilderment. It seems that my lifelong dream conflicts with my adoration for you, Mom. Nothing makes you happier than our unified family. Your joy brightens every room when we laugh together. Your motherly instincts are bold and clear when you teach. Your serenity beams when I sing for you. You are comforted when we are all together at home. I don't want to disturb these feelings you gain from our familial love and devotion to one another.

You are alone when the three of us are away. You work hard to maintain your health and our home. You do so to prepare for the limited communal time we have each day. Kristine comes home. Dad comes home. I come home. You serve dinner and we are able to enjoy each other while savoring your incomparable meals. Your purpose for living is our family. You battle your deteriorating health and fight for precious time with our family. Every shared moment is treasured.

Our love is synergistic. I returned home because I needed you. You needed me to come home. Now that I've healed enough to be independent again, my devotion to you is keeping me still. I know you need me. We need each other. That will never change. I know you would never ask for repayment. Your love is unconditional. I'm having difficulty reacting to your ... faith.

I inhaled. "Is *that* my problem?" I didn't understand until this very moment ... I have conditions. I have conditions if I'm not able to reciprocate and act the same way as you are, Mom. I'm too scared of taking any more away from you than I already have.

"My fear ... I have conditions. Mom, you are showing me faith where I am lacking. You see, Mom? This is your way. I still have so much to learn. I am still too weak and callous to understand how much you truly love me. You love me so much that it doesn't matter what happens to you. Is that what you're telling me? Is that what you truly mean when you say you want me to be happy? Even at the cost of your own life? But ... that is too hard to accept. How can I be truly happy knowing you are suffering?"

Clarity enhanced by unravelling my lack of faith and conditional love. I had always believed my love for my mom is unconditional. I had always believed I couldn't love my mom any more than I already do. I don't want to believe I am lacking, but now I understand a little more.

I am realizing the two influences I thought are opposing ... are not opposing one another at all. They are not fighting nor restraining one another. I now understand that one is willing to let go and set the other free. That is the unconditional love I finally understand and the faith that is crucial for that unconditional love to be. Mom has faith in me and I must have faith in her.

"Does this mean that I have to let you go and set you free too, Mom? Does this mean I cannot fear the unpredictability of your situation? Must I have faith in our bond, no matter the circumstances? As long as I am happy, you are happy? And, if you are happy, I should be happy too? Is that your contentment? Is that how it goes?"

"If so, then ... my sadness is your sadness. My frustrations are your frustrations. Your empathy for me ... you've been consoling me by trying to take my feelings upon yourself, believing your efforts will help alleviate my burdens. That means I am causing you more sorrow. If this is so, then I know what to do."

"I need to tell you, Mom. I need to tell you with all my heart. I've found my purpose. When I come home, I'm going to give you the biggest hug and kiss you on the cheek. We can walk arm-in-arm … like we do … but from now on …" Silence. The words didn't form, but the feeling is undeniable. "It's the unconditional love I am still learning from you." Tightening my muscles, I exhaled everything until nothing remained. Vibrations wracked my body before I was forced to breathe, invigorated by the sensation of letting go. "I have a little more to iron out and then I'll return home. *I know, Mom*. I'll tell you soon." Harmony cleansed me as an unprecedented baptism, elation resonating throughout. Revelation is broadcasting loud and clear. My spirit is overflowing, brimming with newfound resolve. I whispered to all, "I am ready."

XVII

Cleansing Breath

RAIN FROM A cloudless sky sprayed my arms and legs. It was a blanketing mist. Unsteadily raising my head, my eyes opened through crusted tears. Muting contemplation was disintegrated by pressing danger. The aggressive action of waves rhythmically crashed into the jagged remains. The chaotic collisions fused air with water. It had already begun; the churning, the ocean ferociously invading the Devil's Punchbowl or as it was once known as Satan's Cauldron.

I instantly stood to assess the situation, my back against the wall. The sand is entirely submerged and about one-third of the rocks are under frothing water. The waves are freely flowing through the north entrance of the punchbowl. My time is rapidly flowing out.

Adrenaline took over. I moved and concentrated on the north opening. Looking at its base, I see the water has not yet risen to a frightening level, but rising rapidly with each undulating pulse. My fear is that the area beyond the bowl is going to reveal a tide level too high for me to wade through. The thought alarmed me enough to falter and buckle from weakened knees, but I kept moving. I'm going to carefully cross this mess without getting too injured and do so as swiftly as possible. I glanced at my bleeding shins from my reckless movements earlier.

"Whoa!" … I slipped and slipped some more. The camcorder in my hand is a bit of a problem. I should abandon it, but I can't. A foolish part of me wants to videotape this ridiculous situation, but I need both arms to manage my balance over this seaweed and algae. I stooped and cautiously continued with haste. I'm a crab traversing this obstacle course, low to the rocks to catch myself more readily if and when I … "Whoa!" some more.

Steadily crawling along the wall, I kept my center of gravity low. Baby steps and my left hand gave me three points of stability to move towards the opening. Occasionally, my right forearm supported me against the punchbowl, scraping along the way.

I tried to keep an eye on the water level, but slipping and looking down to negotiate my footing drew most of my attention. Nonetheless, I kept darting glances toward the opening and with confirmation that water is filling my passage out, my determination intensified. "Stay calm. I'm getting out of here."

Halfway to the opening, I paused on a portion of a large boulder still above the water level, but beyond this area, the water has risen enough for my feet to go under. The spray is intense! It's hard to believe I'm face-to-face with this. Hesitation cost me precious seconds and I stepped in. Denying the shock from the cold salt water into my open wounds, I continued as my shins went under, but thankfully, I feel sand.

With reassured footing until the exit on the north side of the punchbowl, I hurriedly paced the second half to the opening and turned the corner to see just how much I had to fear. Seeing the ocean flowing through this wall-thick tunnel made it appear longer than it really is, especially when the sand is not visible. I don't have visual reference for depth, but the good news is that the rock platform on the north side is still exposed. The bad news is that the area leading me back to the ramp appears to be completely under.

When I first entered the water, the tide was roughly thirty inches above that walking surface. At this point, I'm praying that it's not higher than five feet or else I'm going to shout for help. My pride is still unscathed though, so I can't let all those people be right. I will make it out of here by my own effort. Otherwise, "I told you so" is going to ring through the air.

The incessant roar is fearsome in this cavity. I ran through the mouth and abruptly stopped on the other side where I anticipated the sand to end at the base of several large boulders. The reflections within the shadows are playing tricks with my perception. It's also difficult to distinguish anything beneath the water's surface with sand swirling around my sandals.

"Sandals …" my eyes widened. "I'm such an idiot!" I hastily took off my sandals and stuffed them down my shorts. Feeling the surface with my bare feet should help me move faster. The algae are slimy. Some rocks are a bit rough and the barnacles too, but I don't have time to fret.

On this north side, most of the larger rocks are still exposed above the ocean's surface. Daylight is helping me analyze the situation more accurately and it's not reassuring. Water is flowing northward because of the pressure from the waves through the west opening. Water is being forced to drain out of this northern exit until all the openings are submerged and the tide levels are equal. I moved.

Before this plight, I would witness the brutality of the ocean, exhilaration sending shivers throughout. I could avert my attention, always from a safe distance. I'd rebalance emotions when I became uncomfortable, but right now I have nowhere to turn. I am in danger. I am currently at the mercy of the ocean's inhumanity. I still have about one hundred feet to get to the ramp where the rock platforms protrude. I can't see the ramp, but those rocks are my marker. Water is flowing freely in the direction I'm moving. Everything here will soon be consumed by the incoming tide and I'll be wading through a lot more water than I did going in.

Every second is drawn out … ninety feet or so. One careful step at a time, I inched closer to the ramp. I hear the waves sloshing about within the punchbowl behind me. The cave mouth is vehemently projecting the action. Eighty feet … I focused on forward progress. My fear surged with each step. Observing the water level made me hesitate as if I could stop and wait. Seventy feet … the water is rising. I now see the extent of area I'll be wading through before getting to that first rocky toe remaining above the water's surface … for now.

Growing anxiety forced me to breathe sharply. "*I'm scared.*" I whimpered. "Okay … I'm okay, one … careful … step … at a time … careful steps." Because of the reflections and shadows, I can't move confidently around the rocks with my bare feet. I shuffled and nudged each one with my toes. "I'm so pathetic." It isn't the uncertain path that's causing my fear to swell it's the view of an unknown distance between me and that first rock to safety. "It looks so far away."

Instead of focusing on the distant marker, I diverted my attention to the rocks indicating the top of the ramp about thirty feet away. The ramp is progress, but that's where I will be trekking through deeper water. I shuddered. Walking barefoot was a good choice and combined with the deluged surface, my stability and movement are more reliable, but I definitely can't be relieved yet, not until I get to the shore beyond the megalith.

Several forces are at work here. Time is causing friction. Each grueling moment is resisting my progress. My harried breathing and the pressure of my concentrated movement keeps building. As afraid as I am for being in this predicament, this is all my doing. I'm responsible. I'm accountable for my actions and at an appropriate time, I'm going to give myself a hefty lecture about my insignificance in this world. I have no right to trouble others with my selfish acts. Right now, I'm proving to myself that I made the right choice in forcing these circumstances, but I will never do this again. Better methods for forcing my own hand must exist. Under these circumstances, I just went with the flow and this is where I ended up being. Prideful and in danger, that's where I'm at now.

Revelations bestowed upon me must be shared, but not only that, I'm going to live this personal enlightenment. In order to live it, I will overcome this physical ... emotional ... spiritual challenge. Every step is adding to my determination ... my will. I am barely controlling my fear, but I know if I looked into my own eyes right now, I'd see the burning desire to reach my goals.

This fear is not going to deter me. I'm fired up. I have much to accomplish. I've just begin. I must keep encouraging myself with these pep thoughts and I'll make it.

During this entire escape, I've held my right hand above my head to protect the camcorder as best as I can. It's been doused a few times, but I'm hoping it's durable enough to dry out and work later. I'm not giving up on it, convincing myself that I'm not a materialistic guy. I have precious memories on the tape. Those memories must be preserved.

Finally, arriving at the rock platform at the top of the ramp I had to calm myself once again. This is it. This is the last leg of my return to the shore beyond the megalith. I'm about to find out how deep the water is. "Cleansing breath … cleansing breath," I repeated the chant of "cleansing breath" as I walked down the ramp. I gauged something in the range of fifty feet on the way in, but this looks much farther than fifty feet. The only reference I have is that toe within the shadow of the megalith. I'm going to that rock.

I'm walking on sand here, but moving slowly, each step leading me into deeper water. "The water is so, *so, so, so cold, cold, cold* …" forget the shins. I didn't move very far and the water level is already at my waist. "Cleansing breath," I focused on breathing with each step. A few more steps and my stomach went under. The water pulsated with the tide, but thankfully, the force is relatively low. I couldn't help but look towards the ocean and gave thanks that most of the tidal force is still being dispersed by the reef I recognized earlier. Without that reef, I'm not sure if I could do this. A few more steps and my chest went under. Both of my arms went above my head and I turned to face the wall, deciding it is best to shuffle sideways.

I remember a log around here somewhere. A few cautious lateral steps and my ankle hit the log. That would normally hurt, but I didn't have time for pain. Instead, I was grateful for the guide. I brought my left arm down to try and touch it, but the log was too low for me to reach without dunking my head. I used my legs against the log to guide me instead.

The pulsing tide made me move with the flow. By this time, my shoulders were nearly under. I dare not think too much. The water level is as high as I can manage. If I slip, I'm going completely under. My footing is stable though. I'm really hopping from side-to-side now. I can't even look down, doing my best not to swallow salt water.

Fifty feet, was it? I closed my eyes periodically to soothe myself. My body kept moving. Progress is key. I maintained a rhythm of cleansing breaths with each side step. The thought of swimming lessons infiltrated my thoughts, but I pushed them out. I couldn't swim with the camcorder, anyway. Swimming lessons are still probably a good idea, though. The tide steadily pushed and pulled. The reaction of water hitting the rugged surface of the megalith gently splashed back onto my face.

The log ended and I felt a large boulder that forced me to move away from the wall. Slowly, I navigated around the protrusion without support and instinctively raised my left hand for leverage when I returned to the wall. That rocky toe must be close. With the undulating tide, I bounced with each incoming wave, propelling myself sideways. I'm taking some risks, but a few more bounces and I'll be there. My chin submerged momentarily with each bounce, but I didn't lose control. I repetitively hopped until I touched the rock.

Grateful that I've managed the tide level to this point, my energy deflated upon realizing why fifty feet looked much farther than it had appeared before. Most of the rock is already submerged. Not much area remains above the ocean's surface for me to climb upon. During my progress, I couldn't avert my attention away from each step. Otherwise, I would have noticed earlier. I'm glad I didn't monitor the rocks being consumed by the rising tide. That would have frayed my nerves. Now that I'm here, I'm not sure if any advantage remains for climbing on top of it.

However, I turned to face the toe and wedged the camcorder between the rock and wall. Next, I tried to move into a position that would allow me to climb. I tried getting my toes onto the surface of the rock, but couldn't manage with sandals down my shorts. "Seriously?" I should put them on so I can climb this rock with mobility. Making sure that the camcorder is still secure, I grabbed my sandals and went under. I used the rock for reference and stability, leaning with my left hand that held a sandal. Blindly slipping on sandals with straps was challenging as I rose out of the water for a deep breath. Without hesitation, I exhaled and went under once more, fumbling with the other sandal before rising again.

I was afraid of losing my sandals, but I stayed calm in my struggle. Staying calm is essential here. Maintaining my balance with the pulsating current and putting my sandals on while being completely submerged within these frigid waters? For one who is deathly afraid and in awe of the ocean, never in my lifetime would I imagine I'd be in this situation, but here I am.

Clearing salt water from my hair and face, I renewed the effort to climb again with a series of cleansing breaths. Each time I was denied. The rock itself is coated with so much algae, I can't get a foothold anywhere. I felt around the surface to locate any cracks I can wedge my sandal into, but nothing is available.

"*Come on!*" The tide is rising. "I can't find a way onto this ..." I exhaled frustration. I kept feeling the boulder's surface under water without luck, but as I slid closer to the wall, I felt rough areas where my right foot moved.

Immediately turning my effort towards the wall, I raised my foot to find anything I could use to prop myself up. With a sigh of relief and salt water spittle, I gave myself a heave, pushing as steadily as I could upward with one foot. My first attempt wasn't enough. I tried again, but to no avail. "I'm running out of time here. Come on, man. Stop being afraid. Just do it already."

I palmed the lingering portion of rock as best as I could with one hand and grabbed the edge against the wall with the other. I found the most stable position for my right foot on the wall's surface. I started to bob up and down, going partially under with each bounce. On the count of three, I'm going to put as much force into this effort as I can muster.

I held my breath and counted in my head with each dunk. One ... Two ... Three and *Push.* My hands remained firmly in place and my foot didn't slip. The force propelled me up and out of the water, but the camcorder was in my way. I knocked it aside and I fell back into the water. I instinctively reached out with my right hand and stopped the camcorder from falling off the rock. "Is this really happening?" I stared in disbelief.

I laughed as I leaned on the rock. The pressure from my chest on the rock's surface made my entire body convulse erratically. This is quite the mess I'm in. I remained hugging the toe for a while longer and decided to abandon a path over the rocks. I'd have to hop onto each partially submerged toe and that might be more dangerous, anyway.

Confidence remained with me. I am nearly at the beach. I'm going to pass these toes and I'll reach the sand. If I remember correctly, as

I peered into the water on the way in, the area around these toes are covered with debris, so I'm relieved that I put my sandals back on. Sure enough, a few steps around the first toe, I kicked a good-sized rock with my sandal that not only gave me decent footing, it also gave me a bit of elevation too.

Keeping in mind that, with the camcorder back in my right palm, slipping and going under is still a threat. Returning would have been so much easier with both hands free. People are going to laugh at me if they ever find out about this. It's kind of comical, actually. With both arms in the air, I faithfully took one step forward while gauging the base of each toe.

The tide kept swaying me and I froze, counteracting the current. I transferred the camcorder to my left hand above my head. I decided to use my right hand to stabilize movement along the toes. Advancing, I meticulously felt around for each jagged rock with my feet. Every step kept my shoulders above the water, hoping I can maintain this height until I get to the sand.

Tenacious efforts strengthened my confidence. I could have easily given in to fear at any time, but I refused. I wholeheartedly refuse. Adrenaline pushed me through this rising tide. Only a little further to go. I relied upon the megalithic toes for stability. My right hand stayed submerged during this final obstacle. I rounded the last rock and stood upon a clear path to the shore. I made it back.

My heartbeat flew towards the sight of freedom. My legs followed after. "This is breathtaking. Wow!" I could have fallen just from the discovery of this stunning scene. Most of this area of the beach has been reclaimed by the ocean. The crack between the megalithic toes is gradually filling, the grotto too.

Re-emerging from the ocean … I don't believe I'll ever feel this way again. In fact, I hope to never feel this way again. Almost completely out, my legs are feeling incredibly heavy. It's either from fatigue or this feeling is coming from a wave of relief … I think it's gratitude.

The adrenaline started wearing off. Stinging sensations began tingling my ankles, shins, forearms, and elbows. I stopped and leaned over to rest my hands on my knees, observing the abrasions exposing my arms and legs. After identifying most of the pain, I squinted and gazed up towards the sky. "Thank you … Thank you … *That was really stupid.* I swear that wasn't a test, but I needed that … Thank you."

I moved further until my feet rested on the shore and turned around to witness the path from which I came. I shivered from deep within knowing that circumstances could have been different. I could have drowned for any number of reasons, but I didn't. My emotions remained within the current; my gaze fixed towards the open ocean. In my heart, I spoke to my dear friends … "Randy … Patrick … I won't be joining you today. I will keep my promise."

The wind surprised me with a few gusts and my teeth started chattering. Thoroughly drenched and soaked through, I studied my open palms … well, my left hand held the camcorder by the strap, but open palm still. I closed them and formed fists. I opened them again. "Yup. This is *really* me … I have much to do."

I just shook my head and with one last cleansing breath, I headed back towards the trail. I couldn't take my mind away from the sand as I made footprints with each step. I stopped to take my sandals off and continued walking barefoot. The warmth under my feet is comforting.

When I reached the trail that was cut through the wild brush, I looked up to scan the beach one last time. I sputtered to a halt. A surge of welling emotions … joy, sadness, kindness, shame, compassion, remorse, gratefulness … obscured my vision through instantly cascading tears.

I lifted my left forearm to wipe them aside and I raised my right hand to make the peace sign.

Roughly a stone's throw away stood a man with hands on his hips. He faced me squarely. His wife was halfway turned to monitor their two children, but her attention was on me. The two little ones with boundless energy ran circles around them, playing a game of tag; the sand angel kids.

Neither the dad nor the mom spoke. They both remained motionless. They awaited my return.

I couldn't speak to express my apology. My feelings were beyond description. I held the peace sign a moment longer and as I dropped my arm, the dad also offered me the peace sign. I whispered, "*Thank you* …" and silently walked off the beach.

For your freedom ...
And for my freedom too ...